The Dynamic Decision Maker

Michael J. Driver
Kenneth R. Brousseau
Phillip L. Hunsaker

The Dynamic Decision Maker

*Five Decision Styles
for Executive and Business
Success*

toExcel

San Jose New York Lincoln Shanghai

The Dynamic Decision Maker
Five Decision Styles for Executive and Business
Success

For information address:
toExcel
165 West 95th Street, Suite B-N
New York, NY 10025
www.toExcel.com

Published by toExcel, a division of Kaleidoscope Software, Inc.

Marca registrada
toExcel
New York, NY

ISBN: 1-58348-005-6

Library of Congress Catalog Card Number: 98-88900

Printed in the United States of America

0 9 8 7 6 5 4 3 2 1

Contents

i

Contents

Appendixes

List of Figures

List of Tables

Preface

Things are changing fast in the world of management and leadership. Popular notions about what constitutes effective management and leadership behavior are undergoing a tremendous upheaval. Concepts that you may have been taught and methods that you may have used as a manager or leader are now seen as outdated, inappropriate, or downright wrong.

You are told to be participative. Motivate and inspire. Think strategically. Be visionary. Be a coach. Be a team player. And last (but you know not least), get results!

Since we originally published *The Dynamic Decision Maker,* the pace of change in management philosophies seems to have increased. The management and business sections of bookstores have exploded with books that sport such titles as *How to Do Everything Well in Ten Seconds* and *The Management Secrets of Ghengis Khan,* all of which purportedly offer sage advice on succeeding and prospering as a manager or leader in today's organizations.

We cannot promise that, if you read *The Dynamic Decision Maker,* you will become an unqualified success as a leader and manager in ten seconds or less. But we do promise that you will be more successful in your career if you apply the insights that this book offers.

Purpose of the Book

The Dynamic Decision Maker introduces you to a framework for understanding in detail the ways in which people differ in their styles of decision making. It arms you with useful tools for evaluating your own styles and those of others. It also provides specific techniques for using your understanding of decision styles to manage your own styles, deal with subordinates, manage your relationship with your boss, make judicious task assignments, and build high-performance teams.

When we write about *decision styles* we just as accurately could refer to *decision habits*. Styles are simply habits that people acquire and that get reinforced or modified throughout life. When we say that you must manage your styles we mean that you must move beyond mere reliance on habit. You must become aware of your styles or habits and then be able to overcome them when necessary.

In applying the techniques we present in this book, you will be joining the ranks of a growing population in the United States and in other places such as Australia, Sweden, and the United Kingdom. Since we developed the dynamic decision style model in university behavior research laboratories, we have applied the model and the techniques presented in the book to companies large and small in the aerospace, automotive, banking, computer-systems, construction, machine-tools, petroleum, pharmaceutical, and shipping industries. We also have applied the model in government agencies as diverse as NASA, the U.S. Navy, and the New South Wales Department of Corrections. In addition, an increasing number of business schools are including the model in their graduate management education programs.

Audience

The Dynamic Decision Maker was written especially for managers and executives whose jobs require managing people successfully. However, even if your job does not formally include the title of manager, but you nevertheless are keenly interested in human behavior, this book is for you, too. Anyone—consultants, advisers, business students, or members of working teams—who must make decisions that involve other people can benefit from the insights and techniques offered in this book.

In particular, for those who work in teams, there are a few facts that we believe you should keep in mind to benefit most from what we have to say:

- Organizations are relying increasingly on team performance rather than individual contributions.
- Working effectively in teams brings you into close contact with people who think and feel differently from you and from each other.
- There is no one way that teams or individual team members should think and behave. Team thinking and team behavior should vary according to the needs of different situations and different tasks.
- Teams that support individual differences in thinking and behavior have greater potential to survive and succeed than those that press for uniformity.
- As a team member, you must be able to manage how you think and make decisions rather than blindly rely on habits that may have worked for you in the past. You must be capable of dealing with the diverse styles of thinking and decision making of other team members and to adapt to the demands of different tasks and situations.
- As a manager and leader, you must help team members work together cooperatively, and you must help your team to actively benefit from style differences among team members.

All of these facts remain true, regardless of whether your team consists of pipeline engineers, a group of sales associates, a shift of control-room operators, the crew on a ship at sea, or the top management staff of a multinational business corporation.

Overview of the Contents

The first few chapters of *The Dynamic Decision Maker* introduce you to the basics of decision-making styles and then to the subtle yet important characteristics that, beyond mere stereotypes, constitute the dynamics of everyday behavior.

The basic decision style model is disarmingly simple. It consists of two parts that each deal with an essential part of decision making and problem solving: analyzing information and generating solutions. Chapter One shows how these two aspects can be combined to describe five fundamentally different styles. As you will see, the styles account for differences in speed of decision making, openness to information and varied points of view, inclination to focus on one subject at a time versus many, propensity to change one's mind, and values related to efficiency, adaptability, quality, and creativity.

Throughout the book, we have included examples describing the behavior of real people to illustrate the different styles. In Chapter Two we draw on famous personalities and well-known leaders to present in-depth portraits of each style. This chapter provides a real feeling for the underlying "personality" of each style and demonstrates the range of behavior that decision styles influence.

The next two chapters, Chapters Three and Four, explore the dynamic aspects of decision styles. Even though people tend to use a particular style more frequently than others, very few use only one style of decision making. Most people shift their styles frequently, even during the course of one working day. Sometimes the shifts are dramatic, going from a very analytic and exploratory style to a very fast and focused style. Chapter Three shows how these style shifts follow a predictable pattern linked to the ebb and flow of pressures in various situations.

How many times have you been misled by a first impression of a person that later proved incorrect or at least superficial? Chapter Four points out the reasons behind mistaken views of other people, when those views are based only on the behavior seen in meetings, interviews, or other relatively formal situations. In particular, the chapter shows how the styles we use when we are most self-aware or self-conscious often differ markedly from the styles we use when we focus our attention outward on a task or a problem. Do not be surprised if some lights of self-insight start to flash as you read this chapter.

Decision styles influence how we behave in various circumstances, from a boardroom presentation to a crisis to a family vacation. As you will see, our own and others' styles influence behavior in many kinds of situations. Chapters Five and Six provide an in-depth tour of the varieties of behavior that reflect decision styles and show how you can use these varied clues to assess your own styles and those of other people.

Inasmuch as interpersonal relationships are powerfully shaped by decision styles, the next three chapters show how to use your understanding of styles to manage different kinds of relationships. Chapter Seven deals with relationships among peers or people of relatively equal status and authority. The particular focus in this chapter is on techniques for adjusting your method of communication to accommodate the styles of others. We describe the quirks and biases of each style and offer specific suggestions for ways to keep yourself on a positive footing with that style.

In Chapter Eight we shift the focus to relationships with subordinates. We show the style-related pitfalls that await bosses whose notions about managing people fail to include adjustments for different decision styles. We point out the kinds of behaviors that bosses exhibit that irk people with different styles and we make suggestions about assignments and supervisory techniques that best fit each style.

Chapter Nine addresses the topic of getting ahead in management, which leads us to talk about adjusting to, or otherwise dealing effectively with, the decision styles of your superiors. However, in Chapter Nine we also talk about the style requirements that frequently characterize jobs at different levels of management, from the shop floor to the executive suite, and in different functional areas such as marketing and finance. We give you some guidelines for anticipating the style requirements of jobs at different levels of management to help you more smoothly manage your career. In effect, this chapter lays out a map that can become an important guide for you to use in making it to the top, if that's your inclination, or, if it isn't, for finding the best place to jump off the fast track.

Suppose, after sizing up your own style and assessing your career objectives, you decide that you need to develop a different style or at least moderate your use of a particular style. How should you go about doing this? That topic is covered in Chapter Ten, where we talk about the process of style change. If you decide on a course of action that requires you to modify your style, you should proceed with your eyes wide open. So we give you a framework to help you objectively assess the strengths and weaknesses of each style and provide specific recommendations for actions that can either increase or decrease the use of each style, whichever your choice may be.

Even if you do not yet know much about decision styles, your own experience may have already told you that they heavily influence how people behave in work groups and teams. In Chapter Eleven we look at how each style expresses itself in small groups in terms of such behaviors as communication frequency, leadership methods, goal setting, and inclusion of other people. Then we suggest roles that each decision style is best suited for in a small group. We also look at the "personalities" of groups and teams whose makeup causes them to lean toward a particular style, such as groups in which a majority of members share the same decision style. We point out the particular strengths and weaknesses of these groups and suggest the types of situations and special purposes for which they can be used most effectively.

Suppose you find yourself at the helm of a new group, perhaps as an outcome of your being promoted into a new job or because of some organizational change. You look around and see evidence of different styles among your staff and little evidence of effective functioning as a team. You suspect that this band of people could be woven together to produce a high-performing team, but you aren't sure how to do the weaving. This is the subject of Chapter Twelve, the final chapter in this book. In it, we offer suggestions from our team development experience as management consultants. We show you how the decision style model and style assessments, combined with individual and group feedback, are extraordinarily powerful tools for building high-performing teams.

Teams need different styles, but the very differences that hold the keys to team success often become stumbling blocks to effective teamwork. Armed with knowledge of decision styles, you need not settle for this state of affairs. Chapter Twelve shows you how you can turn style differences into a sturdy foundation for a winning team.

A Word About Terminology

As you read *The Dynamic Decision Maker,* you will find that we used some new terms such as *satisficing* and *integrative.* We chose to use special terminology to communicate about decision styles because common, everyday language is notoriously imprecise in its meaning. Words that mean one thing to you may mean something different to someone else. For example, just ask a few people what *good judgment* means and see how many different interpretations you hear of this commonly used term.

Such lack of precision does not make for good communication when very specific ideas need to be communicated. The terms that we selected seem to work. We have used all of them many, many times in seminars and workshops on decision styles; in fact, they actually represent a specialized mini-language for talking about decision-making behavior. We find teams and whole organizations still using this language long after we introduced it to them. Even though some of the terms and words we use may seem unusual at first, they should become more normal and meaningful as you read the book.

Applying What You Learn

Decision style concepts can benefit anyone, from the new management trainee or MBA student to the CEO at the top of a large, expanding firm. The trick is to use the techniques properly with the right people in the appropriate situations. The model is no panacea, but understanding, experience, and professional training can augment current methods and ways of thinking. Where possible, professional assessment techniques for personnel and job analysis should be conducted for best results in job profiling, selection, and placement. However, the primary career and management benefits can be gleaned from understanding and applying the concepts you are about to read in the following pages.

As you read, constantly think of how the concepts and examples can apply to you in your situation. Teach to others what you learn at work or even at home to reinforce your learning and to help others better understand themselves and what you are trying to do. Try the ideas at every opportunity to see whether improvements can be made and be alert for feedback about how to modify and improve your approach. If you do, we believe that you will experience fewer career and interpersonal problems, increased effectiveness in accomplishing your work objectives, and more satisfying and productive relationships with other people.

Los Angeles, California   MICHAEL J. DRIVER
August 1993   KENNETH R. BROUSSEAU
                                             PHILLIP L. HUNSAKER

Acknowledgments

Associates, friends, and clients have said that we should have written *The Dynamic Decision Maker* long ago. We could have written a book on decision making styles before now, but it would not have been this book. We learned a great deal during our research, and we attempt to convey the results of this learning in this book. The concepts that we write about originated in theory, were tested in the lab and in the field, and then were tempered, refined, and enriched further by years of practical application in many organizations.

Many people have contributed to this book in many ways. We wish to thank at least a few. In particular, we wish to acknowledge our gratitude to several colleagues and associates who have contributed so many of their own insights to our understanding of styles: Hussein Alawi, Jim Boulgarides, Mike Coombs, Jack Lintott, Naj Meshkati, Ted Mock, Tom O'Connell, Tom Olson, Bill Owens, Mike Perrault, Harold Schroder, Dale Schutt, Sigfried Streufert, Pete Suedfeld, Diane Sundby, Abe Tesser, and Ward Testerman.

We never would have been able to expand our practical applications and understanding of styles without the assistance and cooperation of thousands of people in many companies. For their

enthusiastic support, we especially are indebted to Steve Markoff of
A-Mark Financial Corporation; Jack Halgren of Gibson, Dunn,
and Crutcher; Ken Johnson at Main Hurdman; Brita Murphy, Dave
Rowley, and especially Ed Calkins of Rockwell International; Max
Weiss and Jim Coge at The Aerospace Corporation; Shurl Curci,
Peter Adams, and Max Nardoni of Transpacific Development Cor-
poration; Norm Ryker, Dave Christensen, Ken Mayne, and Frank
Tisch at Pneumo Abex Corporation; Jim Pruneski, Al Indelicato,
Rich Conners, and Guy Gentry at Abex Friction Products; Steve
Winters at McDonnell Douglas; Bill Fello and Bill Kendall at
Xerox; Steve Loizeaux, Linda Pemberton, and John Thomas of
American Honda; Adnan Zainy of Abar and Zainy; Dave Peters at
Eli Lilly; Bob Bartz of The Corporation for Society; Dan Waters and
Norm Buehring at the Los Angeles Department of Water and
Power; Harold Heinze, Ron Remick, Jerry Aspland, and Jack Beal
of ARCO Transportation Company; Ed Conn of Kal Kan; Don
Layden and Chuck Austin at United Parcel Service; and Ed Holman
and Jay Fogg of Carter Hawley Hale. We wish we had the space to
thank personally each of the many others in these and other com-
panies who have supported and encouraged our work.

Much of our work was facilitated by colleagues at the University of Southern California. In particular, we wish to express our
appreciation to Warren Bennis, Ten Brannen, Larry Greiner, Steve
Kerr, Ed Lawler, Barry Leskin, Chuck Maxey, Jim Stevenson, Mary
Ann Von Glinow, and, most recently, Larry Pate and Al Patz. We
also are grateful for the support of Jim Burns and the Research
Committee at the University of San Diego.

Books such as these are seldom written during normal working hours. This one was no exception. For their understanding,
patience, and support beyond the call of duty, we wish to express
our special thanks to each of our families.

M.J.D.
K.R.B.
P.L.H.

The Authors

MICHAEL J. DRIVER is cofounder and chair of Decision Dynamics Corporation, a consulting firm offering state-of-the-art consulting in human resource management, strategic planning, and information systems. His research on decision making, human resource management, information processing, and careers has resulted in two books, more than ten chapters in books, and more than twenty journal articles. He is also professor of management and organization at the University of Southern California. Driver received his B.A. degree (1958) from Fordham University in psychology and his M.A. and Ph.D. degrees (1960, 1962) from Princeton University in industrial-social psychology.

KENNETH R. BROUSSEAU is the cofounder and president of Decision Dynamics Corporation. Formerly, Brousseau was a member of the faculty in the Department of Management and Organization at the Graduate School of Business Administration, University of Southern California. He earned his B.A. degree (1971) at the University of Washington in sociology and his M.A. and Ph.D. degrees (1973, 1976) at Yale University in organizational behavior. He is the author of numerous publications in the areas of careers, job-person dynamics, and decision making.

PHILLIP L. HUNSAKER is professor of management and director of management programs in the School of Business Administration at the University of San Diego. He is also a faculty member of the Institute for Quality and Productivity and of the Leadership and Management Program at the University of California, San Diego, as well as a consultant to management with Decision Dynamics Corporation. An internationally recognized consultant, seminar leader, and speaker, Hunsaker frequently delivers presentations on the topics of management and organizational development. Hunsaker is author of *You Can Make It Happen: A Guide to Personal and Organizational Change* (1977), *The Art of Managing People* (1986), *Managing Organizational Behavior* (1986), and *Strategies and Skills for Managerial Women* (1986). He has also authored numerous articles in academic and professional journals.

The Dynamic Decision Maker

1

The Dynamic Decision Style Model

Joe just can't understand it. How can a man like Dave be so successful—a senior vice president for a major corporation? Even worse, how can he, Joe, ever be successful working for Dave?

Meanwhile, down in the corner office, Dave is wondering, How can I manage a guy like Joe? How did he ever get as far as he has? He's stubborn, argumentative, obsessed with getting everyone doing things the same way, in lock step—and right now! Everything has to be done with lightning speed, according to Joe. He can't seem to accept the need to lay the groundwork, to develop relationships, before acting. Also, he can't seem to accept the idea that different people will do the same job in different ways and still get the job done. When someone resists one of his policies or procedures, he becomes combative. He's like a bull in a china shop. And I think he's trying to turn people against me here.

Joe can't help wondering if Dave ever got anything done—especially by himself. The most you can expect is for him to appoint a "task force" to come up with some recommendations on some "issue." You can never tell where he stands on anything. He says one thing today and another tomorrow. He seldom seems to be upfront with his opinions. What does he care about? He never seems

1

to get upset. Nothing ever worries him. Problems come and go without being resolved, except by default. That means that the outcomes often are way out of line with what they should have been, costing the company money, creating problems for employees, and setting bad precedents for the future. If he would just take a position of some kind, even if it's not one that I would advocate, I could live with that. I could do my job. But you never can pin him down. Something has got to change around here, fast.

Dave and Joe are two real people: one is an officer on the executive staff of a major corporation, and one reports to the other. By a quirk of corporate politics, these two men, each successful, find themselves thrown together in a new situation where they are expected to work cooperatively with each other.

The problems these two executives experience in working together illustrate a style clash created by profoundly different habits of decision making. Inasmuch as their *styles* of decision making differ dramatically, it is a virtual certainty that they will experience conflict and tension. Ultimately, the conflict itself comes to overshadow the capabilities that each of them brings to his work.

Spotlight on Decision Making

In many companies, your management level can be formally defined by how much decision making you do. The *scope* of your decisions—the range of people and events affected by your decisions—is a particularly important measure of your position in management. A good indication of decision scope is how much you can decide without someone else checking up on you and your decisions. In fact, it's been said that your real management level can be measured very simply by the amount of time that you can be absent from your office before anyone notices!

The contrast between Joe and Dave highlights our main concern in this book: differences in how people make decisions. The way managers make decisions is central to their effectiveness and their personal success. Time and time again we see managers who fail not because they make the wrong decisions but because the way they decide creates problems. Sometimes they take too long to act; sometimes they jump too fast. Sometimes they put all their eggs in one (wrong) basket; sometimes they try juggling too many eggs and trip over the baskets.

Our point is that to be effective and successful, managers must

1. Understand their own styles of decision making
2. Know how to identify, understand, and work with the varied styles of other people
3. Match their own styles to the types of jobs for which they are best suited

The Two Key Factors in Dynamic Decision Style

Basically, the term *style* means learned habits. So *decision style* refers to learned habits of decision making. Like all of our styles—writing style, style of talking, dressing, or of playing games—we learn to make decisions in school, at work, in leisure time activities, and from following the examples of others. Because of diverse backgrounds, people learn varied styles of decision making.

There are many ways in which people's decision styles differ. Some like to take risks; others go to great lengths to avoid risk. Some like to go it alone, while others seem to want to make decisions only in groups. Some people rely heavily on intuition; others proceed only on the basis of detailed analysis. Some are speedy; some are slow. Some people seem certain of just about everything; others see the world in shades of probabilities and possibilities rather than hard facts.

Because of their effect on performance, culture, and career development, these decision style differences have been a major concern for many large corporations. We have invested years of research in exploring the underlying factors that account for these differences. Two aspects of decision making appear to provide the greatest power to describe the key differences in decision styles. They are

1. *Information use:* the amount of information actually considered in making a decision
2. *Focus:* the number of alternatives identified when reaching decisions

These factors capture two key stages of decision making: analyzing the situation and formulating a solution. The factors are completely independent of each other. How much information a person uses has nothing whatever to do with how many alternatives a person typically identifies. One person uses a lot of information and identifies many alternative solutions, while another person also typically uses a lot of information but seldom identifies more than one solution.

Put together, the two key factors account for a remarkable range of human behavior. Let's have a closer look at each of these two factors. Then we will put them together and let them describe some very different approaches to decision making and problem solving.

The First Key: Information Use
(Maximizers and Satisficers)

People differ markedly in how much information they use in decisions. We all know people who seem to jump into a situation apparently on a whim and some who won't move without a thorough analysis.

As contrasting examples, consider J. Paul Getty and Howard Hughes. Hughes liked to analyze everything in detail before he acted. For example, before taking his epic airplane journey around the globe, he considered virtually every possible situation he might encounter on the trip. He even built special equipment for straining oil in case he was forced down in an area of Siberia where only a certain grade of crude oil was available.

In contrast, Getty acted much more on the spur of the moment. For instance, he once bought some land for oil exploration that could be accessed only through an extremely narrow isthmus. When asked how he would get equipment onto the land he said he'd "work it out later." When later arrived, he simply ordered a narrow-gauge railroad built to haul heavy equipment onto the land.

We term the fast-action, worry-about-it-later type like Getty a *satisficer*. The more analytic type we term a *maximizer*. The satisficer pattern describes a range of styles in which people use only enough information to get one or more "good enough" solutions to a situation. Satisficers aren't dumb (despite what some maximizers are tempted to think). It is not that they can't process large chunks of information; they just want to get on with things. They feel a need to keep moving and not spend time overanalyzing things. Their nightmare is to fall prey to "paralysis by analysis."

In contrast, maximizers want to get all relevant information before making a move. They know that important points sometimes are subtle and easily overlooked, causing massive problems later. They act when they are sure they have not overlooked some key detail. They want to be sure to have a winning, high-quality solution even if it costs time or money.

Most people's information-use habits typically fit one of these two patterns in greater or lesser degrees, most of the time. People can shift patterns as the situation changes. We have more to say about shifting patterns later.

Figure 1.1 illustrates the differences between satisficers and maximizers. As the figure shows, the first information you receive about a problem generally is most valuable to you as a decision-maker. When you know almost nothing about a problem, those first few pieces of information can be real eye-openers. Later, after you already have gained a lot of knowledge about a situation, new items of information are much less likely to add to, or alter, your understanding of the situation.

Looking at Figure 1.1, you can see that satisficers tend to limit their information use to information that contributes most rapidly to their understanding of a problem. Once they feel that they have enough information to choose one or more workable solutions, they stop looking for more information. Usually, they know that more information is available, but they feel it would not be worthwhile or practical to take the time to consider it.

Maximizers, on the other hand, typically go on using information until they are sure that there really is no new information available that could give them any new insights into a problem. Typically, they remain open to any information that could add further to their understanding of a situation.

There are some people who fall outside these two broad categories, however. Examples are *searchers*, who suffer "paralysis by analysis" and never seem to get enough information, and *lurchers*,

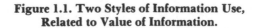

**Figure 1.1. Two Styles of Information Use,
Related to Value of Information.**

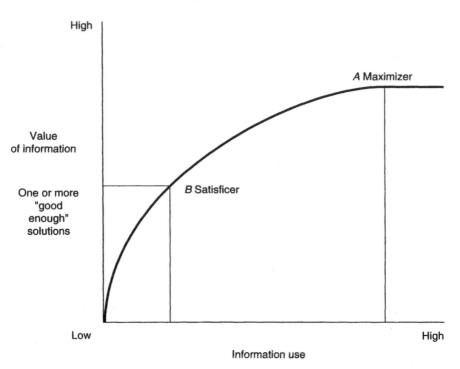

who seem to jump to conclusions with almost no information at all. Since people at these extremes do not have successful careers in organizations and are only very infrequently found among managers, we do not look at them in any more detail in this book.

No One Best Style

How about the satisficers and maximizers? Is one of them better than the other as a decision maker? You may tend to like the one closest to your own style. We all tend toward this. But objectively we suggest that there is no best style. Whether a particular style is better or worse than any other style depends on the characteristics of the specific situation in which it is used. Some key questions to ask in determining the most appropriate style for a given situation are

> Is there time pressure?
> Is the decision critical?
> Is the information complicated?

If there is high time pressure and not much importance or complexity, the satisficer style clearly is best. Conversely, if time pressure is absent and one is deciding an extremely complex lifetime issue, the maximizer is best.

For instance, if you were to select a person to design a space vehicle to take you personally to the moon, which style would you pick? How about a satisficer who tells you the landing module will "probably" work? Or the one who tells you that you might encounter some problems but that "we can work them out later"?

On the other hand, whom would you select to pilot your spaceship? Particularly, whom would you select to pilot the landing module on your descent to the lunar surface? A maximizer might still be studying blueprints while a malfunction needing immediate action caused disaster. In fact, one study of air force pilots demonstrated that virtually all pilots—at least those still with us—were satisficers.

The key point is *contingency*—it all depends. There are many jobs where the satisficer style is essential for success. For instance, we once helped a company select traders for precious metal markets. By now, you shouldn't be too surprised that we found the maximizers still trying to analyze the first moves in the market after fifty swings in prices. Satisficers were in heaven dealing on the spot with rapid price fluctuations. On the other hand, maximizers performed extremely well when asked to prepare long-range financial projections.

Another company set up a system for selecting sales reps responsible for selling costly (five-hundred-thousand dollars-and-up) computer systems. The satisficers charged out expecting to pop a couple of sales in their first few weeks on the job. They became very frustrated and demoralized when they found that they were going to be lucky to close only a handful of sales in any one *year*.

The maximizers, on the other hand, targeted a few high-probability prospects and made careful plans for laying the necessary groundwork with each prospect, identifying "hot buttons," surfacing objections, and negotiating the final deal. "Patience, planning, and persistence" was their credo.

The important point here is fit. You must know your style and either fit it to a job well suited to that style or change your style to fit a job that you want but that requires a different style. The tragedy of a person trying to maximize in a satisficer job—or vice versa—is one of the prime causes of dissatisfaction and poor performance in management or, for that matter, any other career.

The Second Key to Decision Style: Focus

When faced with a problem to be solved, some people use information to come up with one solution, one course of action for dealing with the problem. Others see information about the problem as leading to a variety of solutions—different alternatives for handling the problem.

These two patterns stem from focus differences. As illustrated in Figure 1.2, the *unifocus* pattern uses information to produce only one definite course of action. In contrast, using information to come up with many alternatives is the *multifocus* pattern. Contrary to what the unifocus person may suspect, the multifocus pattern is not one of making no decisions. The multifocus person often tries to put a variety of courses of action into motion at once.

For example, in deciding on personal investment strategies, the multifocus pattern sees value in a highly diversified portfolio. Consequently, the multifocus person's decision might be to invest money in a combination of real estate, CDs, bonds, domestic stocks, foreign stocks, and so on.

In contrast, the unifocus pattern would be to study investment information and then select the type of investment—say, a growth and income mutual fund—most likely to meet a specific investment objective. The unifocus pattern essentially would put all investment eggs in one basket—perhaps a very safe basket or perhaps a very risky basket—instead of choosing the diversified, multifocus strategy.

Figure 1.2. Solution Focus.

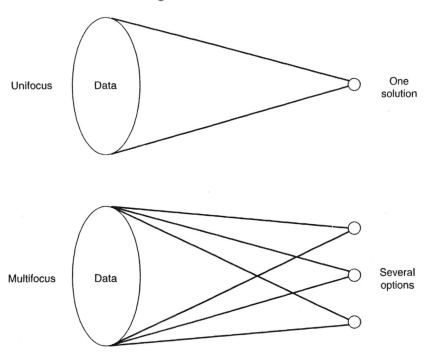

Among executives, you can see both focus patterns at work. We mentioned J. Paul Getty earlier as an example of the satisficer. Now contrast his multifocus pattern with the unifocus pattern of Thomas Watson, the founder of IBM. Watson spent his entire life building an empire focused exclusively on selling business office machines. Getty, on the other hand, used his successes in the oil business as a springboard into a wide range of new business and personal interests in such unrelated areas as hotels and fine art.

Often, focus patterns work their way into the management culture of a company. This was recently manifested by the executives of a new corporation formed as the result of a merger of two very different companies. Let's call them company A and company B. Both were holding companies with subsidiaries. But unifocus was the dominant pattern in the decision styles of executives from company A, whose businesses were concentrated in just two industries. Company B executives, on the other hand, overwhelmingly showed the multifocus pattern in their decision styles; and not surprisingly, they operated a real agglomeration of domestic and international businesses in an assortment of industries.

Focus Differences and Interpersonal Conflict

As we saw in this merger situation, things get interesting very fast when people who are highly unifocused get together with people who are very multifocused. Unifocused people usually have very definite ideas about how things ought to be done. Multifocused people tend to see more pros and cons in any course of action or any state of affairs. The immediate response is that tempers flare and blood pressure levels soar. These reactions often signal forthcoming problems in working relationships that can have dire personal and organizational consequences.

So how does the unifocused person describe a multifocused coworker? Certainly not as "that nice, multifocused guy down the hall." Instead, you are likely to hear loud complaining about "that wishy-washy, flaky jellyfish who can't even write his name the same way twice!" That's just for starters.

Meanwhile, the jellyfish down the hall is thinking of the unifocused person up the hall not as "that unifocused fellow," but as "that tunnel-visioned, rigid fascist who hasn't done anything different since Herbert Hoover was president!" And that's just for starters, too—while folks are still feeling polite.

As you might suspect by now, focus differences have a big impact on relationships between people—even more than information-use differences. It's difficult to work well with people if they strike you as confused jellyfish or rigid fascists.

Focus differences were largely at the root of the problems between Dave and Joe in the opening vignette. Joe was always looking for the right way to get things done, while Dave was off somewhere exploring different options for getting things done. Joe always had a very clear idea about what specific goal he wanted to accomplish, so he could quickly judge a solution as good if it appeared to lead directly toward the goal or bad if it didn't.

Dave, on the other hand, usually had several quite different goals in mind. Consequently, he could judge almost any solution as having some good points (by serving some desirable objectives) and having some bad points (by not accomplishing others).

This kind of reasoning, of course, never failed to raise Joe's blood pressure. Joe's resistance to new ideas, on the other hand, never failed to disappoint and frustrate Dave.

These style-related differences are often responsible for informal groupings that develop in organizations. One day during lunch, for example, it was apparent that all of the unifocus executives were seated at one set of tables and all the multifocus people were sitting together at a separate set of tables. Communication, needless to say, was absolutely minimal between the two groups.

The conflicts that these style differences create are natural, but they are not necessary. In most cases, they can be reduced or controlled. In fact, the differences themselves can form the basis of extraordinarily productive relationships. Later, you will learn about techniques for transforming tension-ridden situations into highly collaborative working relationships.

Putting It All Together: Five Basic Decision Styles

Combining information use and focus gives us the framework for defining the five basic decision styles shown in Figure 1.3. In general, we find that each person tends to use one of these styles most frequently, but we can see a bit of each style in our behavior from time to time.

People vary in how strongly they rely on a given style. Some people use a particular style so often and so strongly that they almost caricature the style. Others may use the same style only moderately, even though it is their most frequently used style. Chapters Two and Three elaborate on the differences between a person's dominant and backup styles and explain how shifts between the two occur with changes in information-processing demands.

Let's take a quick look at each of the styles, then we'll visit each one in more detail with examples. To give you a feel for how they differ, we talk about each style as it shows up in the behavior of people who use the style frequently. So, for example, when we

Figure 1.3. Five Decision Styles: Amount of Information Use.

	Satisficer		Maximizer
Unifocus	Decisive	Hierarchic	Systemic
Multifocus	Flexible	Integrative	

describe the decisive style, we talk about *decisives*—people who use the decisive style more than the other four styles.

The Decisive Style

Decisive is a satisficing and unifocus style. Decisives use a minimum amount of information to rapidly come up with a clear solution for a problem. Decisives prize action, speed, efficiency, and consistency. Once they decide on a course of action, their tendency is to stick with it. Rather than analyze a situation further, or look for other alternative solutions, they typically shift their attention to other situations that require action.

In dealings with other people, the hallmarks of the decisive style are honesty and loyalty.

A vivid example of the decisive style in action was Truman's decision to drop the bomb on Hiroshima after only a brief review of issues. Other classic examples of this style include the tough, action-oriented, and straightforward cowboys portrayed by John Wayne, and Lee Iacocca's tough, no-nonsense, behaviors of honoring commitments and meeting deadlines.

The Flexible Style

Flexible is a satisficing, multifocus style. Like the decisive, the flexible moves fast. But here the emphasis is on adaptability. Any piece of information is seen as having several meanings or implications. Faced with a problem requiring action, flexibles rapidly identify a line of attack; if it appears not to be working, they quickly shift to a second course of action. At any moment, the flexible will drop one tactic in favor of another, often with bewildering speed as the situation changes.

A key issue for people with this style is to keep options open—never get trapped by overcommitment to a particular course of action.

In dealing with other people, the flexible person is very engaging and supportive. Conflict is always avoided. Fast-paced variety is the conversational trademark.

The wily television characters of Bret Maverick or Jim Rockford portrayed by James Garner are perfect illustrations of the flexible style. In business, Donald Trump's wide-ranging set of interests, fast-moving entrepreneuring activities, and personable interaction style all represent a flexible decision style.

The Hierarchic Style

Hierarchic is a maximizing and unifocus style. Hierarchics use lots of information to evaluate a problem and then to carefully construct a very detailed and specific plan for handling the problem. They prize thorough analysis and quality. Consequently, their search for a solution for a problem becomes a search for the best solution, not merely the most expedient. To find the best course of action, they feel, requires using an appropriate method of analysis to study all of the relevant facts that will lead logically to the highest-quality solution.

Socially, hierarchics form relationships based on mutual respect. They usually prefer deep, long-term friendships rather than a wide range of acquaintances.

In motion pictures, the Sherlock Holmes character—particularly as portrayed by Basil Rathbone—superbly illustrates the hierarchic style. As a real-life example of the hierarchic style, Howard Hughes is hard to beat. Consider Hughes's search for a method of launching an airborne radio antenna for communicating with his airplane during his round-the-world flight. First, he tested hundreds of kites on a Los Angeles lakebed. Then, after selecting the winning kite, he made sure that it was backed up by helium balloons—just in case.

The Integrative Style

Integrative is a maximizing and multifocus style. Like their hierarchic cousins, integratives also use a lot of information to evaluate situations. However, rather than zeroing in on a single solution, their tendency is to explore a problem from many perspectives to come up with a variety of alternatives for dealing with the problem. In many cases, the integrative's preferred solution is to pursue several courses of action simultaneously.

Although integratives may value efficiency, quality, and adaptability, these considerations tend to pale in significance compared to the importance that they attach to creativity and exploration. Methods and plans are never fixed or final. Why? Because no two situations are the same and because situations change, says the integrative.

In conversations, the integrative style is easy to recognize. Integratives are usually thinking on several tracks simultaneously, but unfortunately are equipped with only one mouth. They frequently interrupt themselves, saying, "On the other hand, . . ." and then a little later, "But, of course we shouldn't forget that . . ."

The integrative style is particularly well suited to working in groups: integratives love varied ideas. They thrive best in an atmosphere of cooperation and trust.

A good historical example of the integrative style is Thomas Edison. The sheer magnitude of his personal creativity and his development of research teams to further the application of his inventions aptly illustrate both the intellectual and social characteristics of the integrative style. The character of Obi-Wan Kenobi played by Alec Guinness in the epic *Star Wars* trilogy illustrates the style rather well. In business, Steve Jobs, founder of Apple Computers, demonstrates the integrative's team orientation; creative talents; preference for decentralized, organic, fluid organizations; and need for high use of information.

The Systemic Style

The systemic style is a relatively recent addition to our decision style model. We came to recognize the systemic style as we began to notice that some decision makers make frequent use of both the integrative and hierarchic styles. A closer look at these people brought to light a two-stage decision process.

First, the systemic approaches a problem as an integrative would, using lots of information, sizing up the situation from different perspectives, and laying out alternatives for handling the problem. Then the systemic shifts into a more hierarchic mode and orders or evaluates the alternatives according to one or more criteria or values. This style is very methodical, yet it often gives the outward impression of greater "looseness" than the hierarchic style.

The final result of the systemic thought process is a prioritized set of strategies for dealing with the situation, not just a collection of alternatives or a single, elaborate plan. Systemics typically define situations more broadly than do other people, seeing them as consisting of multiple, interrelated problems that must be considered together. So any action that the systemic takes usually has multiple objectives. And each of those objectives is eventually attacked with a variety of actions.

A splendid example of the systemic style in the business world is Harold Geneen, former CEO of ITT. Under Geneen, ITT was a maze of information networks and staff operatives whose purpose was to take information from the company's many subsidiaries around the world to Geneen's office in New York. In television, Peter Falk's character Colombo illustrates the loose, seemingly scattered yet structured and tricky aspect of the systemic style as he gathers, analyzes, and orders information on crimes while appearing to be just poking around and then springs a complex solution at the end.

Once Again: No Best Style

None of the styles we just described is better or worse than any of the other styles in an absolute sense. There is no Superman style here, nor is there a failure style among the five. Each of the decision styles has its own strengths and weaknesses "built in," so to speak. We point out each style's major strengths and weaknesses when we describe each of the styles in depth in the next chapter.

But bear this in mind: whether a strength is a strength, and whether a weakness is a weakness, depends on the circumstances in which a style is used. Until a style meets a situation, strengths and weaknesses are potential strengths and weaknesses. If a particular style doesn't fit the demands of a job, a task, or a decision situation, its potential strengths don't matter nearly as much as its weaknesses, which no longer are potential.

In general, the decisive and flexible styles have the edge when things have to be done now, particularly when the issues that must be considered are relatively simple and clear. The hierarchic, integrative, and systemic styles excel when problems are complex and decisions will have costly, long-term consequences.

The decisive and hierarchic styles have the advantage in highly structured or regulated situations, where experimentation or exploration cannot or will not be tolerated. But on the other hand, the flexible and integrative styles are superior in highly changeable situations where there is a lot of new territory to be covered.

Summary Guidelines

This chapter started out with the real-life examples of Dave and Joe who simply could not see eye to eye on anything. Now that you've read about the dynamic decision style model, you probably understand why the stand-off developed between them. You can now begin using the model to better understand everyday relationships in your own work life.

When trying to understand the sources of interpersonal conflicts, like the Dave and Joe situation, ask yourself the following questions. What are the decision styles of the people involved? Are they in conflict over solutions or over how they reached their conclusions and how they would implement their respective courses of action?

Try using the style model to gain insights into people's information-use habits. Which do they lean toward—the satisficer or the maximizer patterns? How focused are they in their recommendations or preferred solutions for problems? Do they zero in on one clearly defined course of action? Or are they always willing to consider a new tactic, a different strategy?

Joe and Dave are not heavy information users, but they are

light years apart on focus. So what they display is a classic conflict between the decisive and flexible styles. Once you pinpoint the decision styles that may have contributed to a conflict situation, you have set the stage to manage the situation effectively. You will learn about how to deal effectively with style-related clashes in later chapters. But first let's take an in-depth look at each style in the next chapter. Then you'll be in a much better position to develop constructive methods for dealing with the varied styles around you.

2

Understanding the Five Decision Styles

*T*o appropriately apply decision style concepts to yourself and others you need a thorough understanding of each style's strengths, weaknesses, and other characteristics. This chapter provides a closer look at each of the five decision styles and illustrates them in action by describing the behaviors of well-known leaders.

These decision style characteristics provide the necessary base for applications to improve communication, planning, goal setting, leadership style, and team building. As you read, think of yourself, or someone else who possesses the characteristics being described, and consider how you can apply this new understanding to improve task and interpersonal performance.

The Decisive Style

Major business and political leaders, as well as leading characters in television series or motion pictures, often portray the five decision styles in action. Just tune in to any late-night John Wayne movie for a close-up glimpse of the decisive style in action. You'll find no mealy-mouthed mumbo jumbo and no beating around the bush—just straight talk, then straight action. Decisive players from business include Lee Iacocca and H. Ross Perot; from politics consider Harry Truman and Ronald Reagan.

The decisive style is a get-things-done-now style. The focus is on deciding for today, not planning for the next five years. And what's wanted for today is to get lots of things done per unit of time or cost—or better yet, per unit of time *and* per unit of cost—to maximize both productivity and efficiency.

Long-range studies and five-year plans are considered pointless exercises that squander time and resources. Why waste time trying to peer into the murky future when things probably will change? Better to get things going now and deal with the future when it arrives and you can see it clearly.

Decisive communication is short and to the point. You don't have to guess about what's being said. There are no hidden messages or subtle innuendos to interpret. Decisives say what they mean and mean what they say. Such was the tough, direct approach of Lee Iacocca as he charged ahead to turn around Chrysler Motor Company.

If you are decisive and you want someone to do something, you go directly to the person who should do it and you tell him or her what needs doing. You don't worry about chains of command or elaborate protocol, and you don't rely on lengthy memos. You go direct, even if you are the CEO and the person you will deal with is three, four, or five levels below your position. Your concern is getting the job done—now.

There is perhaps no better example of this aspect of the decisive style than the actions of billionaire H. Ross Perot, recent candidate for the president of the United States and founder of EDS. Some years ago Perot became concerned about the possible failure of a major Wall Street firm, DuPont Glore & Forgan—an event he felt would have disastrous effects on the U.S. economy. Perot felt that he couldn't just stand by and watch this happen. So he acted. He bought up a controlling interest in the firm and quickly moved in his people and methods. Then he visited all 112 of the firm's offices and *personally* explained his requirements to all 4,800 employees: honesty, hard work, perseverance, and achievement. Failure would be met with termination. Books would be closed, balanced, and the results wired to headquarters each day.

More recently, the same behavior occurred following the

merger of Perot's company, EDS, with General Motors. Shortly
after the merger, Perot began showing up unannounced in dealer
showrooms to get a firsthand look at what was happening where
the rubber meets the road.

It should come as little surprise that with their emphasis on
action, decisives have little tolerance for committees. Meetings
should be short, follow a clear agenda, and end on time with decisions made. Without reaching a closure on at least one decision,
the decisive feels that a meeting has been a total waste of time—and
wasting time is a serious offense. This unifocused, satisficing style
is what led the decisive Perot into a head-on collision with GM's
chairman of the board, Roger Smith.

For another decisive example, consider Harry Truman, our
the-buck-stops-here president. Once, when recalling a meeting with
Winston Churchill, Truman said that he told Churchill, "I did not
want to just discuss. I wanted to decide." Churchill responded by
asking if he "wanted something in the bag each day?" As far as
Truman was concerned, Churchill was as "right as he could be. I
was there to get something accomplished, and if we were not to do
that, I meant to go back home."

Decisives prefer working in organizations where jobs are
clearly defined. Ideally, each person has his or her objective, and
nobody's job overlaps with anyone else's job. Fuzzy objectives, overlapping responsibilities, and duplication of effort are sources of real
irritation. When channels of communication are short and direct,
you know immediately where to go and with whom to talk if you
need information to get something done fast.

Multiple goals and objectives are disliked. Decisives prefer to
do one thing at a time, often with high intensity and persistence.
Only after things are clearly resolved are they inclined to shift attention to new challenges.

The management style of the decisive boss is a blend of au-
tocracy and delegation. Decisive managers are highly directive and
autocratic in defining subordinates' goals, objectives, and timeta-
bles. So if you work for a decisive boss, uncertainty about what's
expected of you will be the least of your worries. But once your
decisive boss is satisfied that you know what you are supposed to
do, you will be left alone to decide how to get results. There may

be some simple rules that you are expected to follow, but achieving results will be your responsibility alone. You won't have to worry about close supervision. In fact, attempts by you to get more guidance probably will be met with signs of growing impatience.

Here again Ross Perot provides a good illustration of this management style. His theory of management is simple: pick the right people, give them resources, motivate them, and then leave them alone to do their jobs. At EDS this theory was enforced. Corporate executives who violated the rule by giving too many orders to managers working in the field, who presumably knew their situations better than those at headquarters, were subject to sharp tongue-lashings on the spot by Perot, regardless of who was present.

Loyalty, consistency, and perseverance are qualities that decisives look for in other people. People who act in ways that are seen as disloyal or who appear to "say one thing and then do another" get written off very fast by decisives. If you cannot be trusted, then you will not be tolerated.

When decisive bosses run out of tolerance, this generally means that someone will leave soon. Consequently, when General MacArthur, during the Korean War, wrote to Congress publicly disagreeing with Truman's decisions, he had behaved disloyally— not so much to Harry Truman as to the president of the United States. So Truman fired him abruptly, American hero or not.

This same pattern was obvious in the actions of the CEO of a large graphic arts company. Within his company, the CEO was known as the "fastest gun in the East." If you got results, fine. But if results were slow in coming, you could be sure that you would be fast in going. No hard feelings, nothing personal, just no results; next problem, please.

This also shows how decisive managers motivate subordinates: by handing out immediate rewards for success and immediate punishments for failure. Mr. Fast Gun was widely respected in his company as a man who always let you know where you stand and for giving credit where it was due. Managers working for him were richly rewarded with large bonuses if they achieved the results that were expected. Those who failed to achieve expected results were dismissed.

Decisives win the respect and admiration of others by being

honest, forthright, and aboveboard. They shun corporate politics, at least insofar as scheming behind closed doors is concerned. If they are against you, you and everyone else will know it because they express it.

People can count on decisives to do what they say they will do when they say they will do it. They are results oriented. So when situations need fixing fast, decisives are often the people to send in to do the fixing.

Our example of Joe is a case in point. Even his critics had to admit that Joe got things done. When he hired on with the company, he took over a function that had been neglected for years and was badly in need of fixing. Joe quickly introduced simple, easy-to-follow rules and policies everywhere. Chaos and disorganization were eliminated. Joe turned the situation around.

Not surprisingly, this results orientation often earns decisive managers reputations as "turnaround artists," especially when situations have become messy out of sheer neglect. But it also can earn them reputations as intolerant and even ruthless. And when situations change to the point where new solutions must be found for new problems, they run the risk of being seen as rigid and unreasonable.

Joe again provides an example. He insisted on adherence to rules. Those who violated policies were fired—no exceptions. This frustrated other managers who, from time to time, felt that extenuating circumstances and unique business considerations should have been considered before taking action. Following a merger, Joe came to be seen as a bully when he insisted that newly merged units immediately adopt the rules and policies that he developed years before. Managers in those units deeply resented that he showed little inclination to take into account the unique qualities of their businesses and organizations before imposing his rules.

As you have seen in the previous discussion, the decisive style has a variety of both strengths and weaknesses. This is true with all the decision styles. The advantages and disadvantages of the decisive style are illustrated in Table 2.1.

The Flexible Style

Johnny Carson represents the characteristics of the flexible style. He is easygoing, personable, nonconfrontational, and jumps around

Table 2.1. The Decisive Style.

Advantages	Disadvantages
Fast	Rigid
Consistent	Avoids change
Reliable	Avoids complex data
Loyal	Inflexible
Orderly	Shortsighted
Obedient	Low empathy for others

from one unrelated topic to another. In the business world, J. Paul Getty and Donald Trump represent flexible styles, as does FDR from the political area.

Flexible managers use moderate levels of information, as do decisives, but they interpret the same information in different ways at different times depending on the point of view they currently hold. Flexibles value action, speed, adaptability, and variety, using these attributes to gain acceptance from others and consequently a sense of security for themselves. By being able to quickly adapt to the expectations of others, flexibles almost guarantee acceptance. It's like the politician who says, "Some of my friends are Republicans, and some are Democrats, and by God, I'm going to stick with my friends."

In our study of precious metals traders, flexibles were most effective in dealing with the market dynamics that required on-the-spot decisions in response to rapid price fluctuations. Their willingness to accommodate the wishes of others also gives them the advantage as campaigners for political office in communities consisting of constituents with diverse needs and interests. Being able to see things from many different perspectives allows flexibles to select the interpretation most appropriate for the group they are currently interacting with, but still shift to another point of view if people or circumstances change.

Flexibles prefer not to plan, because planning makes them feel hemmed in, trapped, and unable to exercise options. Flexibles often use their intuition to "play it by ear." They are like travelers on summer vacation who would rather buy one-way tickets to Europe and "wing it" than purchase guided tour packages that promise to help them plan every minute of their time from departure until return. Their motto might be, "If it feels good, do it."

As managers, flexibles pursue many goals. Their objectives, however, often reflect what they think others want; therefore, like some politicians, they frequently change direction depending on who is present. This tactic is designed to provide acceptance rather than consistency or advocacy.

Flexibles prefer loose, fluid organizations with little structure and few rules. They are comfortable with fluidity and lack of structure because it gives them the ultimate ability to exercise their creativity and adaptability. They dislike structure and rigid rules and regulations, preferring to adapt as the situation evolves.

In contrast to decisives, flexibles prefer vaguely defined jobs that allow them to deal adaptively with situations as they arise without worrying about stepping on someone else's turf. Flexibles often work effectively in jobs such as sales or fashion design that permit or even require them to exploit changing circumstances and to express themselves freely.

In Chapter One's introductory vignette, it isn't surprising, then, that Joe's flexible boss, Dave, objects to Joe's attachment to uniform rules and policies, simple as they are. Dave's inclination is to permit wide latitude to operating units to decide for themselves on policies affecting their operations. Dave's approach to the development of corporate policy is to form task forces consisting of representatives from operating units who were charged with the responsibility of formulating policy recommendations. This, he feels, avoids the problems of "straightjacket" rules that are never truly accepted and that ignore the peculiarities of situations calling for decisions.

Like decisives, flexible managers prefer brief, concise communications and reports and dislike long-winded discussions and analyses. However, they also prefer a variety of briefly stated solutions from which they can choose. This contrasts sharply with the decisive's preference for a single solution.

Flexibles also like spontaneous interaction between people. Their decisions are based on participation that takes into consideration both the needs and feelings of everyone concerned. Since all people involved in a decision seldom completely agree, flexibles must move fast and tactfully to "stick with their friends" when they hold varying opinions. Their adeptness at shifting perspectives rapidly helps them accept the most recent idea in the discussion.

As managers, flexibles win points and influence through popularity and charm. Their influence is reinforced by using positive incentives and by staying in touch with the feelings and needs of their subordinates. They often gain additional acceptance and popularity by allowing subordinates to participate actively in decisions.

William Durant is a good overall example of a flexible manager. He built several companies, but he is best known as the builder of General Motors. Durant's values displayed highly flexible patterns. His goals and plans were in a constant state of change. He was exceedingly concerned with sales volume—a short-term measure of results as compared with longer-term reports of profits.

Durant made decisions through intuition and flashes of insight, even though some of his more hierarchic successors, like Alfred Sloan, felt that his decisions were often hasty and based on inadequate data analysis.

Durant did not make formal plans, and he was even less concerned with controlling than with planning. He did not see how accounting would help production. He was opposed to inventory control because it was constraining. Durant ran a loose organization and delegated extensively to his subordinates; however, he reserved final decision-making power for himself.

Durant's behavior illustrates several of the advantages and disadvantages typically manifested by managers with flexible decision styles. He was spontaneous, adaptable, and responsive to short-run changes. These very qualities set the stage for one of the most successful companies in U.S. history. On the other hand, Durant's lack of long-range planning, concern with outward appearance, and lack of, or hasty, data analysis, sometimes led to oversights and problems. The advantages and disadvantages of the flexible style are summarized in Table 2.2.

The Hierarchic Style

We now turn from the fast-paced, satisficing decisives and flexibles to the maximizing styles, which are prone to long-range planning and complex data analyses. The hierarchic style makes maximum

Table 2.2. The Flexible Style.

Advantages	Disadvantages
Intuitive	Short-term perspective
Fast	Lack of planning
Adaptable	Inconsistent
Entrepreneurial	Short concentration
Likeable	Resists structure
Opportunistic	Unreliable

use of all information to reach the best single conclusion. Howard Hughes acted in a truly hierarchic fashion by tracing everything back to one factor: quality. He made certain that every issue was thoroughly analyzed before deciding on the best alternative for the best possible result. This attraction to quality was seen very clearly in the way Howard Hughes ran RKO Studios. In his classic aviation picture, *Hell's Angels,* Hughes refused to film scenes with simulated rain. Only genuine downpours would do. Similarly, models or mockups of planes were not acceptable. When a huge dirigible was to go down in flames, Hughes had a real dirigible built and crashed it at a cost of a half million dollars.

This quality focus clearly fits the basic aspects of the style: high data use is dictated by the desire to leave no stone unturned; no detail that could lessen the quality of a product is ignored. And once the information is rigorously analyzed—often in quantitative fashion—the resulting plan is complex but highly focused. There is clearly a "best way" to do things. The usual hierarchic plan is a masterwork of detail and tries to anticipate all sorts of possible contingencies.

Here again, Hughes supplies an excellent example. At one point in his career, he was offered a chance to question a senator during a hearing but had to prepare questions in advance. His questions correctly anticipated the senator's responses to the point that the man became trapped in a hopeless box, creating a public spectacle and destroying his subsequent bid for reelection.

In control over operations, the quest for quality is also seen in the hierarchic style. Hierarchic control is often very close both on methods used and results expected. The philosophy that underlies time and motion study engineering, with its emphasis on precise delineation of tasks and physical motions, is quite hierarchic. The assumption is that thorough analysis will yield the one best method of performing a job. Here again, Hughes illustrates the style in an extreme form. He was notorious for trying to control all aspects of an operation—even to the point of arguing with workmen at Hughes Aircraft about the proper way to use a wrench.

Given this intense quality focus, there is an obvious issue of delegation in the hierarchic style. Delegation can be a real problem for highly demanding people who feel the best way to do something right is to do it themselves. As you might expect, at RKO Hughes often ran the camera himself. But this real problem of delegation is a potential pitfall that hierarchic managers must guard against and develop some countermeasures for if they are to be successful.

While strongly tending to control others, hierarchic style people often resent attempted control from others. Hughes spent years fighting control—the censorship, for example, of his more controversial movies such as Jane Russell's *The Outlaw*. During World War II he even resented the FBI's monitoring of secrecy in his aircraft plants.

Because of their tendency to control, it is sometimes difficult to communicate ideas to a hierarchic listener. Trying to communicate to hierarchics as they communicate to you is not the answer to the communication issue. The hierarchic communication style is to wait until most people have their say, if in a meeting, and then to deliver a long, carefully thought-out summary of the issues—as the hierarchic sees them—with a proposed solution as the finale. There is also a great delight in elaborately staged debates, as long as personal attacks are avoided. There is a strong emphasis on an orderly presentation—stating a problem, its background, relevant studies, data, and finally a solution.

However, if one tries a hierarchic presentation on another hierarchic, the result is often total noncommunication. There must indeed be evidence of thoughtful definitions and research data—it is only through demonstrating a high-quality thought process that you gain respect. If your presentation is too perfect, however, there is no opening for argument or for adding the listener's viewpoint— and there is no engagement of the hierarchic listener.

One good example of this lack of communication occurs at

high-tech board meetings where often extremely hierarchic scientists deliver perfect orations that are never heard by other scientists because no option for argument is given and each one is too busy perfecting his own oration to listen to the other anyway. To engage this style, one method of communicating to a hierarchic is to deliver an almost perfect presentation. Some hook must be included—like an uncertain area or something needing input—if contact is to be made and cooperation established.

In general, the secret of getting along with this style is to build respect based on the quality of your own intellectual processing. Charm and social chitchat are usually not valued. Hughes, for instance, used to bitterly complain that he lost contracts because he did not wine and dine the military brass. He felt he should win based solely on the quality of the ideas in a proposal.

Hierarchics focus on quality and perfection. The ideal hierarchic organizational structure is probably found in the ideal bureaucracy. Ideally, a bureaucracy selects and promotes on merit, has jobs carefully designed and clearly controlled, and uses information maximally to reach rationally developed goals.

A very hierarchic human resources executive, with whom we worked some time ago, provides a good case in point. Previously, he had introduced a new selection process involving elaborate and extensive testing and background checking. After carefully evaluating numerous assessment programs, he selected one that, although very complex, boiled everything down to one "go"-"no go" recommendation on job candidates. If the recommendation was "no go," then the candidate was not hired, no matter how loudly the hiring managers or recruiters who had brought in the candidate protested.

When hierarchic managers find a bureaucracy failing to live up to their rational ideals, and when their formal authority is limited, there is a strong tendency to use individual political processes to attain power "behind the throne." General Gunther, the maximizer who analyzed information for President Eisenhower, demonstrated this pattern. He attained power by becoming the information analyst and filter for the more action-oriented, decisive Ike. Henry Kissinger's career has similar patterns, as evidenced in his roles where he analyzed and organized material for less complex people like Gerry Ford.

Given the opportunity, though, hierarchics are quite willing to move to the top of the organization, as evidenced by individuals such as Howard Hughes, David Rockefeller, Woodrow Wilson, and Richard Nixon.

Because hierarchic managers insist on quality and are inclined to work out plans in great detail and logic, they sometimes find themselves becoming deeply committed to visions of what the future could and should hold. When they are at their best, their plans become challenging and highly inspirational visions of excellence. Because they so clearly see the beauty and logic of their visions, and the strategy for bringing them to reality, they are capable of stimulating great enthusiasm, energy, and support from others. A splendid example was President Kennedy's launching of the Apollo moon program, which became the most dramatic peacetime technological adventure in history.

Hierarchics also provide rational and thorough controls to ensure high-quality output. They emphasize ideas rather than politics and inspire the highest effort in otherwise sluggish organizations by setting high standards that they follow themselves in order to provide an example for others.

At worst, the style can sink into a self-absorbed micromanagement dictatorship that stifles initiative and blocks creativity in entire companies. An example is the F.A.O. Schwarz Company president, who controlled everything, demanded all details, insisted on tight organization, and left notes on subordinates' desks on how to do their jobs.

These disadvantages can be controlled or eliminated by hierarchic managers themselves through the development of self-awareness of their own styles. Considering the strengths of the hierarchic style, we see self-aware hierarchic managers as having a vital role to play in restoring the United States' prominence as a purveyor of quality goods and services to the world. A summary of hierarchic style advantages and disadvantages is provided in Table 2.3.

The Integrative Style

Steve Jobs, of Apple Computer fame, typifies the creative, open, complex, integrative style. The maximal-information-seeking, consensus-

Table 2.3. The Hierarchic Style.

Advantages	Disadvantages
High quality	Overcontrol
Thorough	Lack of delegation
Precise planning	Resists others' influence
Logical	Overinvolved in details
Inspirational	Rigid
Good follow-through	Argumentative

seeking decision style of John F. Kennedy during the Cuban missile crisis is another example.

Like hierarchic managers, integratives use masses of information, but they generate as many solution alternatives as possible. Integratives habitually produce a wide variety of possible interpretations of information about situations simultaneously. This differentiates them from flexibles, who also generate a variety of interpretations but do so sequentially, one after the other, based on limited information. Contrast the research biochemist trying to integrate all available information into a wide variety of possible new drug compounds in hopes that one will result in a cancer cure, with a floor trader buying and selling stocks during a volatile market on Wall Street.

Integrative managers value exploration and creativity. Some managers with different styles may see them as indecisive and unable or unwilling to meet deadlines. But this doesn't much deter integratives from their collection of more, and more varied, information to add to their already comprehensive store of information.

Integratives generate long-range plans based on detailed analyses of data, but their plans are constantly being altered and revised, especially as situations change. This causes frustration for the nonintegrative managers with whom they work, who become irritated with their apparently greater interest in thinking and analyzing than in action and follow-through. Although decisions and actions do eventually occur, they are constantly open to change, if necessary.

Consequently, organizations like the Rand Corporation have been established to allow integrative thinkers an open and empathetic environment in which they have the time and cooperative support to explore multiple options without anxiety about producing immediate concrete results. Even in organizations less dedicated to creativity, departments requiring levels of information analysis can locate their integrative staff in positions that are removed from the daily firefighting activities of line managers.

Integrative managers are concerned with numerous personal and organizational goals, which they often try to make compatible. Several goals are often pursued simultaneously, which may have ramifications for the person, the organization, and other entities outside of the institution. Consequently, integrative styles are often exhibited by philanthropists, who must consider the effects of their decisions not only on their own personal sense of contribution but also on the organization receiving the gifts, on those who did not, and on various related components of society.

Integratives do not like being limited in rigid, hierarchical organizations, preferring relatively loose, fluid environments that can be adapted to the demands of changing circumstances. The matrix organization structure found so frequently in aerospace companies fits these requirements because it emphasizes both team process and rotating job assignments.

Preferred communications for integratives are long and elaborate, with quite involved discussions. Brief reports are shunned in favor of complex analyses from many points of view to generate a wide variety of possible conclusions. For example, President Kennedy preferred the reams of complex data presented by Secretary of Defense Robert McNamara so that he could review decisions and be sure no alternatives were overlooked.

President Kennedy provides a particularly interesting example of what appears to be a style shift during his administration. During his early political career and the beginning of his administration, Kennedy's behavior appeared quite hierarchic. But in the later portion of his presidency, particularly after (perhaps because of) the Bay of Pigs fiasco, he showed the typical integrative preference for advisory committees and consensus decision processes that bring many, many conflicting, points of view to bear on problems and generate numerous ideas for potential courses of action. This integrative process may have been a primary contribution to the success of the Cuban missile crisis decision.

Kennedy's increasingly integrative communication preferences contrast sharply with those of his predecessor, Eisenhower. Ike's preference was to have his staff screen out superfluous information for him by preparing highly summarized reports on issues, preferably with action recommendations.

Integratives develop considerable power and influence because of their information-processing habits and the confidence others have in their expertise and breadth of vision. Because their broad "peripheral vision" leads them to notice things that others ignore or dismiss as irrelevant, they frequently are able to quickly develop a revised strategy when a situation changes unexpectedly. This makes the integrative manager indispensable in rapidly changing situations.

As managers, integratives want peers and subordinates to participate in decisions. Feelings, facts, and opinions are all equally admissible as information to be taken into account. Consequently, other people become willing to contribute their feelings, facts, and opinions because of the integrative manager's openness and empathy.

Thomas Edison's approach to decision making is a good example of the integrative decision style. Valuing information and variety, he read voraciously. As a child, he read the entire local library from A to Z. His diverse knowledge was used productively as he integrated different pieces of information to reach new and innovative conclusions. Much of his creativity was generated by his need to explore the unknown, and this led to a vast array of inventions from light bulbs to cameras. Edison was very influential, not only because of his tremendous knowledge and reasoning ability but also because he valued the feelings and ideas of others, leading them to trust and admire him.

Although Edison is generally regarded as a positive example of integrative characteristics, some of the negative aspects of this style have been alluded to earlier. An example is the integrative's tendency to ramble on and on, which may create listening problems in others, especially decisives, who want the bottom line as soon as possible. Table 2.4 summarizes both.

Table 2.4. The Integrative Style.

Advantages	Disadvantages
Good listener	Ambiguous communicator
Sees big picture	Indecisive
Creative	Unable to meet deadlines
Empathetic	Overintellectual
Informed	Passive attitude
Open	Slow

The Systemic Style

Of the five basic decision styles, the systemic style is the most complex and difficult to grasp. This is because the style combines qualities of both the integrative and hierarchic styles. It is a maximizing style, but it is both multifocused and unifocused. At times systemics appear multifocused and exploratory, and at other times they appear unifocused and rigid. Examples include the apparently scattered detective Columbo, who amazingly puts all his seemingly unrelated questions together to solve a mystery, and ITT's Harold Geneen, who, although much more organized, operated the same way in the business world.

The systemic version of planning is very elaborate, with a heavy emphasis on producing multiple, prioritized, and detailed strategies for dealing with problems. Despite the hierarchic part of the systemic style, the systemic plan may not be very long-range. Generally, the plan has a vaguely stated, overarching goal that may be quite far off in time. But for the near future the plan includes a multitude of very concrete and measurable targets and detailed operating plans for hitting the targets, all of which lead toward that distant goal.

The systemic plan is both unifocused and multifocused. It is unifocused in terms of the single, distant unifying goal, but it is multifocused in that it will contain many different subgoals or targets that lead toward the distant goal and many tactics and strategies for hitting those targets.

Harold Geneen's reign as CEO of ITT graphically illustrates the workings of the systemic style. When Geneen took over as CEO in 1959, ITT was generating revenues of about $760 million a year as a struggling telephone equipment company. Eighteen years later, ITT was generating over $16 billion, employing over three hundred thousand people in 250 profit centers operating in every country on the planet outside the Communist bloc. No longer was the company's business limited to telecommunications. It was into a bewildering array of businesses, including bakeries, car rentals, parking lots, lawn seed, industrial equipment, cosmetics, insurance and financial services, and hotels. This represents the epitome of complexity, both created and managed by a systemic.

Geneen insists that two-year, three-year, and five-year plans should be sketched out but that detailed plans are laid out for the year ahead. These one-year plans include anticipating problems that are likely to occur and formulating plans for avoiding them or, if they cannot be avoided, determining what will be done to deal with them if they do occur. And for each of those situations, backup solutions should be ready and waiting in the wings if the first solutions don't succeed.

For the systemic, information is precious; it's something to be collected regularly and carefully and then used extensively. You must make sure that you get information, even if doing so means that you put in place overlapping and duplicate information collection systems. After all, it's better to have too much information than too little. Few things are worse than being unprepared or uninformed.

A cardinal rule is that you never do anything that might discourage other people from giving you information. This means that you cannot be intolerant of mistakes. You cannot be feared because people who work for you might be tempted to distort or screen out information in order to hide their mistakes and deprive you of the information you need to take corrective action.

The systemic manager questions and probes to find out what's going on. But the questions must not put others on the defensive. You must be like Columbo, the self-effacing and rumpled TV detective portrayed by Peter Falk. Your questions must not send people running in fear that they are being judged. If mistakes in judgment are revealed, they must be used to learn from experience, to find better solutions the next time around. Questions must encourage thinking and contribute to the big picture.

Systemics place heavy emphasis on process and methods. The organizations they design reflect this fact. Usually, they consist of many parts that are linked together in multiple ways. At ITT, for example, Geneen used a combination of traditional hierarchic structure and reporting relationships superimposed with several nontraditional structures designed to produce a steady flow of accurate and timely information between headquarters and the operating centers. Staff members from headquarters roamed freely in the field and were authorized to have access to any operating information they wished to see. They were expected to report any significant information to Geneen and his staff, on condition that they tell operating managers what they were reporting.

Financial managers in the units were required to report all financial results directly to headquarters at the same time that they reported to their operating bosses. Geneen also held monthly general management meetings at which results and plans were reviewed in detail. Often these meetings surfaced problems that would be analyzed in depth and for which solutions were generated.

As Geneen's examples show, delegation is not a systemic's management style. How can you know what's going on if you delegate important tasks and problems to others? Suppose that the person to whom you delegated something important leaves the company before the something is done? What can you do then if you don't know the details of the situation?

Systemics exercise influence by controlling information. Their style leads them to use information to understand situations broadly and in detail. Consequently, compared to managers using other styles, they are likely to know more and understand more about the business problems they face. This gives them power.

Diagrams, maps, pictures, "war room" paraphernalia depicting the marketing campaign or the production process and schedule—any graphic representation that tries to depict the "big picture" in all its intricacies are telltale signs of the systemic style at work. For example, during a project to produce a job profile describing the ideal sales representative for a large automobile company, one of our office walls was decorated with a five-foot flow diagram depicting the entire sales cycle from beginning to end. The diagram was crammed with decision nodes, feedback loops, and alternative strategy routes to be taken in case of many, many contingencies. We had been given the diagram by a quiet and unassuming sales support manager, who when tested later—surprise!—turned out to be a high systemic.

Systemics sometimes get themselves into trouble in the communications department. We have seen a number of cases where systemics were thoroughly misunderstood by their coworkers and bosses. Others may have the impression that systemics have nothing going on in their heads. Why? Because they say little, particularly when in large meetings. No one can tell what they are thinking, so they assume that they aren't thinking anything. Yet if called on, they give a complex and rambling discourse that few can follow.

The problem here is that systemics frequently find it difficult to communicate the complexity that they see in a situation to other people—particularly if the others are decisive or flexible. They try, but the response is usually not favorable, so eventually they give up and keep their mouths shut.

One of the techniques that systemics tend to use to get a point across is to tell anecdotes or stories that in effect are parables. The stories are fascinating, but they test the patience of others who may tune out before the story is told and miss the point.

Systemics generally like to be right. They hate being caught without having done their homework. So when putting together plans, they may fall into the habit of keeping silent about what they are contemplating until they have all the details worked out. This can create real problems if they are working for a decisive boss who may conclude that they are doing nothing at all. This can put them in a real no-win situation. On the one hand, they feel that they must not lurch into a situation and then make a foolish blunder, and on the other, they probably find that their decisive boss shows no appreciation for what appears to be a hopelessly overcomplex plan when finally they come forward to present it.

It doesn't take too many situations like this before systemics begin to become secretive and "crafty." Feeling that they can't get the reasoning across to justify the actions they want to take, they put on a facade and then go about quietly implementing their plan. If successful, they can end up exercising heavy influence without anyone's noticing.

Table 2.5. The Systemic Style.

Advantages	Disadvantages
Sees the big picture	Manipulative
Handles complexity	Information hoarder
Strategic planner	Needs to be right

This can be risky, because if caught doing something that they haven't gotten approval for and for which they are unable to offer an understandable rationale, they may be seen as manipulative, sneaky, or dishonest (see Table 2.5). And, as you have seen, when working with some of the other styles, that could spell the end of a relationship.

To be most effective and to gain the benefits of their style, systemic managers especially need to maintain close contact and communication with others whom they must deal with on the job. This will help prevent them from getting so far out in their thinking that they become isolated from others. In particular, the need to be right must be controlled. Otherwise, they run the risk of finding themselves increasingly socially isolated and receiving only a fraction of the respect and recognition that they may deserve.

Finding the right fit for your own and other's styles can go a long way toward enhancing personal and organizational effectiveness. This section has demonstrated how decision styles match up to different jobs. Later chapters in this book explore how style differences can help individuals plan, communicate, lead, and relate to others more effectively.

3

Style Dynamics

*T*he decision styles of some people are so easy to read they might as well be written on their foreheads. As you read the style descriptions in the preceding chapter, you probably thought of people you have known who seem to be walking and talking personifications of the styles.

On the other hand, the behavior of some people does not seem to fit clearly any one style description. You can see elements of different styles in their behavior. This simply reflects what you probably already realize: most of us have more than one style. Even though we may be in the habit of using one style more than others, we also use other styles from time to time.

Perhaps you know someone who seems very decisive—fast acting, focused, tenacious. Yet you probably can think of many times when this same person has seemed very integrative—contemplative, exploratory, willing to reconsider decisions and try new approaches. As it turns out, using different styles is not all that uncommon; many people adapt their styles to suit environmental and personal conditions.

The shifts in style that people often experience as they move from situation to situation are not random; they follow predictable patterns. One pattern is the ebb and flow of stresses in the immediate environment. In this chapter, we examine these stresses and how they affect our thinking. Another pattern arises when we behave one way when we are aware that our behavior is being observed and another way when we concentrate on tasks and information instead of on ourselves. We have more to say about this phenomenon in Chapter Five.

Environmental Load and Information Processing

On a short-term, day-to-day basis—or sometimes from one hour to another—people shift from one style to another as conditions around them change. When you work under "normal" conditions—that is, when conditions are as you experience them most often—you tend to use one particular decision style most frequently. As conditions change, however, you gravitate toward a different style, and then as conditions return to normal, you shift back to the style that you normally use. You may shift back and forth between these styles many times during any one day.

The term that we use to describe conditions that influence style shifts is *environmental load*—that is, anything that increases a person's sense of pressure. Environmental load factors include frequent deadlines, uncertainty, complexity, and the prospect of important consequences, good or bad. Situations having many of these factors represent high environmental load. High load creates a feeling of being under pressure, and low load feels like the absence of pressure. Table 3.1 summarizes the major factors that contribute to high and low environmental load.

How does pressure influence the amount of information that you use in decision making? Do you use more or less information as pressure mounts? When we ask people these questions, we get different answers. Some people assert that people use less information as pressure increases. Others say that people use more information with increasing pressure. Which answer is correct?

As it turns out, both answers are correct. People use more information with increasing pressure, if they are moving from a low-load to a moderate-load situation. But when they move from moderate-load to high-load situations, the amount of information

Table 3.1. Environmental Load Factors.

Low load	High load
No deadlines or time pressure	High time pressures, frequent deadlines
Simple tasks	Highly complex tasks
Predictable events	High uncertainty, unpredictable events
Unimportant or trivial consequences	Important consequences
Neutral emotional environment	Highly charged emotional environment (positive and/or negative)

they process begins to fall off. Figure 3.1 shows the basic inverted U-shaped pattern that describes information-processing habits of most people under conditions ranging from low to moderate to high environmental load. You most likely would see this pattern if you closely watch your own and others' style shifts.

As you look at the inverted U-shaped curve in the diagram, you can see that most information processing occurs under moderate load conditions and not the extremes of high or low. In other words, a person is likely to give most thought and consideration to an issue when load is moderate. Some people view this upside-down U-shaped curve and say, "Wait a minute. Don't people do most of their thinking when load is low?" This might be so if time pressure was the only load factor. But load is low also when a task has little complexity, little importance, little uncertainty, and no risk.

Most of us have faced tasks that seem little more than busy work or make-work projects or routine chores, such as tying up loose ends on a project that has already been 95 percent completed—especially when the loose ends were left by somebody else. Or we may be asked to prepare a routine report but know from experience that the report will be filed and probably never even read.

If you have faced such situations, you may have found it difficult to motivate yourself to do the work: there was nothing in the tasks to stimulate much concern or interest. When you actually did these chores, you probably didn't give them much thought. You may have merely gone through the motions necessary to get them out of the way.

Figure 3.1. Environmental Load and Information-Processing Behavior.

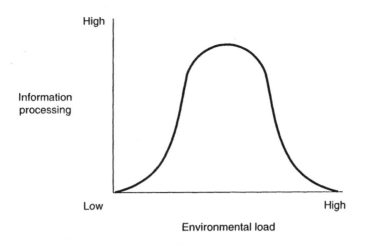

On the other extreme, in high-load territory, tasks are marked by high complexity, uncertainty, importance, risk, and time pressure. Some of these tasks call for a great deal of thought and careful consideration of information. Despite whatever might be required however, under high load you are unlikely to be able to process much information. You may feel overwhelmed, perhaps even bewildered, by the barrage of information and impressions coming at you from all sides. When these conditions prevail, you are likely to grab an item of information and act on it.

Figure 3.2 translates these patterns into decision styles. When pressure is very low or very high, virtually anyone will use one of the satisficing, low-information-use styles—flexible or decisive. Virtually no one is willing or able to use a maximizing, high-information-use style under these conditions. However, when environmental load is moderate, conditions are right for using one of the analytic, maximizing styles—hierarchic, integrative, or systemic. For example, suppose that you are called on to draw up a plan for the reorganization of several departments that might take place next year. This is an important issue and could affect many people, and it is moderately complex because quite a few considerations must be taken into account. There is some uncertainty: the plan might not be implemented. Time pressure is relatively light,

Figure 3.2. Environmental Load and Decision Styles Used.

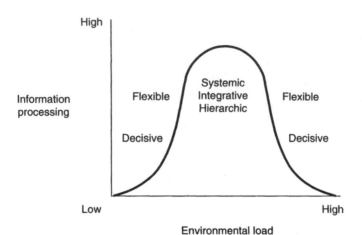

inasmuch as no decision will be made for at least several more months. In this kind of scenario you most likely would use one of the more complex styles, such as systemic. When load conditions get high enough or low enough, even the most die-hard, analytic maximizer becomes a pragmatic, action-oriented satisficer—at least temporarily. Likewise, most committed satisficers become maximizers under the right, moderate-load conditions.

Environmental Load and Focus

An inverted U-shaped curve relationship also exists between solution focus and environmental load. Essentially, as pressure increases from moderate to high, people become more unifocused. For example, we might move from integrative to hierarchic or from flexible to decisive. Under very high pressure, almost everyone continues steaming in the same direction. Peripheral vision decreases to the point where we seldom notice other possible avenues.

Under very high pressure we might abandon one track for another, but we are likely to change directions only if pushed by other people or circumstances. When we feel that the time for exploring new alternatives and other options is behind us, we are most likely to say, "Damn the torpedoes, full speed ahead!" We then have no appetite for creativity; our interest in "getting on with things" is at its peak.

Several years ago we were doing some work for a public accounting firm in New York City. Tom, the CEO, was exceptionally integrative—very conceptual, exploratory, and creative. He had been elected in a landslide vote by the partnership to bring about some needed changes in the firm's strategies and policies. You could talk to him at length about virtually any idea or topic. Nothing was too outlandish for him to consider—except on Friday afternoons, when he transformed into a virtual caricature of the decisive style. Load seemed to hit its zenith for him then as everyone scrambled for his input or approval on decisions that needed to be settled before the weekend or before Monday morning staff meetings. On those Friday afternoons, no one seemed able to speak fast enough for Tom, no one seemed able to recall decisions that already had been made, no one appreciated cost considerations or the need for forward motion. By Monday morning, however, Tom could be counted on to be back in his integrative style.

When load goes from very high to high to moderate, and pressures ease, people generally shift from unifocused to multifocused styles. If a person thinks decisively under high pressure, that person tends to move toward and then pass through the flexible style as pressure eases. In this case, the person who seemed all action and no nonsense might become surprisingly open-minded and tolerant of novel or unusual ideas.

Figure 3.3 shows the most common pattern of style shifts that occurs as people move from moderate- to very high-load situations.

Figure 3.3. Environmental Load and Shifts in Focus.

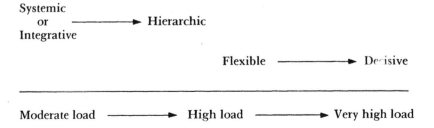

This is the range of load conditions most common in management jobs. Relatively few management positions spend great amounts of time in low-load territory.

Primary and Backup Styles

People use different styles in different situations, but most of us develop a greater affinity for one decision style than for the others and use that style more often and in more situations than the other styles. We are creatures of habit, and styles are habits. Some habits are stronger than others.

The style that you are in the habit of using most often is your *primary style*. The style that you are most likely to use when not using your primary style is your *backup style*. For example, if your primary style is decisive, you might use an integrative backup style.

You are likely to use your primary style under the broadest range of load conditions. If your primary style is decisive, and your backup style is integrative, then you probably behave in a decisive way in more situations than a person who has a primary style of integrative and a backup style of decisive. Even though the inverted U-shaped relationship between load and style holds for both of you, you would behave in a fast and focused, decisive way in the kinds of situations in which your counterpart with the integrative primary style and decisive backup style behaved in an analytic, exploratory, integrative mode. In other words, your "decisive window" overlaps with the other person's "integrative window."

Figure 3.4 shows this graphically. The top curve shows the relationship between styles and load for a person with a primary style of decisive and a backup style of integrative. The bottom curve represents the style behavior of a person with the reverse combination of styles—a primary style of integrative with a decisive backup. The curves are shaped somewhat differently, but the basic upside-down U-pattern describes both curves. You can see that even though both people are likely to behave in a decisive way when load is very high and in an integrative way when load is moderate, the person with the top curve is likely to use the decisive style under the widest range of load conditions and in fact will still behave quite decisively

**Figure 3.4. Examples of Two Different Primary
and Backup Style Combinations.**

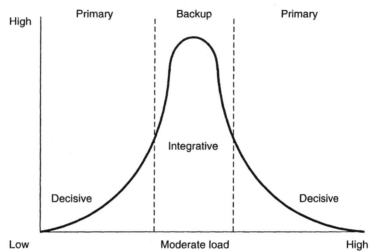

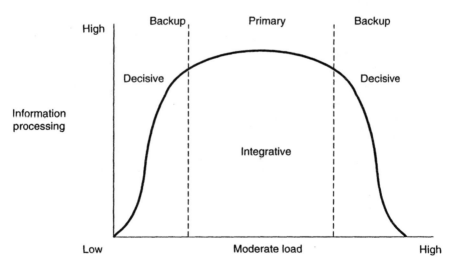

when the person with the bottom curve has shifted into integrative gear.

Developing a Primary Style

How does one person develop a primary decisive style while another develops a quite different style, such as integrative, as a primary style? The answer appears related to the levels of environmental load that we face daily. A person who constantly faces high levels of load tends to develop a satisficing style as a primary style. A person who works under conditions where load usually is moderate tends to develop a maximizing style as a primary style.

For example, suppose that you are working as a supervisor in a mass production manufacturing operation. One of your chief responsibilities is to keep the production line moving steadily. Production delays are deadly, because they reflect poorly on you and have bad repercussions all the way down the line. Efficiency is king. Time is of the essence. This is a job in very high-load territory. The high load frequently pushes you into decisive mode to the point where the decisive style becomes your primary style. Furthermore, because your fast-moving decisive style is likely to be a good fit with the demands of your job as a production supervisor, you are rewarded for your decisive behavior, which reinforces your decisive style even further.

Suppose that because of your top-notch performance as a production supervisor you come to be seen as a "good guy" by the bosses upstairs. What happens to good guys? Why, they get promoted, of course. You are promoted to the rank of manager, but not of production operations; that job wasn't open. Instead, you were made manager of manufacturing engineering, with four supervisors reporting to you.

Now things are different. You aren't on the firing line quite as often. Whereas before you were making instant decisions about how to keep things moving, now you establish policies for ensuring that new designs can be manufactured according to high quality standards and within reasonable cost constraints. You find yourself looking at designs that are on the drawing boards or CAD screens months or even years before they will ever see the shop floor.

This job is definitely in moderate-load territory. What happens to your heavily reinforced decisive style? The chances are that you will continue using your decisive style but with decreasing frequency. If you are more self-aware than the average person, you may see clearly that your new job calls for a different way of dealing with decisions and problems. Even so, your old style habit that was so heavily reinforced probably will keep you in the decisive style in some situations where a more maximizing style would be more appropriate. Even if there are no really noticeable negative consequences in these situations, you may begin to feel that things work out better all the way around when you step back and take a longer-range and a broader view of things—when you let things "simmer" for a while and take time to look at some alternative ways of handling problems.

Besides, you don't have anyone barking at you to keep things moving. In fact, your new boss seems to like thorough analyses and a variety of alternatives to choose from when the two of you talk about decisions. Little by little, you begin using the integrative style more frequently. In fact, you notice that even when you go to the grocery store now, you stop more often to read labels and look at other choices, whereas before you simply would have grabbed your usual brand and headed for the check stand.

You have, in effect, developed a new primary style. Looking once more at Figure 3.4, the top curve could represent your styles as production supervisor and the bottom curve could represent your styles four years later as manager of manufacturing engineering. This sort of style change appears to take place relatively frequently as people move from job to job; a backup style becomes a primary style, and a former primary style moves to backup position.

Using Style Dynamics to Your Advantage

Because a person's primary and backup styles often are very different, dealing with the same person in primary and backup styles can be like dealing with two different people. However, without knowledge of decision style dynamics, people often attribute these shifts to unpredictable moods. These style shifts, however, follow patterns that you can learn to read. When people behave in very different ways in different situations, knowing something about the pattern that governs style shifts can greatly increase your chances of working effectively with them.

Our earlier example of Tom, the accounting firm CEO, illustrates this pattern. At first, unwary associates found their heads spinning after a Friday afternoon encounter with an unexpectedly very decisive Tom, but associates and partners soon learned to take advantage of Tom's style shifts. They found that if they wanted to get a quick response to a relatively routine issue, Friday afternoons were the ideal time to see him. At other times, when Tom was in his characteristic integrative style but they only wanted a quick yes or no, they would expect a lot of questions, a lengthy discussion, and possibly a whole new set of issues to investigate. If they wanted to bring up a touchy topic with some risks and unknowns involved, Friday afternoon definitely was the wrong time; they learned to discuss these fuzzier, sensitive issues during early morning, mid-week meetings when Tom was likely to be most integrative.

Different people experience pressure differently. For Tom, Friday afternoon was a high pressure point. For others, Monday morning or any two days preceding a board meeting might be more pressure packed. With a little systematic observation and practice, you can learn to read the times and conditions that trigger style shifts among the people with whom you work. If you factor these observations into your interactions with them, you can anticipate their styles and adjust your plans and behavior when dealing with them. We have more to say in Chapter Eight about adjusting your style to deal with others. For the moment, however, we simply want to point out that better reading and understanding of others' styles and style shifts can give you an extra margin of success in your dealings with them.

You can expect to benefit especially from any insights you gain into your own style dynamics. For example, we recently heard from Jack, an executive in an aerospace firm who attended a decision style workshop about six years ago, that insights into his own style shifts have made a big difference in his career. Jack tended to slip into the flexible style as pressure in his work environment increased, although he felt that most of the time the systemic style he used under moderate load was a better fit with his job as a program manager of advanced technology programs. He learned to manage his environmental load to keep pressures in the moderate range as much as he could. He even had the door of his office moved to the other side of the room so he wouldn't be distracted and pressured by people constantly hovering in his outer office hoping to catch "a minute" of his time.

Jack was interested mainly in keeping himself in his maximizing style. But another person could use the same principles to push himself or herself periodically in the other direction, toward a satisficing style. This could be done by *increasing* pressure or load. If, for example, you find that you sometimes need to cut short an analysis of an issue and turn your thoughts to action, you could help yourself make the necessary shift by imposing deadlines on yourself, making commitments to others about completion times, arranging to reward yourself for task completion, or even establishing penalties for slow progress.

Managing with Style Dynamics

Managers who use their knowledge of style dynamics can shift course or try new strategies as situations change. One of the most difficult things for many people to do as managers, however, is go against tradition. Even when traditional methods are not working well, embarking on a new course of action often means sailing into uncharted waters with an uncertain destination. At such times, it is comforting indeed to have solid guidelines to navigate by. Here is where your knowledge of style dynamics can help.

Consider the following example of a situation where navigating by style dynamics showed that traditional methods were counterproductive. An information services company shifted its strategy and introduced a relatively complex, high-cost software product to augment and eventually replace the dwindling revenues it was receiving from sales of the modestly priced service on which the company had been built. However, the software sales were extremely sluggish, jeopardizing the whole strategy.

Analysis of sales representatives' decision styles and sales records showed clearly that the best combination of styles for sales success was an integrative primary style with a hierarchic backup. However, analyses of previous service sales records showed that successful sales representatives in the past had been fast-moving, action-oriented flexibles.

In the face of slow sales growth and a sagging market in the industry, the company's sales managers were putting pressure on sales reps to increase their sales by closely monitoring sales contacts, requiring frequent activity reports, and placing reps on "performance plans" with thinly veiled threats of dismissal if sales were not achieved within relatively short periods of time.

On the surface, these actions seemed to make sense, right? Put the fear of God in these people. Make sure that they are out there hustling up business as fast as they can. Looking at this situation from the perspective of style dynamics, however, can you see how these actions contributed further to the sales problem? The company should have been reducing pressure on sales reps. The increased pressure pushed sales reps further into the satisficing styles that worked in the past, when they should have been moving in exactly the opposite direction toward the maximizing styles.

Some Common Primary and Backup Style Combinations

Although an individual may have a particular primary decision style, a backup style also influences how he or she works with other people. The behavior of a person with a primary decisive style and a hierarchic backup style is quite different from the behavior of someone whose primary style is decisive but whose backup style is integrative.

Although in our work we have seen just about every conceivable combination of primary and backup styles, some combinations are more common in management than are others. For an idea of how these combinations influence behavior, consider the following brief portraits of several of these combinations. Please note that for convenience we often use a shorthand to indicate primary and backup style combinations. For example, to indicate a systemic primary style and flexible backup style combination, we write *systemic/flexible*.

The Decisive/Integrative Combination

This is an interesting combination because the primary and backup styles contrast so sharply, yet it is relatively common in management, particularly among CEOs. People with the decisive/integrative combination often like to kick around new ideas and keep the big picture surrounding any problem in mind, but their focus is on action. After toying with a few alternatives, they often suddenly land on one with little forewarning and take off with it. At this point, the case usually is closed. If you want to kick around some more new ideas with this person, your best bet is to bring up a new issue rather than trying to reopen an old issue.

The Flexible/Systemic Combination

This is another combination of contrasting styles. Its hallmarks are exceptional speed and fast maneuvering. However, the maneuvering is contained within a larger, grand plan. People with the flexible/systemic combination rapidly grow impatient with long, drawn-out analyses or rambling conversations. The flexible/systemic combination often confuses others who see the person as unpredictable and yet sharply opinionated. Very often the grand plan within which he or she is maneuvering is never fully articulated to other people.

The Hierarchic/Decisive Combination

With considerable justification, we could easily denote the hierarchic/decisive combination as hard-driving. It is a very tough style combination. People with the hierarchic/decisive combination insist that all things be planned and that all plans be carried out. They are highly organized, determined, and dedicated to very specific goals and targets. They feel little tolerance for any behavior that strikes them as vacillating or confused or as indicative of partial commitment to goals.

The Integrative/Hierarchic Combination

People with the integrative/hierarchic combination never lack a plan of action, but the plan should not be taken literally. They see plans as best guesses of what should be done at any particular point in time. When situations change or unforeseen circumstances arise, they adjust the plan or pursue a modified strategy that they have had in mind all along. Although they usually are willing to modify any part of a plan, including strategies and even priorities, they rarely simply throw away a plan and go off in an altogether different direction.

The Systemic/Decisive Combination

The systemic/decisive combination is similar to the hierarchic/decisive combination, but this combination does not have the same hard-driving edge to it. Moreover, the plans developed by people using the systemic/decisive combination are more multifocused and all-encompassing. They want very much to see their plans implemented, but they want them carried out carefully in the right way and in the right sequence. Moreover, they want others to comply willingly with their plans. They often invest considerable energy in persuading others to see the logic of their plans or in leading people indirectly to see things in the same way that they do.

These short sketches indicate how different combinations of styles influence behavior. If you understand the dynamics of your own styles and can detect the style combinations that other people around you use as well as the circumstances that trigger their style shifts, you will be exceedingly well prepared to excel as a manager. As you will see in Chapter Four, however, reading people's styles can be tricky unless you have the opportunity to see them (or at least hear about them) working and interacting with people in a variety of situations.

4

The Dynamics of Role Styles
and Operating Styles

We were waiting for Bill in his office when he arrived for our meeting. As he entered the room, we noticed the easy self-assurance and sense of command that he carried with him, even though he had been promoted to president of this subsidiary of a much larger company only six months previously. The company had fallen on hard times in recent years. Many felt the company was adrift in increasingly stormy seas. Bill's predecessor had the reputation of being a loner, a "bean counter" who had kept close to his chest his plans for reviving the company—if he had any, which most people doubted.

Bill, on the other hand, was seen as just what the company needed. We already were impressed by the fact that just about every manager we interviewed—and this included almost all of the key players—had independently described Bill as a charismatic leader. "Bill knows what we should be doing, and he's not afraid to stand up and say exactly what it is," we were told. "He's clearly confident that we are going to succeed here," said another. "Bill gets us excited. He's so sure of himself and of us," echoed another manager. Others pointed out that Bill was making important changes. "He isn't afraid to shake things up. People know they have to perform."

"You've got to watch out. Bill is fair, but he doesn't tolerate stupidity or excuses."

Bill joined us at his small conference table where we were seated. Everything about him looked fresh-pressed and military sharp. His image clearly was the decisive leader, the man of supreme self-confidence—determined, tough, yet fair.

The purpose of our meeting was to give Bill a progress report on the project he had hired us to conduct. As he sat down, Bill smiled, glanced at his watch, and said, "Sorry I'm late. We'd better get started. I can't give you more than forty-five minutes. So tell me, in a nutshell, what have you found so far?" There was no question about it. Bill wanted a short and to-the-point report, highly summarized with highlights and bottom-line implications only—a decisive report. So that's exactly what we gave him.

Bill listened intently. Then he sat back, looked thoughtful for a moment, and said, "Tell me more about . . ." And then there followed a long series of "What if . . ." and "I wonder what . . ." questions. The briefing became a highly interactive conversation that took many twists and turns, far beyond our findings from the project. The meeting broke up three hours later.

That's the way it was with Bill. A former Marine Corps officer, he walked the halls of the company as a virtual paragon of the decisive style. But within his inner chamber, except for the first five minutes and times of extreme business pressure, Bill seldom showed anything but the integrative style. Those who saw him mainly in the halls and staff meetings would hardly have recognized him.

Here again a CEO is showing both decisive and integrative styles. However, in this instance, the distinction is not between primary style and backup style but between *role* style and *operating* style. Understanding the difference between role and operating styles represents a great challenge in the art of reading people.

Disentangling Role and Operating Styles

Before we go any further, let's think about your decision styles. By this point in the book, you probably have formed an opinion about your own styles. Pause for a moment, and jot down answers to these two questions: Which style do you use most frequently? How sure are you about your answer to the preceding question?

After you jot down your answers, set them aside. They later may lead you to some revealing and surprising insights into your own styles. By the way, how long did it take you to decide about your style? Make a note about that, too.

At this point, the style you identified as the one that you use most often is likely to correspond more closely to your role style than to your operating style. On the other hand, how sure you are about your answer, and how long it took you to reach it, are likely to point to your operating style more accurately than the particular style you identified. We will have more to say about this distinction later.

A person's role style is the style that he or she uses when conscious of the need to create a favorable impression. For this reason, we often use the term *public style* interchangeably with *role style*. For example, a person is in role style when making a speech, when making an important formal presentation, or when delivering a briefing in a staff meeting. This is when the person attempts to behave as he or she believes one should behave.

A person's operating style, on the other hand, is adopted naturally when the individual is least self-conscious or self-aware and is focused on a decision that must be made or on a task immediately at hand.

When Bill marched into his office in the decisive mode, he was in role style. But as he listened to our report and began thinking about our findings, his awareness of his position and his motivation to project a favorable image as CEO began to fade. His attention shifted from himself and us to the problem and issues that we were discussing. As his focus of attention shifted, he moved out of his role style and fell naturally into his integrative operating style.

Bill is in no way unusual. A person's role style and operating style often differ—sometimes dramatically. This is why we are often puzzled, confused, or disappointed—or perhaps even pleasantly surprised—when our first impressions of other people turn out not to be accurate. It is also one of the chief reasons why interviewing for hiring purposes has such a dismally bad record of success.

Creating a Role Style

Our role styles usually reflect our views about how a person ought to behave. Not surprisingly, these views in turn reflect the norms, rules, and standards of the social environments in which we live and work. We learn our role styles from other people who are influential in our lives.

Consequently, when we want to create favorable impressions with other people, we tend to rely on our previously acquired views about good behavior. These views start affecting our behavior and actions when we become aware of the need to do something "the right way." The presence of other people who might evaluate our behavior sparks this awareness.

When people meet for the first time, or when they deal with others in formal circumstances, they quite naturally want to create favorable impressions of themselves. This is when they are most concerned about, and aware of, the quality of their relationships with other people. Even though the impression that they project at these times may be quite different from the one they project when they are less aware of their image and behavior, they are not "faking it" with people; they simply are behaving as they feel they should behave.

Most of us are scarcely aware of the "shoulds" and "oughts" that color our role styles. We tend to carry around notions about how we ought to behave, but we seldom consciously examine them. Even though we may not be aware of these notions, they directly influence how we act when we are aware of the need to project a favorable image or merely to do a good job in our own eyes.

Role style behavior is not insincere behavior. As far as those acting in role styles are concerned, they are only "acting natural" and merely doing what comes naturally when the spotlight shines. Most of us are unaware that we behave differently from one situation to another. We may be completely unaware that what comes naturally when we feel the spotlight on us may differ radically from what comes naturally when we are unconscious of the effect of our actions.

Shifting Between Role and Operating Styles

As you might guess, most people are unaware of when they move from role style to operating style or from operating style to role style. To shift from role to operating style, a person simply needs to feel unconcerned for the moment about how his or her relationship with another person is faring. Even when a person behaves in two different ways within a short time span, he or she is unlikely to be aware of that fact. It is not that people think they are behaving the same way as always when they are in operating style; they simply are not thinking about how they are thinking or coming across.

When Bill began to be involved in our briefing, he was psychologically "rolling up his shirtsleeves" and going to work without paying attention to himself, his position, or to his relationship with us. This moved him into his operating style.

The same is true for you. When you feel in any way that other people are attending to you and your behavior, your tendency will be to adopt your role style. As the attention moves from you to other people, things, or issues, you will tend to slip into operating style. You are most likely to be in your operating style when you are working alone or with people with whom you are comfortable and familiar.

Self-Perception, Role Styles, and Operating Styles

From what has been said thus far, you may have the impression that a person's role styles and operating styles always differ, but this is not always the case. Some individuals' role styles perfectly match their operating styles. These people see themselves with unusual clarity. But they are the minority. For most of us, clear self-perception is a goal yet to be achieved.

Earlier in this chapter, we suggested that you write down the style that you believe you use most often, how sure you are about your choice, and how long it took you to make up your mind about that choice. We said that your answers would provide clues to your styles, but not necessarily in the way that you might expect them to. Let us explain.

As we discuss in the next chapter, our decision style assessments are designed to identify both role styles and operating styles. Over the years, we have conducted many assessments. Consequently, we have accumulated a database consisting of thousands of style assessment results.

Many of the assessments were done for training purposes, usually in a workshop that introduced people to the dynamics of decision styles before we gave them feedback on their assessment results. Once we make a presentation on decision styles, we ask people to identify their own styles—much as we did with you earlier in this chapter. Time and again, we find that the answers people give correspond more closely to their role style scores (determined by our style assessments) than to their operating style scores. When we ask people to identify another person's style, however, answers tend to correspond to the person's operating style scores—particularly when the person is well known by those who are asked to describe his or her decision style.

Operating Styles: Looking at One's Deeper Self

If you are like most people, your role style is part of your self-image. You see your role style but are much less likely to recognize your own operating style. People who work with you, however, do see your operating style.

We believe that perceiving one's own operating style is important. Most of us are in operating style as much and even more than we are in role style. Yet the style scores in our database indicate that not only are we blind to our operating styles but we also tend to systematically misperceive our operating styles.

Recently, we statistically analyzed the relationships between role style scores and operating style scores for a sample of people we assessed over a two-year period. The correlations between role style scores and operating style scores were very small—that is, if you identify a person's role style, you still know very little about that person's operating style.

Nevertheless, even though the operating style and role style correlations were small, they did show some interesting—and surprising—patterns. Here is what we found when we looked at the data to determine how people with different operating styles see themselves:

> People with decisive operating styles are most inclined to see themselves as integrative and least inclined to see themselves as decisive.
>
> Operating flexibles tend to see themselves as decisive. Compared to people with any of the other operating styles, they are least likely to see themselves as flexible.
>
> Operating hierarchics tend to see themselves as flexible, although they aren't very sure about this.
>
> People with integrative operating styles are pretty certain that they are not integrative, but beyond this they are not very sure about their styles.

We found that if you feel sure that you know your style, you are most likely to have a decisive operating style—that is, unless you are sure that you are decisive. People who are convinced that they are decisive are most likely to have a flexible operating style.

Although we talk more in the next chapter about assessing your styles and other people's styles, you can use these findings to roughly identify your role and operating styles. For example, when earlier in the chapter we asked you to jot down the style you believe you use most often, if you were absolutely convinced that your style is integrative, you instead are most likely to have a decisive operating style. Nonetheless, at least you are likely to be right about your role style. It is likely to be integrative.

People in general have a slight tendency to systematically misperceive their styles. As yet we have been unable to discover an adequate explanation for this.

We don't know why people who see themselves as using one style are most likely to have nearly opposite operating styles. One possible reason is the need people have for balance and wholeness in their self-image. Because many of us like to think that we embody all the good qualities of all styles, perhaps we "make up" for qualities missing in operating styles by "putting" them into role styles.

For instance, although operating decisives may be very stubborn, they may wish they were more flexible (a good thing) and so stress it in their role styles. The fact that, in general, people who are convinced that they know their styles turn out to have decisive operating styles does make sense. Being certain about things is a decisive trait. Despite these possible correlations, however, you should keep in mind that role and operating style relationships generally are weak no matter which way we look at them.

Origins of Role and Operating Styles

The two types of style often differ because they stem from different sources. Role style is heavily influenced by both national and organizational cultures. Operating style most often reflects the task demands of a particular job.

Culture determines role style because culture very strongly establishes your values or what you think right behavior should be. Culture is a rich source of the oughts and shoulds that you carry in your head and that guide your behavior. These cultural forces are strongest when circumstances force you to become aware of how you should act. It is usually when you are in formal communication settings that you are most sensitive to the cultural values you work with. You are aware that if your behavior deviates from the cultural norm, your communication is likely to fail.

It is not yet clear what type of culture most strongly affects role style. For some people, national culture has an overpowering effect; for others, organizational culture outweighs national factors. For instance, we have noticed that a very strong national culture favors the hierarchic style in Japan, whereas Americans seem more sensitive to diverse organizational cultures. We have worked in companies with very strong decisive cultures—so strong that employees carried this culture with them out of the workplace, even when temporarily assigned to work in other organizations with integrative cultures. We also have seen highly focused organizational cultures, in each of the main styles, where the strength of employees' role style scores in the culturally preferred style correlated powerfully with the number of years in the firm. In one study we found that over a period of a few years, company socialization had reduced a highly diverse set of role styles among new hires to a very homogenous pattern.

The degree of cultural impact on role style seems to depend on how persuasive, consistent, and powerful national or company cultures are. We suspect that where national cultures are long established, very homogenous, and very strongly felt and national pride is high, national cultures are vital in influencing role style.

Where societies have diverse, pluralistic values or are developing new values, national cultures may have a weaker impact. The same may be said for organizational culture. If the organization is ingrown (that is, promotes from within), engages in frequent socialization (orientation, training, a company newspaper), is a successful player, and has a fairly focused, singular product or service, company culture can be very potent. Where products and services are very diverse, training is weak, and people are going in and out of jobs constantly, the company culture is weak.

Finally, we note that many people try to serve many masters. The result may be a pattern where three and even four role styles are exhibited by a person.

The driving forces behind operating style are subtle. Thought processes are constantly being shaped by the tasks you perform—often without any conscious awareness on your part. For instance, it is known that doing dull, routine tasks produces a profoundly depressing effect on one's thinking and diminishes the capacity to handle change or complexity. Conversely, doing varied or complex work seems to create greater complexity of thought process. This effect may even be reflected in the structure of the brain itself (Kohn and Schooler, 1981; Brousseau, 1984).

We see operating style as reflecting the cumulative effects of your task history. It is affected by education, which provides you with content in the way of knowledge and also gives you intellectual skills that affect operating style. We continually see operating style differences relating to level of education and type of education. For example, college education generally induces multifocus thinking.

Work also alters operating style. We believe that the four factors in environmental load can strongly affect operating style. Time pressure and information complexity can transform operating style, and so can uncertainty and the emotional demands of a job. We have seen repeatedly how changing a job subtly affects style.

As a new operating style is learned, the previous style may retreat to a backup position. For instance, an engineer who was using a hierarchic style as a technical worker and who is now building up a decisive style as a supervisor may return to the old hierarchic style as a backup style. Some individuals develop a capacity to work in three styles that reflect their work histories. Although it is rare to find someone facile in all four styles, adaptive persons have moderate tendencies to use all four styles.

The impact of work on style seems to diminish with age and experience. Our studies show that style change is easier for young people, which follows from the idea that styles are habits and habits become harder to change with repetition. It is easier to change your style when you are younger; it is more feasible to change the job as you grow older. There are, however, exceptions to this pattern. For instance, people with moderate tendencies toward a style seem to adapt more easily than those with strong tendencies. For people with strong style tendencies, a style may become part of their self-definition and may be difficult to change.

How Different Role Styles Feel

Role styles are tied closely to our personal values about how people ought to behave, so when we are in role style we are basically playing out our values. Just as we can sense these values in our feelings about how we should behave, so, too, there are different sets of feelings associated with different role styles. Let's have a look at how different role styles "feel." (Incidentally, as far as we can see, the systemic style is strictly an operating style and not a role style. So we don't comment on what feeling systemic is like.)

Feeling Decisive

Many people who have decisive role styles have picked up the idea that speed is a very good thing. Being slow and hesitant is bad; being able to respond quickly is good. Very often, the assumption is that speed is a sign of intelligence—of being quick witted. So, of course, good people have their wits within easy reach.

If your role style is decisive, you want to come across as a person who can state a clear point of view quickly. Very likely, you are a believer in the KISS principle—keep it short and simple. The last thing you want is to be caught in a situation where you find yourself hemming and hawing, unable to voice a clear opinion or respond speedily to a question.

As the KISS dictum demands, you must respond rapidly, and you must be able to deliver your message in as few words as possible. You must be able to "net it out" quickly. If you get too wordy, and if you get into a lot of depth and detail, then you are violating the KISS dictum. After all, you may feel, if it can't be said quickly and succinctly, perhaps it isn't worth saying at all.

Feeling Flexible

People in flexible role style also value speed, but more important, they loathe debate and confrontation. They want to make a decision and get on with things. Debates bog things down. Flexibles do not like things to get bogged down and "heavy."

If you are in flexible role style, the last thing you want is to be seen as argumentative or rigid. Even if you have strong views, you are not going to defend them with lengthy speeches. For you, it is bad form indeed to be seen as "beating an issue to death." If you find yourself running into resistance, your tendency is either to switch topics quickly, before others get opposing views staked out, or to reach a quick compromise with another person's views. Or you try to lift the tension and "keep things light" with a funny remark or a joke.

Feeling Hierarchic

If you are in hierarchic role style, you are likely to feel that it is very important to be seen as a person who has definite points of view— points of view that you can explain, defend, and back up with facts and logic. To be put in a situation where you cannot justify a position with information, to be caught unprepared, to be unable to answer a technical question will seem like nightmarish scenarios to you. Even worse would be to present a point of view and then be proved wrong by information or logic presented by someone else.

If and when you find yourself in hierarchic role style, unlike your decisive counterparts you place relatively little value on making speedy responses. Your tendency is to think out what you have to say before saying it. Your aim is to impress others with logic and data. This, of course, is just how you expect others to behave if they are explaining something to you.

Points of view that sound like conjecture or mere assertions that are not based on information and logic have little value for you. Rather than keeping things short and simple, you want instead to communicate your point of view along with as many of the facts and as much of the reasoning that influenced your conclusion as you can. After all, that's nothing more than you expect others to do when communicating with you.

Feeling Integrative

If your role style is integrative, you want others to see you as open and creative. Unlike your flexible cousins, you don't mind a little debate. In fact, you find yourself stirring up debate when things seem to be too cut and dried. This brings out different points of view—points of view that may be new and stimulating.

You don't mind when people express views that are different from yours. In general, you want others to see you as a person who sees new ideas as interesting and worthy of consideration. Your tendency is to incorporate a new idea with your point of view to come up with a third idea.

Naturally, you expect others to react with interest to your ideas, so your tendency is to toss other people's ideas back to them with a few new twists. You're disappointed if they seem annoyed by this, as your more decisive and hierarchic counterparts are likely to be.

You value a little friendly debate, but you don't enjoy heated debates in which the participants stake out strong positions that they then defend tenaciously. Instead, you like a game of give and take that ends with consensus.

If your role style is integrative, you have trouble with the decisive's KISS dictum. To respond quickly with a simple response may seem inappropriate and undesirable to you. You don't want people to see you as not thoughtful or as pedantic or overly conventional.

Applying Role and Operating Styles

We have found that people use two very different types of style. Role style reflects various cultural values and is used when one is self-conscious, usually when interacting with important others. Operating style is affected by tasks at work and is displayed when one is not self-conscious; it is the more "natural" style. The two styles are more often different than similar. Both show the pattern of change from dominant to backup style as environmental load levels change. Both are used frequently and are critical in understanding style behavior.

Each of these role styles has its own set of logic and values. If you can understand the behavior of people acting out any one of these styles by recognizing the values that underlie the styles, you can interact more effectively with people who are using styles that differ from yours. You will be able to anticipate how they will respond and why. Armed with this information, you will be able to adapt your own approach in a way that increases the chances that your interactions with others will result in constructive outcomes.

You also will better comprehend the dynamics of your own behavior. Instead of seeing your own and other people's behavior as absolutely good or bad based on whether it meets requirements that you may be only vaguely aware of, you will be able to make reasonable and conscious choices about how to behave to reach productive outcomes with other people. You will be less a creature of habit and more a person of choice. In short, you will be better able to consciously manage your own style.

5

Assessing Your Role Style

Chapters Five and Six discuss how to assess decision style in yourself and others. Understanding your decision style is a bit like observing yourself in a rose-colored mirror. There is a well-documented tendency among humans to distort self-perceptions in a socially desirable direction whenever possible (Secord and Backman, 1964; Miner, 1988). Because most of us would rather think of ourselves as witty, attractive, and influential than the opposite, we need to avoid self-inflating biases when examining our decision styles.

A second problem runs even deeper. Although researchers are far from unanimous, most scientific opinion suggests that we have great difficulty understanding our own unconscious thought processes (Penfield, 1952; Boddy, 1978). Unconscious aspects of our decision styles may be beyond our capacity to describe.

Of the two very distinct types of decision style—role and operating—operating style is most likely to be unconscious. When most people describe their style, they refer to their role style—the style they think they *should* use. The exceptions are when a very strong operating style (coupled with a weak, ill-defined role style) leads someone to use the operating style as the basis for self-

66

description. With these cautions in mind we now look at how you can assess your style.

Assessing Style: A Catalog of Methods

The three major approaches to style assessment are (1) validated measures, (2) the perception of others, and (3) your own self-judgment. The most accurate method of analysis uses the two validated psychological measures of style: the Driver Decision Style Exercise (DDSE) to measure operating style and the Driver-Streufert Complexity Index (DSCI) to measure role style (see Appendixes B and C). Both measures have been tested for reliability and validity over a period of fifteen years and give an accurate picture of style. Each requires about thirty minutes to complete. (Copies of these measures can be filled out and sent for scoring as outlined in Appendix D.) These measures are discussed in detail below.

The next most accurate style assessment method is the judgment of others. For reasons described above, others can often see unconscious behaviors that we do not observe in ourselves. They also may be freer of bias—although others sometimes allow their feelings to cloud judgments. A good procedure is to select several individuals who know you well to rate your role and operating styles using checklists outlined below. You can average their judgments for a fairly accurate view of how your styles appear to others.

Finally we come to self-perception. Despite all cautions, everyone forms an impression of his or her style and the styles of others when he or she encounters this model. Rather than leave this process to a random set of factors, we present below a structured guide for assessing role styles. Chapter Six discusses how to assess operating style.

Guidelines for Assessing Role Style

Your role style today is the product of previous experience. Many experiental factors help give shape to that style. In this section, we lay out a framework showing how various experiential factors link to each role style, and we provide you with cues to help you size up your own style and the factors that have shaped it.

Background Factors

Role style can be shaped by personal background factors such as national culture, class, sex, occupation, organization, and family. Table 5.1 summarizes the probable connection of these factors with role style. For instance, in U.S. culture the preferred role style seems to be decisive for males and flexible for females. In non-U.S. cultures the preferred male role style appears to be hierarchic. There are no clear cultural biases toward integrative role style that we can document at present, nor do we have a clear fix on non-U.S. female cultural role concepts. As with all background factors there are many exceptions to these generalizations, but responses to these factors provide one set of style indicators.

To use Table 5.1 check the style that *best* fits each background factor for you. For example, if you are a U.S. male, put a check in the Decisive column for row one. Non-U.S. females should put no checks in this row.

We have found some affinity between economic status and role style. For example, low economic status fosters a tough, action orientation linked to decisive style. Flexible style seems more common in the lower middle economic class, where slightly higher income levels produce a more adaptive pattern. The increasing resources of middle to upper levels of the middle class can support a thinking-oriented maximizer style (integrative, hierarchic, systemic). The very wealthiest level of society tends toward decisive and can achieve what they want with minimal analysis.

The religion of one's parents is linked to role style. The simple, conventional faiths generally support a clear, uncomplicated decisive manner. Unconventional faiths, such as Unitarianism, or agnostic views are more likely to develop a nondecisive role style. In this row, you can check either the decisive column or all of the other three style columns depending on your parents' religion.

Other parental values have been correlated with role style. Placing value on legitimate authority is an obvious link to decisive thinking. We also find that high income is stressed in homes producing decisive children. In homes emphasizing the importance of

Table 5.1. Background Factors Relating to Role Style.

Factor	Decisive	Flexible	Hierarchic	Integrative
1. National culture	U.S. males	U.S. females	Non-U.S. males	(No score)
2. Social class	Lower or upper	Lower middle	Upper middle lower upper	Upper middle lower upper
3. Religion	Conventional	Unconventional or no religion	Unconventional or no religion	Unconventional or no religion
4. Parent values	Economic authority	Popularity	Thinking and academic	Thinking and popularity
5. Family emotional climate	Strong positive and negative feeling	More positive feeling	More positive feeling	More positive feeling
6. Family size	Small to medium size (2–3)	(No score)	Only child	Large family (4+)
Sum:				
Divide by:[a]	6	6	5	6
Average = score				

[a]Decrease this number by the number of rows in each column you do not use.

popularity, we see a bias toward flexible style. Households concerned with thinking as a value as well as academic achievement tend to produce hierarchic children. Thinking values combined with popularity lead to integrative style. You should check off the values that best characterize your background.

The family's emotional climate factor has been tied to style. In general, a strong emotional climate, in which positive and negative feelings are common, tends to produce a decisive style. A positive climate with low levels of negative feelings fosters nondecisive styles. Here again, check off all three other styles if the climate was positive but not negative. If the climate was neither—that is, cool emotionally—check no style in this row. If no emotional climate description is checked, reduce the division factor at the bottom of each column by one.

Family size also relates to style. The only-child status connects to the hierarchic style, whereas being in a large family relates to integrative role style. (Chapter Six discusses a completely different implication of large family size for operating style; for operating style large family implies a decisive style.) Complex social interaction favors adoption of a fluid, complex role style. Medium to small families foster a decisive attitude. We find no clear connection between family size and flexible role style.

In order to determine your role style score, add up the checks in each column and divide by the number indicated (such as 6). This number corrects for rows that can't be scored for certain styles. If you cannot check any style in a row (in the case of a cool emotional climate, for example), divide your sums by the number of rows in which a style is checked. The resulting means indicate the role style for which your background has predisposed you. This result should be combined with other checklists, as we show you below.

The checklist in Table 5.1 can be used to determine your role style and also to assess other people's styles. If you cannot assess certain factors for others, such as parent values or emotional climate, simply check factors you can assess and divide by the number of factors you have used. For instance, if you can't check off parent values, divide by 5, 4, 5, and 4 in each column, respectively.

Occupation Factors

Certain occupations have affinities for role style. They stress certain role behaviors as part of occupational membership, independent of organizations. Table 5.2 summarizes our present understanding of this relationship. In general, conventional occupations with well-defined work roles, relatively simple tasks, and stable environments relate to decisive role style. We give several examples in Table 5.2. In addition, occupations stressing practical, hands-on action also suggest decisive style. If your occupation fits these types, you probably are encouraged to act decisively.

A large class of occupations comprises a social contact group. These occupations tend to stress accommodation to customers and emphasize flexible roles.

We can make no distinction between hierarchic and integrative style concerning occupation at present, but we list several types of occupations linked to both maximizer styles. A strong connection exists between psychologically oriented work and maximizer styles.

Table 5.2. Occupational Factors and Role Style.

Decisive	Flexible	Hierarchic	Integrative
Conventional occupations (banker, veterinarian, clerical) —	Social contact occupation (sales, entertainment, service) —	Psychologically oriented occupations (psychiatrist, counselor, psychologist, social work)	—
Practical occupations (farmer, carpenter, printer, production, surgeon) —		Investigative occupations (biologist, lawyer, CPA, computer programming, scientist, professor)	—
		Public administrator (school principal, personnel director)	—
		Technical occupation (engineer)	—

Equally strong is the link with investigative occupations that stress analysis. We also find a connection between maximizer style and public administration and technical fields.

To use Table 5.2, locate your occupation in the most appropriate category. If you have any doubts, ignore this approach. This method can be used equally well for assessing your style as well as others' styles, but it should be taken as merely one factor influencing role style. It is not definitive and must be used with Tables 5.1 and 5.3.

Other Factors

Other forces shape role style, and one such force is the culture of an organization. Our research finds that the style emphasized by an organization—particularly by its top management—is a major source of an employee's role style. We have found pervasive role styles in many companies. For instance, in aerospace and other engineering-driven firms, a decisive/hierarchic combination role style dominates. The influence of the CEO even in large firms is impressive. In one very large computer company we have seen how a shift in role style by the CEO from decisive to integrative slowly penetrated the entire management level of the company.

We cannot offer a simple chart on organizational style culture, but using the methods discussed below (Table 5.4) to assess senior managers in an organization can help you understand your organization's role style culture. Table 5.3 can also be used to examine the effect of organization on role style. Several factors, easily determined, concerning company properties are related to role style in Table 5.3. For instance, in the first row we relate company form and size to style. We have found that, all else equal, small sole proprietorships and small corporations (or large corporations with highly decentralized, virtually autonomous small operating units) foster decisive role style. If your company fits these patterns, check the decisive column. Small partnerships tend toward flexible style, while larger partnerships lead to integrative style. Strongly participative units in conventional corporations often require integrative style. Large centralized corporations favor hierarchic style. Check off the best fit for you or a person you are interested in.

Table 5.3. Company Type and Role Style.

	Decisive	Flexible	Hierarchic	Integrative
1. Company form and company size	Sole proprietor — Small corporation — Decentralized large corporation —	Small partnerships —	Large, centralized corporations —	Moderate-large partnership — Highly participative corporate units —
2. Product service	Transportation — Manufacturing (not high tech) — Retail —	Sales — Service — Entrepreneurial —	Financial — R&D — High tech — Engineering —	Marketing — Advertising — Consulting — Real estate development — Computers —
Sum:	—	—	—	—

The second row deals with the primary product or service of the unit in which you or a person of interest works. These categories are self-explanatory and quite broad. If you cannot locate your company's service or product in Table 5.3 or have doubts, it is best not to use this table. If both rows in Table 5.3 agree, the style implication is clear; if they disagree, there are mixed style pressures present.

You can combine the results found in Tables 5.1, 5.2, and 5.3 in evaluating the forces that have shaped your role style or that of another person. If they agree, they indicate a clear pattern. If they do not agree, you can infer conflicting forces (not uncommon). Sometimes a dominant force can be seen among conflicting patterns. For example, background and occupation checklists may favor decisive style, and yet the organization checklist may lean toward integrative style. Unless the minority factor, in this case organization, is central in shaping style, you can assume the most frequent style in the three tables—decisive—is dominant. However, if no style dominates across the checklists, or you are unclear of the relative force of background, occupation, and organization, you should turn to Table 5.4 on self-concept as the best single non-test indicator of role style.

Additional role style issues concern line versus staff work and a position's hierarchic level in an organization. Line positions generally require a decisive style, whereas staff positions benefit from hierarchic style if they provide expertise and from flexible/integrative style if they provide service to the line. First-level and senior managers are often expected to seem decisive (in U.S. culture), whereas middle managers can be more integrative or hierarchic (see Chapter Nine). Finally, entrepreneurs are often expected to be flexible.

The complexity of these influences precludes any simple measure. You should consider them, however, in reconciling the results of background and occupation analysis with the self-concept to be discussed below.

Self-Concept

Although background is important, a second (and more important) approach to role style measurement is via self-image. A number of key indicators of role style self-image are listed in Table 5.4. All these factors show how a person *wants to be seen* by others. To use Table 5.4, review each row and check off the description that best fits you or another person being evaluated. Some factors need discussion with another person if you are evaluating others (such as preferred organization form). Most factors can be directly observed.

In some cases you may see some mixed patterns. For instance, a person may express liking for well-defined roles but also for informal teams; a desk may be sometimes neat and sometimes messy. Try to select the *most* typical pattern for yourself or another in these cases and avoid checking more than one column. If you cannot resolve a choice in some cases, check both columns.

Most of the factors in Table 5.4 are self-explanatory, but a few comments may be helpful. In the first row, *span of control* refers to how many people report directly to a person. The *matrix* system is an organization design in which people report to several bosses—such as a department manager and a team leader. *Rational role assignments* means a preference for objective assignment to jobs based on measured competence.

In evaluating office appearance, caution must be used. Company rules sometimes overwhelm individual role style; if company rules on desk appearance are explicit, a strong role style message is being sent. We recommend that office appearance be included except where it differs from other factors *and* you know company policy has produced the difference. A similar caution may affect personal appearance, although we believe the categoric descriptions here are broad enough to conform to most company policies. For instance, in a company that stresses neat clothes, the integrative role style could shine through by being *somewhat* less neat in attire than a decisive role style.

On the facial and physique factor, some allowance must be made for genetics. We are not concerned with absolute attractiveness but rather with fitness and grooming. The terms describing physique need explanation: a *mesomorph* has a medium muscular build; an *endomorph* has a heavy, plump build; and an *ectomorph* has a light, lean build.

Information storage refers to all forms of storage and not just

Table 5.4. Self-Concept Checklist: Role Style.

	Decisive	Flexible	Hierarchic	Integrative
1. Preferred organization form	A few well-defined roles; clear authority; small span of control	Informal teams; informal power; changing roles	Rational role assignments; clear authority; wide span of control; well-documented formal procedures	Participative management; matrix systems; changing roles and rules
2. Office appearance				
a. Desk	Clean, neat	A few articles/magazines strewn around	Considerable material neatly organized in folders; baskets	Apparently disordered "piles"
b. Decor	Very spartan; some awards or progress charts	Fairly simple; some trendy artistic effects	Complex; bookcases, file cabinets, award plaques	Complex like hierarchic but some non-task-related art, books
c. Reading material in sight	Very little; company brochure	Some magazines on varied topics	Stacks of journals in professional area	Considerable array of varied books, magazines
3. Personal appearance				
a. Face; physique	Neat; strong features; intent expression; good shape; mesomorphic	Focus on looking attractive; relaxed, humorous expression; endomorphic	Thoughtful, serious expression; ecto-mesomorph	Somewhat amused, animated expression; ecto-endomorph
b. Clothes	Conventional; simple	Trendy; aesthetic; casual	Neat, formal, elaborate; status symbols; elegant quality	Less neat; unconventional; creative

4. Information storage (file cabinets or computers)	A few files on current issues	Not much; "circular file"	Elaborate files; well organized	Pack rat; many files; apparent disorder; stacks close at hand for interactive use
5. Formal communication				
a. Listening	Short attention span; wants "bottom line"; eyes "glaze over" if input too long or rambling	Short attention span; likes humor; likes many alternatives	Long attention span; likes to see data; likes organized approach; wants to argue or correct	Long attention span; wants to "build on" ideas; likes long discussion
b. Preferred sending mode	Written summary; charts with "bullets"	Verbal dialogue	Lengthy, data-based written reports; briefing with data slides	Written "think pieces" followed by group discussion
c. Participation in groups	Wants agenda; brief comments; keeps to point; little small talk; time keeper	No agenda; brief comments; frequent topic change; agrees a lot; injects humor	Wants agenda; long speeches; argumentative; cites/queries data; status references; may wait till end to speak	Wants several objectives; long statements; interruption; building on others; looping
6. Formal controls	Impersonal checks; results only	Personal checks; exceptions only	Interpersonal checking system; result and methods	Interpersonal discussion is checking system
7. Relations with superior	Loyal supporter; wants clear direction of goals	Friend; tries to give desired input	Wants to be intellectual advisor; produces data; political	Wants to be colleague; seeks frequent dialogue; new ideas
Sum:				

filing cabinets. Today, computer files are as critical as older file formats.

In evaluating communication, we stress formal settings—such as briefings and committee meetings—where high-level managers are present rather than informal, one-on-one interactions or group sessions with peers or subordinates. Similarly, we are not interested in informal group behavior in evaluating role style. In the group participation row under Hierarchic, *status references* are comments made by a speaker and designed to give others the idea that the speaker can give them special status in resolving a problem. Mentioning one's engineering degree in a technical debate is a status reference.

Formal control refers to overt methods of controlling work, resources, budgets, and so forth and not to subtle methods of control. In the relations with superior row we describe the role the person wishes to play with his or her superior (such as loyal supporter) and the way the person wants to interact with a boss.

To use Table 5.4, check off the best description in each row, and then add up the checks. The maximum score possible is 12 if one style predominates. You may find that several styles have close scores, which may indicate dominant and backup patterns in role style.

In the clearest cases, background and self-concept results agree on styles. When they do not, give precedence to self-concept data—especially when assessing others (or when others are assessing you). If you are assessing yourself and your background does not agree with your self-image, ask someone to assess you or determine whether other factors, such as company culture, staff or line demands, or level in hierarchy, outweigh other background factors. For instance, if Tables 5.1, 5.2, and 5.3 suggest a decisive style and Table 5.4 says integrative, could you move other background factors toward integrative? Or should you get a second opinion from another? The best resolution of all is to complete the Driver-Streufert Complexity Index for an objective reading of your role style.

The Driver-Streufert Complexity Index

Appendix C contains a specimen copy of the Driver-Streufert Complexity Index (DSCI), which consists of sixty self-description items. (See Appendix D for an answer sheet.)

The computer analysis generates scores for each of the four basic decision styles. The scores are presented in numerical form (as Z scores, which are based on a standard population) and in a simplified seven-point scale format from very low (VL) to very high (VH).

The Z scores compare a score for each style to a standard U.S. population. We calculate a Z score by subtracting your actual score from the sample population mean score and then dividing by the standard deviation of the population (a measure of score dispersion). A zero Z score means your score is at the population mean. A 1.0 Z score means you are one standard deviation unit above the population mean (approximately higher than 84 percent of those taking the test). A -1.0 Z score means you are one standard deviation below the mean. A score of .5 means you are one-half a standard deviation unit above the mean, and a -2.5 score places one two-and-a-half units below the mean. And so on.

From the relative strength of the four scores you can detect your dominant and backup styles, as illustrated in Table 5.5. As can be seen in Case A in the table, most people identify with one style strongly (1.5), moderately with a second style (.8), and reject the other two (-1.2, -5). A few people (such as in Case B) identify with three or even four styles as possible role models. Some people reject all but one style (Case C), and a few reject all styles (Case D), which is often a sign of a career/organization change or identity problems. The feedback on the DSCI includes written analysis of the scores as well as the numerical values. The DSCI has been in use since 1971 in its present form. It has been checked for reliability many times and gives the same scores on repeat use. Test-retest correlations are quite good (.6 to .8).

The DSCI has proven predictive validity; it is a good predictor of occupational choice, work success, and attitude toward school. For instance, the decisive score correlated significantly with being a flight instructor in a study of air force officers (Hager, 1977).

The integrative score correlated well with success as an insurance underwriter, and hierarchic scores related to success as a claims adjuster (Driver and Sundby, 1978). In high school, hierarchic dominant students were scholars, whereas integrative dominant students were leaders (D'Antoni, 1973). Decisive dominant

Table 5.5. Typical Role Style DSCI Scores.

Case	Decisive	Flexible	Hier-archic	Integrative	Dominant style	Backup style
A:						
Z score	1.5	.8	−1.2	−.5	D	F
Verbal score	H	MH	L	ML		
B:						
Z score	.8	.5	1.3	−2.1	H	D,F
Verbal score	MH	MH	H	VL		
C:						
Z score	−.4	−.8	−2.3	.9	I	−
Verbal score	M	ML	VL	MH		
D:						
Z score	−.8	−1.0	−.3	−1.5	−	−
Verbal score	ML	ML	M	L		

people were most happy in high school, and integrative and flexible dominant people felt better in college (Driver and Prince, 1981).

The DSCI also has *construct validity*: it correlates well with other personality factors associated with a given style. For instance, the decisive score correlates with high achievement motivation and aggressiveness. The flexible score connects with being sociable, intuitive, and tolerant of ambiguity. Hierarchic scores relate to dominance and achievement motivation and integrative scores to being empathetic, social, and ascendant.

In sum, we recommend use of this instrument wherever high precision in role style measurement is sought.

Although it may appear fairly obvious how other people make decisions in groups, it is also important to be aware of your own public decision style. Your role style is the way others perceive you in problem-solving situations. Their perceptions may not be apparent to you unless you have very close relationships. You can bet, however, that your decision strengths and weaknesses are known and shared among your colleagues.

It is important to your career success and managerial effectiveness for you to know how you come across to others in decision situations. The best way to make this determination is to directly seek feedback from the others involved. If the political climate is not supportive, however, two validated psychological measures are available to provide an accurate picture of how you make public decisions.

Armed with valid feedback about your role style, you will no longer have blind spots about how you are perceived in decision situations. This improved self-perception can aid you in avoiding your style's pitfalls and capitalizing on its strengths, so that you can enhance your decision making effectiveness with others.

6

Assessing Your Operating Style

*G*enerally speaking, operating style is less apparent than role style. A convenient way to assess operating style is to take the Driver Decision Style Exercise (Appendix B). Another approach is to have one or more people who know you well evaluate you using the tables in this chapter. These people should *not* be your supervisors and should interact with you frequently. Using several evaluators helps balance personal biases.

A third approach is self-appraisal. The two approaches to operating style appraisal offered here look at biographical factors related to operating style and allow you to rate managerial behaviors related to operating style.

Biographical Factors in Operating Style

Table 6.1 summarizes background factors that relate to operating style development. No one factor is dominant. Each factor helps shape the style pattern of a person, and each should be taken as though all else is equal (for research on biographical factors, see Driver, Sundby, and Chulef, 1989).

Family size influences style. Large families tend to favor the decisive style because time pressure is high and time for complex interaction with each person is low. Large families tend to be structured and orderly or to generate overload with many comings and goings (called by one large family the Grand Central Station effect). Structure and overload foster a decisive response.

In contrast, small families or only-child conditions focus much parental attention and concern on the child, permitting highly complex interactions. Often there is also strong control. This formula fits the hierarchic pattern. Moderate family size is optimal for flexible or integrative styles because more give and take and less overload can occur than in a large family, yet parental control may not be as total as in the small family.

The *birth order* effect operates on style development. The only child tends to develop a focused, self-oriented style (hierarchic/systemic) that can digest complex information because social interactions are fewer than in larger families.

The opposite is true for flexible style: the presence of other siblings is important in providing the variety of viewpoints crucial to forming this style. The flexible rarely is the oldest in the family because this style stresses adapting to others rather than taking control.

The decisive is often a younger child who learns to take orders in a chain of command and at times passes down the orders to still younger children. The oldest child is likely to be controlling of others and hence hierarchic or systemic. The integrative is not likely to control but advises others and often is the next to oldest or in an older role.

The general conclusion about *parental style* is that like breeds like. Hierarchic or systemic parents tend to foster children in their own stylistic likeness—as do the other styles. Some variations do occur, however. For instance, extremely hierarchic parents can overload a child and produce a decisive and not a hierarchic. Two decisive (or hierarchic) parents who constantly clash on issues may generate a flexible child who copes by agreeing with both parents.

A family's religious *beliefs* are powerful predictors of style. Strong yet simple beliefs such as fundamentalist Christian or Moslem tend to foster decisive thinking. Complex belief systems, such as the Jesuit approach to Catholicism, induce hierarchic styles of thought.

Table 6.1. Biographical Factors Relating to Operating Style.

Factors	Decisive	Flexible	Hierarchic	Integrative	Systemic
1. Family					
a. Size	Large (4+)	Moderate (2–4)	Small (1–2)	Moderate (2–4)	Moderate-large
b. Birth order	Younger	Not only child; middle	Only or oldest	Older (not oldest)	Only or oldest
c. Parent style	Decisive or very hierarchic	Flexible or decisive/hierarchic with opposed views	Hierarchic	Integrative	Hierarchic or systemic
d. Beliefs	Strong and simple	No clear beliefs or strong conflict	Strong and complex	Many beliefs; tolerance of pluralism	Child allowed to form own beliefs
2. Education					
a. Level	High School	Some college (liberal arts); law school	College (science engineering); Ph.D, esp. science	College (liberal arts); MBA	College (science, technical); Ph.D.

b. Type of education	Action/use emphasis; consistent; authoritarian	Action/use emphasis; not consistent	Idea emphasis; very consistent; focus on one area (e.g., engineering); Socratic method	Idea emphasis; varied fields; participative classes; creative emphasis	Idea emphasis; many areas—individual work emphasis; Socratic method
c. Extracurriculars	Few, a doer; team sports	Varied short-term involvement; individual sports; social groups	Leader in intellectual groups; debater	Many activities; government leader; communications (i.e., paper)	Few; intellectual focus
3. Community					
a. Size	Very small or very big city (over 3 million)	Large city (over ½ million)	Medium size (50,000 to 500,000) (suburbs)	Medium to large (suburbs)	Small or medium (10,000 to 50,000) (suburbs)
b. Number of communities lived in	One	Many to very many	One or two	Many	One or two
c. Job pattern	One occupation area, one job	Many jobs in many areas	One occupation; seeks power	Many areas but stays in each 5 to 10 years	One occupation area; seeks to be "expert"

When a family has no strong beliefs or when beliefs clash in family arguments, the flexible style is favored. If many beliefs are expressed in an atmosphere of tolerance, the result is likely to be integrative style. If a child is permitted or encouraged to examine various beliefs and formulate his or her own strongly held, possibly unique view, there is a strong press toward systemic thinking.

Education also can influence style. High school education seems to generally induce a decisive mind set. Decisive people often identify this stage in education as their favorite or peak education period.

College education with a liberal arts focus seems to generate a flexible style. Law school appears to foster an adaptive, case-oriented thinking style that is primarily flexible (except for those specializing in corporation or tax law). Completion of college in liberal arts and social sciences may tie into a more integrative style. Engineering or technical college graduates tend toward hierarchic style. Both flexible and integrative style people see their college years as their peak educational experience.

Multifocus master's programs such as many graduate business school programs foster complex yet diverse thought processes leading to an integrative or systemic output. This is particularly true in areas such as marketing and management. Master's and Ph.D. programs with an emphasis on rigor and focus foster hierarchic or systemic thought, especially in the financial, accounting, scientific, and technical areas.

The *type of education* one receives is as important as the amount. Schools that emphasize immediately useful, action-oriented material (such as trade schools) tend to foster satisficing styles, whereas schools that foster thinking per se favor maximizing styles. Programs that emphasize concentration in a few areas (such as accounting or engineering) tend toward hierarchic or decisive style, whereas programs ranging over many fields (such as liberal arts) favor multifocus style. Consistency in material presented also induces focused thought. Finally, a unilateral, authoritarian teaching style generates decisive response. A Socratic method that involves participation but in which the teacher has the "right" answer leads to hierarchic or systemic style. A focus on doing one's own work is likely to produce systemic or hierarchic style; a discussion-oriented structure favors integrative thinking.

Extracurricular activities during school can affect style. Participation in only a few activities is found in decisive or systemic pasts. The decisive tends to be a doer in a few groups—particularly team sports. The systemic is often a loner, joining only a few intellectual groups. The hierarchic is likely to be a leader, particularly in intellectual groups, as well as a debater. The integrative is often a school leader and is involved in communication activities (such as school newspapers and yearbooks). The flexible shifts frequently across groups, stressing individual sports and social groups.

The *community* one grows up in can play a role in style development. Very small towns with predictable lifestyles tend to favor the decisive style. Conversely, a very large city may provide so much overload (excessive input) that decisives develop to "close out" the noise. Flexible style also is a frequent response to living in a large city. The other styles are optimally fostered by living in smaller cities or suburbs of large cities that provide complex intellectual stimulation without reaching the overload condition.

Moving from one community to another affects style. In general, frequent moves foster the adaptive flexible or integrative styles, and few moves produce the other styles, particularly the decisive. Note that very frequent moves (as in some military families) may produce overload, which induces satisficing style responses.

One last biographical consideration is *job history* (discussed at length in Chapter Nine). Staying in one job (as a doctor or plumber) supports a decisive style. If one stays put but develops increasing expertise in one area (as a scientist or author), a systemic style is indicated. Staying largely in one area but moving up in power levels suggests the hierarchic style. Movement across career areas at a slow rate (such as five to ten years in an area) is indicative of integrative style, while rapid motion across many jobs and areas suggests the flexible style.

To use Table 6.1 select the box in each row that best fits your past or that of a person you are rating. In some cases, you can check several columns in a row. For example, if you had a moderate size family you would check the Flexible, Integrative, and Systemic columns. Add up checked boxes to find the dominant style in your background. Secondary scores may indicate backup styles. As was the case for role style, it may be difficult to assign others to these categories. Discussions may clarify issues. If not, simply delete these categories.

Managerial Behavior: Moderate Load

A second approach to operating style examines managerial behavior. Managerial behavior can be classified according to behavior occurring under moderate environmental load and under high load conditions. *Load* refers to the combined effects of information complexity, negative stress, positive input, and uncertainty in a given situation (see Chapter Three).

The styles identified under each of these load conditions are candidates for your dominant or backup styles. If you spend most of your working time under moderate stress, the style associated with moderate load is likely to be your dominant style, with the style identified with high load your backup style. If you work mainly under high pressure, the style associated with high load is most likely your dominant style with the moderate pressure style your backup style.

The behaviors associated with moderate load are listed in Table 6.2. For each behavior check the pattern that most frequently describes you when you are *not* trying to impress someone and are working under *moderate* pressure (that is, when information complexity, time pressure, stress, positive input, and uncertainty are not too extreme). For example, for the first factor in Table 6.2—occupational task preference—determine the type of work activity you (or the person you are rating) prefers. Which set of adjectives best describes the work that you (or the person you are evaluating) do most frequently? We provide an example of an activity that illustrates the preferred type of work for each style. Put a check in the column that best describes typical preferences when not experiencing overload.

After deciding preferred tasks, consider how projects you work on are structured. Here again, think of how you (or the person you are analyzing) have been able to structure projects according to your preference. A preference for one simple project at a time, which

Table 6.2. Style Perception Checklist: Operating Style (Moderate Load), Cont'd.

Factors	Decisive	Flexible	Hierarchic	Integrative	Systemic
5 Information search	Familiar area: use experience; unfamiliar area: get one best expert view	Collect ideas from several sources; rely on intuition; most recent data key	Familiar area: rely on past procedure; new area: intense, rigorous data collection; become expert	Collect many data in many ways; try "trial balloons" to gather data; no difference between new and familiar areas	Always conducts rigorous data collection
6. Creativity use	Prefer tried and true	Likes quick intuitive hunches; brainstorming	Highly rational attitude may block creativity; infrequent complex new ideas that "fit" bias	Constant, complex, creative idea generation; building on others	Slow, powerful original creative process; self-generated; creativity evaluated by rational analysis
7. Behavior in informal small groups; 1-to-1 interaction	Task-focused; defers to authority; tense; closes in on objectives	Talkative; uses humor; agrees; changes topic; introduces new ideas; brief statements	Sets agendas; controlling; presents data; argues; status reference; long speeches; summarizes	Builds on others; generates many alternatives; seeks others' views; long comments; seeks consensus	Listens to others; tries to guide others to own view subtly; command of data

Table 6.2. Style Perception Checklist: Operating Style (Moderate Load), Cont'd.

Factors	Decisive	Flexible	Hierarchic	Integrative	Systemic
5. Information search	Familiar area: use experience; unfamiliar area: get one best expert view	Collect ideas from several sources; rely on intuition; most recent data key	Familiar area: rely on past procedure; new area: intense, rigorous data collection; become expert	Collect many data in many ways; try "trial balloons" to gather data; no difference between new and familiar areas	Always conducts rigorous data collection
6. Creativity use	Prefer tried and true	Likes quick intuitive hunches; brainstorming	Highly rational attitude may block creativity; infrequent complex new ideas that "fit" bias	Constant, complex, creative idea generation; building on others	Slow, powerful original creative process; self-generated; creativity evaluated by rational analysis
7. Behavior in informal small groups; 1-to-1 interaction	Task-focused; defers to authority; tense; closes in on objectives	Talkative; uses humor; agrees; changes topic; introduces new ideas; brief statements	Sets agendas; controlling; presents data; argues; status reference; long speeches; summarizes	Builds on others; generates many alternatives; seeks others' views; long comments; seeks consensus	Listens to others; tries to guide others to own view subtly; command of data

8. "Body language"	Serious; leans forward; taps on table; consults time piece; few gestures; stays in one place	Shifts posture, position; smiles; many gestures; doodles	Serious; arms folded; steepling fingers; goes to board; stands up; consults data	Leans back; arms behind head; animated emotion; makes random notes, sketches	Serious; writes down notes for self; backed off
9. Small talk	A few polite remarks	Stream of light comments; humor	"Heavy" inquiry on business issues	Creative discussion of new ideas; questions about other person	Long anecdotes; "guided discussions"
10. Politics and peers	Competitive on task results; dislikes politics; few allies	Competitive; very political; seeks allies; does reciprocal favors	Competitive; subtle politics based on problem-solving competence; expert power	Not competitive; collegial; cooperative; win-win view; advances via creativity	Mild competition; more self-contained; use system-building to advance
11. Leadership a. Relations with subordinates	Results oriented; task focus leader; can be "tough"; delegates; expects loyalty	Relation and results oriented; supportive; exception manager; dislikes conflict; social leader	Method and results oriented; task focus; intellectual leader; status concern; quality emphasis	Relation/process oriented; participative; intellectual leader; emphasis on creativity	Process, method, results oriented; likes to see "big picture"; welcomes input but ultimately wants own way
b. Motivation focus	Relies on position authority; may use threat; gives structure	Uses charm, praise, social interaction	Relies on rational analysis, facts	Tries to discover each person's motives and addresses them	Relies on logic, some sensing of and attention to individual differences
Sum of checks:					

is completed before shifting, sounds decisive. Doing several fairly simple projects by shifting back and forth—always doing one at any one time—suggests a flexible style. In sharp contrast, the hierarchic mode is to have one major project with several related side projects. The integrative style executes several complex projects simultaneously with attention fluidly shifting over projects. The systemic does the same except that time allotted to each project is carefully prioritized. Be careful to check off the pattern *personally* preferred, not the pattern required by an employer.

Next, consider the preferred self-imposed pace or the pace you are most comfortable with under moderate pressure. This factor includes how quickly you work as well as how you handle time in planning. Now consider planning behavior. Is short-range (decisive) or long-range (hierarchic, integrative, systemic) planning favored? Is one "best" plan with many contingency steps to take care of possible problems (hierarchic) developed? Do you constantly reevaluate and change plans as you go along (integrative)? The systemic pattern is like the hierarchic but also includes a priority list outlining how many resources to put on each action planned. The flexible style prefers to "play it by ear"—collect resources and react as the situation evolves; it usually dislikes getting pinned down by too much planning.

A good way to self-assess is to recall how you typically approach the situation in question. In planning, recall some plans you have developed at work. Avoid thinking about situations where your plan had to conform to company norms.

In the area of *information search* (that is, getting input in making decisions) we can also see styles at work. The decisive tends to rely on past experience if familiar with a problem or seek the best expert opinion if in a new area. The flexibles' tendency is to collect opinions from several sources, usually verbally and somewhat casually. They then often rely on intuition to give them insights on problems. Hierarchics' search behavior is objective, scientific, and thorough, unless they are familiar with an area. Systemics are always thorough, even in familiar territory; they always suspect that things might change. Integratives like to collect data and send probes or trial balloons out to "see what happens."

Creativity differs by style. The decisive reliance on past successes often blocks creativity. The hierarchic penchant for rational analysis also usually blocks true creativity, although when rationality fails, creative ideas sometimes do bubble up and are accepted if "reasonable." The flexibles tend toward a stream of quick, simple, intuitive hunches with little prior priming; they are natural brainstormers. The integrative tends to work with others over considerable lengths of time to produce complex group creativity, while the systemic builds complex creative ideas more by study and working alone.

Social behavior under moderate pressure also reveals style. In Table 6.2 we evaluate behavior in small groups, and unlike Table 5.4, here we address behavior in *informal* small groups. The hallmark of informal groups is the absence of high-level managers, formal recording (minutes), and regular scheduled time. Decisive behavior in such groups is to stick to the task, quickly close down the discussion to a solution, and sense what the "most powerful" people want. The flexible pattern is to keep things light and moving.

Hierarchics, even in informal settings, like order and analysis. They will argue ideas, exert control, and often wait until all others have spoken, then "summarize" what has been said. They often refer to past experience or attainments to gain respect (status reference). Integratives are concerned with group process (whether all members in a group are involved), with "looping" from one line of thought to another, and with talking as long as needed until consensus is reached. Systemics engage in a Socratic process where they indirectly guide people toward their views or goals.

A more subtle guide to operating style is *body language*—the posture, movement, and expression people use in interaction settings. Most of the descriptions in Table 6.2 are self-explanatory, but a few may require a comment. For instance, when bored, decisives try to be polite but often glance at their watch, whereas the flexible may do little doodles while nodding at appropriate places. Favorite hierarchic gestures are to "steeple" fingers—an analytic signal—or to fold arms—a signal that a debate is coming. Note taking is found in integratives and systemics; the difference is that integrative notes are sporadic and often put up where all can see (perhaps on a flip chart), whereas systemics make notes on a pad in an orderly fashion for their own use.

In the area of *small talk,* operating styles are clearly visible (except when a VIP is present). This kind of conversation is very difficult for a decisive and a delight for a flexible. The other styles convert casual conversation into a style-revealing pattern. The hierarchic gets into a serious analysis of a job-related issue; the integrative explores new ideas; and the systemics either ramble on with some anecdote or work to guide you toward their objectives.

In dealing with *politics and peers,* style is often very evident. Decisives are rather competitive, are often very achievement oriented, but dislike "games" and office politics. They want to compete on output productivity and do not usually build elaborate alliances.

The flexible competitiveness is channeled into political processes. They develop many temporary alliances, building often on friendship and "log rolling" or mutual benefit. Hierarchics play a less obvious political game, usually building political coalitions centered on their expertise or on their solution to a problem needing attention in an organization ("a cause").

The integrative is the least competitive style. Integratives strongly prefer cooperative, win-win approaches and tend to get ahead based on their group skills and creativity. Systemics also are not very competitive; they are often loners who rely on developing their own systems, ideas, or solutions to advance their careers.

Leadership also reveals style. Decisive leaders are task oriented, want to see results on time, and can be quite tough, even coercive, if it is needed. They delegate and are not usually seen as dictators. They rely on formal "position authority" and expect loyalty. Flexible leaders are more relationship or people centered. They are supportive of subordinates and rarely try to control. When things go wrong, however, they may impulsively get rid of ineffective workers. They often lead by charm and praise.

Hierarchic leaders are intellectual leaders who are task focused. They are methodical and oriented toward detail and quality. They believe in "explaining" how best to do anything. They may overcontrol and have trouble with true delegation. They thrive also on status as a basis for leading.

Integratives also are intellectual leaders but lead more by stimulating creative interaction with others than by marshaling data. They are participative and relationship oriented as well as idea oriented. They try to sense others' motives and relate to them. The systemic seems like an integrative leader in method but is actually more task related and more likely to use "pseudoparticipation" in which the group is led to accept their views via long, consensus-oriented discussions.

To use Table 6.2 simply add up the checks in each column. The style with the most checks is probably the one used most under moderate pressure.

Managerial Behavior (High Load)

Table 6.3 presents some managerial behaviors relating to *high-pressure situations.* Imagine yourself under high pressure—too much complexity, stress, success, or uncertainty. How do you typically behave? Or consider how a person you wish to analyze operates under high pressure. For instance, consider in Table 6.3 how time pressure relates to style. Decisives think well under time pressure; in fact, they often create it if it isn't there. They maintain a sense of high urgency. They delight in closing in on the best solution and then sticking with it to make it work. Flexibles also seem unflapped by time pressure, but unlike the decisive they remain "cool," throwing out several quick solutions. They often try to lighten up the situation.

The hierarchic also seems to keep cool under time pressure, often invoking some contingency plan and moving quickly to a solution if it is a familiar problem. Otherwise they insist on analysis before moving—even under time pressure. The systemic is a more extreme version of the same thing who almost never moves fast; even in familiar areas systemics carefully analyze before moving.

The integrative seems most sensitive to time pressure. They appear disturbed, and may react by hyperintegrative behaviors such as endless circling around or flying off in all directions. Their effectiveness seems to deteriorate.

Reaction to strong *criticism* was one of the earliest situations used to assess style (Schroder, Driver, and Streufert, 1967). It gives

Table 6.3. Style Patterns in Managerial Behavior Under High Load.

Managerial behavior	Decisive	Flexible	Hierarchic	Integrative	Systemic
1. Time pressure reaction	Urgent; closes in fast on one solution to it	Less intense; flips out solutions; humor	Cooler; may move fast like decisive if on familiar ground; otherwise still insists on analysis	Seems disturbed; appears to "circle around" looking at many alternatives; goes flying off in many directions	Very cool, slow, careful analytic response
2. Strong criticism	Accedes to authority; rejects if not from proper authority; may get angry	Evades; appears to agree	Argues; uses data to deny; overcome only by superior analysis	Finds interesting; confronts, willing to discuss, to "solve problem"	Seems to listen, willing to discuss; privately needs to be convinced like hierarchic
3. Failure	Attack source; try again	"Quick fix" or rapids shift to new area	Analyze problem; complex solution; renew effort	Call meeting; analyze problem and entire system; redesign system and objectives	Like integrative except objectives stay same

4. Extreme success	Elation; renewal of energy to continue	Pleased, but time to move to new area	Quiet satisfaction; intensified planning; put resources on successful activity	Interesting; reanalysis of whole effort; support for new ventures as well as old	Careful reappraisal of priorities shifting emphasis to high success area
5. Conflict resolution	Gives in to authority; gives disagreeing subordinates orders to take; integrative view	Smooths over; avoids	Gets data from all concerned; determines "best view" and enforces it on all	Gets all involved together; confronts all issues; works until consensus achieved	Listens to all parties; encourages discussion, then reaches best view; persuades all to accept
Sum of checks:	—	—	—	—	—

a highly reliable estimate of style. The classic decisive response is to quietly reject criticism if it is not too unpleasant and does not come from an authority. Criticism from an authority is taken to heart, while extreme criticism from one with no right to criticize may provoke an explosive, angry response.

Flexibles sidestep criticism; they seem to agree; critical comments make little impact. The hierarchic responds with an intellectual defense to criticism. They love to debate and, as long as emotion stays cool, will enjoy rebutting criticism. They accede to superior arguments. Emotional outbursts are met with quick withdrawal by the hierarchic.

Integratives greet criticism with interest: it is an invitation to a discussion. They analyze the "whole situation" to determine all factors involved in "solving the problem." They confront the criticizer if necessary but avoid angry explosions.

Systemics seem to listen and talk like the integrative. Privately they are rebutting the criticism and need to be convinced by solid evidence, just like the hierarchic.

Failure is also met differently by each style. The decisive mode is to quickly attack the problem at a symptom level. They persistently try and try again when confronted by failure. Flexibles also trie for a "quick fix" in the face of failure, but if again unsuccessful they tend to shift their efforts to a new area.

The hierarchic reaction to failure is an analysis of the entire problem. Causes are sought beyond the symptom level. Solutions are often complex. The hierarchic—like the decisive—does not give up easily but keeps at a problem until resolved.

The integrative response on failing is to call a meeting. The meeting then reviews a total system analysis and often results not just in refining the system but redesigning it and the objectives of the system. Thus the integrative may use failure to induce a change in direction. The systemic approach procedurally is like the integrative; systems might be redesigned but objectives are not likely to change.

Extreme *success* can induce style-related reactions of interest. For the decisive style, extreme success produces overt elation and renewed energy to forge ahead. The flexible is also very pleased but often uses success to trigger a move to a new project or problem.

The hierarchic reaction is quiet satisfaction combined with a careful analysis of what the success can mean to future planning and resource allocation. The integrative success reaction is interest. Success means a chance to reanalyze one's whole effort to develop new systems or new spinoff ideas based on the success. For the systemic, success means a chance to reexamine priorities, possibly shifting emphasis to the successful areas.

A final area is *conflict resolution.* The decisive agrees with authority or, if subordinates are involved, takes the "right side" and demands compliance by all parties. The flexible often denies conflict or agrees with others in order to smooth issues. The hierarchic listens to data from all sides and develops the "best solution," which is then enforced for all. Systemics are very similar except that they *persuade* others to accept the best solution. Integratives can get into fairly heated confrontations but work until consensus emerges.

The best way to use Table 6.3 is to quickly check off descriptions that fit best. Because you are looking at operating style, too much "conscious" processing can bias you toward responding with your role style. For each type of behavior, recall how you or another acted in some recent high-pressure situations and check off the best description. Add up checkmarks to find your typical high-pressure style.

Once you have determined your strongest style in moderate and high load, it remains to find your dominant and backup styles. First determine what the typical load level is in your work. If most of the time you operate under moderate pressure with only occasional peaks of overload, then the style found under moderate load (Table 6.2) is most likely your dominant style, and your high-pressure style is most likely your backup style.

If, on the other hand, you work mainly in a high-pressure zone with only occasional relief, the reverse is true. Your high-pressure style (Table 6.3) is dominant, and the moderate-pressure style is backup.

Ideally, the biographical styles indicated by Table 6.1 agree with your perceived operating style from Tables 6.2 and 6.3. If they do not agree, we suggest (even more strongly than for role style) that you either get others to rate the person in question or rely on the

Driver Decision Style Exercise. This suggestion is particularly urged if you are evaluating yourself.

The Driver Decision Style Exercise

The Driver Decision Style Exercise (DDSE) was developed in the early 1960s with aid of Siegfried Streufert at Princeton University. It was the result of intensive experimental studies of decision making. The DDSE presents a small-scale personnel case to the reader with six pieces of information concerning the case. The reader then decides what the case means and how to use the information provided. It is in effect a miniature decision-making simulation (see Appendix B).

The DDSE is computer scored to generate numerical scores for each style. If a person is systemic, scores are computed for systemic style and not integrative or hierarchic; if a person is not systemic, we compute scores for integrative and hierarchic styles but not systemic. These scores can be converted into a comparative scale from very low to very high, which allows one to determine dominant and backup styles. We also can determine the degree of consistency in the responses to detect effects of inattention, fatigue, or disinterest.

The issue of reliability or stability over time for the DDSE has been documented extensively (Driver, 1981). In general, categorization of a person's dominant style using the DDSE provides good test-retest stability (significances ranging from .01 to .001). Scores for each style also have fairly good reliability (correlations ranging from .56 to .64 for a one-month test-retest interval). There is some variation in style over time, but very often this is not random error but predictable shifting from dominant to backup styles in relation to properties of the environment. It has been shown that most style change over a six-month period was related either to a shift to backup style or to a decisive style under extreme pressure.

For instance, decisive people exposed to a complex "mind expanding" graduate school course shifted to more complex backup styles. People with more complex styles generally showed no style change in this course. Conversely, in a very regimented, decisive course program, the decisive styles stayed stable while weaker integrative and systemic styles tended to revert to less complex backup styles. Interestingly, flexibles (and possibly hierarchics) stayed stable regardless of what course environment they were in.

This suggests that style change is predictable given knowledge of environmental pressure and current dominant and backup styles. This result has important implications for training and development; programs can be built to shift styles (particularly from dominant to backup). This is crucial to using style dynamics in the development of managerial careers (see Chapters Nine and Ten).

The validity of the DDSE has been extensively established. Several experimental studies of decision making have shown that DDSE scores and categorizations predict decision-making behavior. For instance, we found in a study of decision making in a NASA-sponsored lunar colony simulation that decisive dominant persons made faster decisions than integrative or systemic dominant persons but that complex styles used more contingencies and saw more connections among issues in their planning process (Driver, 1970).

In a second series of experiments (Mock and Driver, 1975; Driver and Mock, 1975b) we found that in a business game, systemics remained slow in decision time and flexibles were fast. Decisives were slowest of all; the game in its most complex version seemed to overwhelm them (it was *too* complex), and they virtually tuned it out. A study of decisive learning curves showed no gain over time, unlike all other styles. The systemics, although slow, were high data consumers and "aced" the game. The integratives were not comfortable in a structured game but also did well in its complex version. In a simpler version of the game, decisives did not look bad: in fact, they outperformed other styles, particularly the integratives.

As these studies illustrate, no style is ideal. The style that best fits its environment's demands will be most successful.

The DDSE has also been validated in applied settings. In the simple, time-pressured, predictable world of a supervisor in a state bureaucracy the decisive style was most satisfied and highly rated (Boulgarides, 1973). The integratives and hierarchics were either unhappy or unproductive. In another study (Alawi, 1973), integrative and hierarchic styles were most likely to be found at middle management in a high-technology, matrix-structured aerospace firm. In a more traditional, classic bureaucracy (an airline), however, only hierarchics predominated in middle management. Moreover, complex styles gravitated toward complex jobs and socially complex units in a company.

In a study of air force officers (Hager, 1977) it was found that flight instructors had low integrative scores and physicists tested as highly integrative. And in a study of insurance company positions (Driver and Sundby, 1978; Driver and Testerman, 1979a, 1979b) the hierarchic style negatively predicted success in underwriting and claims representative jobs but positively related to success as an underwriter manager. Financial analysts with a flexible style do best in short-range sensing of market trends (Sundby, 1978). More recently, both integrative and hierarchic styles were positively associated with success in computer sales (Brousseau, 1987).

In addition to being predictive of work behavior, the DDSE also possesses *construct validity*—that is, it relates meaningfully to other personality traits. For instance, data suggest that integratives positively regarded complexity and disliked dependency. Decisives liked solving problems but not thinking for its own sake (Boulgarides, 1973).

Another study (Schutt, 1976) found those with a decisive style to be very concrete and extroverted and those with an integrative style to be intuitive. The flexible style was associated with being unconventional and social. Still another study found the hierarchic style to be quite detail-oriented and the opposite for the decisive (Ridgeway, 1977).

Finally, one study (Meshkati, 1983) found marked physiological differences among individuals with various operating styles. Heart rate analysis showed that decisive persons were highly aroused across many levels of task difficulty. Hierarchics were not aroused by changes in task difficulty. Flexible and integrative persons were at low arousal levels in simple tasks and became more aroused as task difficulty increased.

Further evidence of validity for the DDSE is demonstrated in later chapters, but this brief review should be sufficient to document the powerful validity amassed by the DDSE over fifteen years. We strongly recommend its use for an accurate style analysis.

7

Communication
Between Styles

*T*he metaphor of ships passing in the night describes very well the experience of how people with different styles attempt to communicate with each other—although collisions at sea might describe even better what happens on some occasions. The fact that people do things differently is a great blessing of human nature. But as you are likely to have discovered, applied to communication it definitely is a mixed blessing. You can learn a lot from others whose styles differ from yours, and they can learn from you. For this learning to take place, however, understanding and some element of acceptance are required. And therein lies the rub.

People with differing decision styles communicate and absorb information at different rates and quantities and use different techniques to influence others. Watching two people with unlike styles communicate—or attempt to communicate—is a lot like watching a couple attempting to dance the tango and an elegant waltz at the same time.

This image can be humorous—except when you are one of the dancers or even if only a spectator when your circumstances are affected by the outcome of the dance.

Points of Compatibility and Points of Tension

This chapter focuses on communication among peers and associates—people who are more or less workplace equals. Other chapters deal with communication with subordinates (Chapter Eight) and with supervisors (Chapter Nine). Here we look at how the styles interact and communicate and provide some guidelines that can help you to adapt your style of communication to the styles of those with whom you must communicate.

In communicating with others, each decision style has its own strengths, but these strengths can become obscured by negative qualities. Table 7.1 summarizes the positive and negative elements of each style from a communications perspective. The greater the difference between two styles, the more the tendency to see only the negative qualities of each style's way of communicating, which results in some styles being more compatible with each other than others are.

Decision style compatibility and tensions in communication spring from the same two basic factors that are responsible for style-related similarities and differences in other types of behavior: information use and focus. Similarities in either of these two factors create points of compatibility in communication just as differences create points of tension.

Any one style will have some common ground as a basis for communication with at least two other styles that share that style's level of information use or focus. Finding these areas of common ground can help greatly to facilitate effective communication between you and someone whose style differs from yours.

Compatibilities and Tensions with Decisives

For example, decisives share common ground with both hierarchics and flexibles. They are similar to hierarchics because both styles are unifocus; they like a single, well-defined course of action, which in communication translates as a definite, clearly stated position or recommendation. However, decisives often become impatient and frustrated by hierarchics' tendencies to "get bogged down" or to

Table 7.1. Decision Styles and Communication.

Decisives		Flexibles		Hierarchics	
Positives	*Negatives*	*Positives*	*Negatives*	*Positives*	*Negatives*
Clear	Superficial	Intuitive	Shallow	Thorough	Nit-picking
Concise	Poor listener	Open-minded	Uncommitted	Prepared	Too domineering
Frank	Blunt	Adaptable	Vacillating	Logical	Arrogant
Action oriented	Cocky	Informal	Too nonchalant	Committed	Rigid
	Rigid	Congenial	Too agreeable	Visionary	Too intense
		Humorous	Flippant		

Integratives		Systemics	
Positives	*Negatives*	*Positives*	*Negatives*
Knowledgeable	Too intellectual	Many-sided	Vague
Open-minded	Impractical	Knowledgeable	Arrogant
Good listener	Confusing	Patient	Too slow
Patient	Too soft	Careful	Too conservative
Creative	Disorganized	Thorough	Overly complex
Tolerant		Systematic	Too structured
			Secretive

"belabor things" with lengthy analyses before coming to conclusions. If only hierarchics would come quickly to the point.

Decisives are similar to flexibles in that both are satisficers. In communication, they like highly summarized, short analyses that quickly indicate implications for action. However, decisives often feel frustrated with flexibles' tendencies in conversations and presentations to jump too much from topic to topic, sometimes without appearing to reach a clear decision about what to do.

Compatibilities and Tensions with Flexibles

Even though they are compatible with decisives' preference for quick analyses, flexibles, on the other hand, dislike decisives' tendency to "lock onto" one position and their tendency to want everyone to agree to one course of action. For this reason, flexibles also find some compatibility with integratives, who share the multifocus mode of looking at solutions to problems.

In conversations and meetings, flexibles find integratives to be open to ideas and good listeners who aren't concerned about having everything cut-and-dried and nailed down. On the other hand, they do get impatient with integratives' tendency to overintellectualize issues and their seemingly endless patience with analysis and looking at everything from many different points of view.

Compatibilities and Tensions with Integratives

Integratives also appreciate their flexible associates' willingness to consider different positions and their willingness to explore more than one topic, including some that simply emerge from a conversation or discussion. However, they sometimes feel that flexibles are too much inclined to bounce around without adequate discussion of any one topic. To integratives, this seems shallow and dissatisfying.

Integratives get their need for adequate analysis met in discussions and meetings with their hierarchic and systemic associates. However, integratives chafe when in discussions and meetings they raise what they consider to be interesting points and possibilities and are chided by their hierarchic associates (and sometimes their systemic associates, too) for not being prepared with well-organized data and logic to support their ideas.

Compatibilities and Tensions with Hierarchics

Hierarchics like integratives' willingness to get into the substance of issues without lurching to conclusions, and they often find them to be good sources of information and ideas, although sometimes their ideas strike them as strange, impractical, or confusing. To a hierarchic, it's often not clear what objective an integrative has in mind when raising a point or making a suggestion, nor is it clear what train of thought might have led to the point being made. On this count, they find decisives to be somewhat easier to communicate with because their ideas, positions, and objectives are clear. If only decisives would spend a little more time thinking things through and getting their data in order.

Hierarchics also find systemics to be good sources of ideas and information. They like systemics' thorough analyses of issues, too. However, they find themselves either becoming confused or impatient by systemics' insistence on talking about so many issues at once or by systemics' recitation of long-winded stories or parables to get their ideas across. On balance, they find themselves wondering just what systemics want. Because systemics seem concerned about many issues and objectives, hierarchics sometimes write them off as too impractical or too cautious.

Compatibilities and Tensions with Systemics

Systemics find compatibility also with hierarchics and integratives. They like both for their willingness to talk about issues in depth. They like hierarchics also because of their organized plans and commitment to specific objectives. They appreciate integratives especially for their willingness to look at many issues and objectives and their willingness to adapt plans as circumstances change. However, they sometimes find hierarchics to be too narrowly focused and inclined to be combative and confrontational when disagreements arise about plans and objectives. Integratives, on the other hand, strike them as disorganized and as sometimes too willing to compromise on important issues.

Toxic Relationships

You may have noticed that in the preceding discussion we said nothing about compatibility in communication between several combinations of styles, such as between decisives and integratives. These particular combinations represent what we call *toxic relationships* in the sense that they are difficult relationships and things can easily go sour in them. There are few points of compatibility between these styles; they differ in both information use and focus. If you sense that you are facing such a relationship, beware: land mines surround you. You need to adjust your mode of communicating to bridge the gap between your style and another style without setting off the mines. Let's have a look at these especially sensitive relationships.

Decisives and Integratives

Decisives find communication with integratives frustrating in just about every way. Integratives seem to talk too much about too many things. If you are decisive, you may wonder if your integrative associates even know why they are talking. They seem to circle endlessly, revisiting the same old issue or problem without reaching anything recognizable as a clear solution. Instead, they talk about all kinds of possibilities. Just when you are trying to make your point, they interrupt with some off-the-wall comment or question. Just when you feel that you have reached agreement on what will be done about some problem, they want to take another look at it.

For decisives, integratives seem to want to put off a decision as long as possible. They seem to feel no sense of urgency or practicality. Then, when they do decide, they want to do too many things. They come up with the most elaborate plans. Nothing is ever simple. It often seems that they have gotten their agendas and objectives mixed up. Sometimes, you walk out of meeting with an integrative without any idea about what he or she really wanted to say or do.

Integratives, on the other hand, experience decisives as skipping along on the surface of things, with no sign of giving anything much thought. They feel that decisives simply assert their points as ironclad fact, without reference to any information or logic. And they seem bull-headed—amazingly committed to positions and points of view to which they obviously have given little thought. You can never stray off the beaten path with them because if you do they start acting impatient or confused. Almost before you can get a thought out about some topic, they start talking about solutions. And once they get an idea in their heads about what to do, you can forget about changing their minds, no matter how much information, facts, logic, or questions you use.

As you can see, things can get rough when these two styles get together. In many ways, it is like the Tower of Babel. Neither understands the other's language. The words, the cadence, the rhythm are all different.

Most of us can think of relationships that for us were toxic. We just could not seem to get through to another person no matter how hard we tried, even though this same person seemed to have good working relationships and communication with other people.

Flexibles and Hierarchics

Relationships between flexibles and hierarchics are as difficult as they are for integratives and decisives, maybe even more so. To flexibles, hierarchics seem ponderous and rigid: you can't get a simple answer to a simple question without listening to a long dissertation first. Overkill is the order of the day. They seem to be incessantly concerned about facts, method, and logic. And they always appear to be trying to nail you with a question you can't answer. If they sense an inconsistency in something you have said, they pounce on it and then want to dismiss everything you have said.

Flexibles find it particularly perplexing to try to change a hierarchic's mind after the hierarchic has taken a position on some topic. They always seem to be so serious and so intense about things. You have to build an elaborate case indeed to get their attention. And your facts and logic have to be truly compelling to sway them at all. Otherwise, you can forget about budging them.

Flexibles' views on their hierarchic associates' inflexibility is aptly summed up by the comment we heard a flexible manager make about a particularly hierarchic associate: "It's like the guy is on rails."

Hierarchics are just as perplexed and frustrated by their flexible counterparts. They find it virtually impossible to follow the conversations or presentations of their flexible associates. In the worst cases, they stop trying and just write them off as lightweights. First of all, they feel that flexibles seldom seem prepared to talk about anything in a substantive way. You usually can find flaws in any figures they present if you look closely enough—that is, if they resort to using anything as concrete as numbers, which is seldom. They hop all over the place, from topic to topic. If you challenge something they say, they either act insulted or back off immediately without offering much defense for themselves.

Worst of all is the hierarchic's frustration when attempting to get a flexible colleague to take a stand on something. They get rattled particularly when they feel that they have just identified the flexible's real point of view, only to hear the person say something quite different or apparently agreeing with a very different point of view.

Systemics with Flexibles and Decisives

Systemics tend toward toxic relationships with both decisives and flexibles. Neither of these two styles is patient enough to give a systemic colleague a sufficient chance to explain a point of view in the depth and breadth that the systemic feels is needed to understand his or her position. In fact, the more the systemic tries to explain, the more his or her decisive and flexible colleagues seem to be dissuaded instead of persuaded. Basically, decisives and flexibles feel that a point of view is not worth having if it cannot be explained concisely. Yet the systemic feels that an action is not worth taking unless you understand why it makes sense and what varied kinds of outcomes might be expected from it. Decisives and flexibles stop listening, and systemics scratch them from their lists of worthwhile associates or contacts.

Same-Style Communication

By and large, of course, compatibility in communication is greatest when two people using the same style get together. Then, at least, they tend to use the same words, rhythm, and cadence in their communication. As communicators, of course, they are most likely to see the positive qualities summarized in Table 7.1. Consequently, we often find natural groupings of people with similar styles in organizations, even though these groupings sometimes do not correspond to the organization chart. People gravitate toward others with similar styles. Managers tend to hire subordinates whose styles are similar to their own (even though, objectively, they often should hire someone whose style complements rather than clones their own styles). Likewise, people often want to work for someone whose style matches their own style.

Things do not always run smoothly and conflict-free when people with the same styles interact, however. Decisives can collide with other decisives and bounce apart quickly if they happen to have different goals or if, through different past experiences, they formed different perceptions of business problems and issues. This, too, can happen when hierarchics get together with hierarchics and when systemics get together with systemics, except that they do not bounce apart as quickly. Instead, they tend to engage in lengthy debates, which only increase the distance between their positions.

Nevertheless, even when their views and positions differ, decisives tend to respect other decisives. If they disagree, they understand why. They do not confuse each other. Hierarchics also tend to respect other hierarchics even though their views differ, and if the conflict between them does not degenerate into open warfare, they still may communicate effectively and work well with each other on new issues and problems on which they have not yet taken positions.

In general, flexibles tend to communicate well with other flexibles, as do integratives with other integratives. They are more likely to accommodate each others' points of view and preferences and consequently are much less likely to be polarized on issues and solutions.

Adjusting Your Communication to Others' Styles

To avoid the kinds of difficulties and miscommunication that we have just described, it is necessary on numerous occasions to alter the way our own style naturally leads us to communicate in order to reach meetings of the mind with other people. We assume here that the others with whom you communicate are uneducated in the mysteries of decision styles, their effect on communication, and consequently knowing how or when to alter their styles. In other words, we are assuming that the burden is on you to adjust how you communicate.

If you are wondering whether you should adjust your style to another person's role style or operating style, you should adjust your style to whichever style another person seems to be using at the moment. Later in this chapter we offer some pointers on how to sense which style this is.

To make the necessary adjustments, of course, requires behavioral adaptability on your part. To be adaptable, you first must be aware of your own styles and behavior. As we have indicated in this book, however, decision styles are habits that we may be only dimly aware of. We recommend that you review the material in Chapters Five and Six to be sure you understand your own style before attempting to adapt your style to that of another person. Keep in mind that the material in those chapters can help you to accurately assess another person's style.

If you attempt to adjust your way of communicating to fit a different style and find yourself falling into the same old habits, try using some of the guidelines in Chapter 10 for adjusting and modifying your style.

Let's take a closer look at how each style communicates and then explore some ways to adjust your communications to better fit that style. As you read, we suggest that you periodically look at Table 7.2, which highlights our recommendations for communicating with different styles.

How Decisives Communicate

Decisives are terse in their communications. They like to keep communications short and to the point. Their main concerns are ac-

Table 7.2. Communicating with Different Styles.

Decisives	Flexibles	Hierarchics
Be on time.	Keep things informal.	Be prepared: do your homework.
Minimize chitchat.	Keep an open mind about solutions.	Get and use their input.
Get to the point.	Use humor.	Present information and conclusions clearly.
Be self-assured and positive.	Be willing to shift topics.	Show your reasoning and logic.
Make clear recommendations.	Stress options and choices.	Never "win the argument."
Stress bottom-line benefits.	Don't ask for long-term commitment.	Expect proposals to be "corrected."
Avoid unnecessary detail.	Don't overkill a topic.	Listen well.
Answer questions directly.	Keep conversation moving.	Do not press for quick agreement.
		Allow time to "mull things over."
		Be willing to share credit.

Integratives	Systemics
Share information from varied sources.	Get them involved early in problem solving.
Solicit their ideas and information.	Stay in touch: communicate often.
Invite participation in problem solving.	Present lots of information and ideas.
Communicate hunches.	Find connections with their interests and goals.
Explore positives and negatives of proposed solutions.	Stress the "big picture."
Be willing to modify your ideas.	Emphasize multiple benefits.
Avoid absolutes.	Allow for modification of your ideas.
Do not press for quick decisions.	Allow lots of "mull over" time.
	Go out of your way to give credit for their ideas.

tions and their benefits, and the benefits they value most are efficiency, productivity, and quick results. When they speak, they tend to say first of all what they intend to do, with a very brief summary of why, pointing to a few essential facts. They may begin a presentation or meeting with one or two short jokes, but then they settle down to business. In short, they strive for clarity.

Rather than attempting to motivate and persuade others on the basis of information and logic, decisives are inclined to emphasize the value and "rightness" of a particular course of action. They prefer to get their points across without a lot of interruptions and questions.

How to Communicate with Decisives

In communicating with decisives, you must keep things moving. Your first step should be to make clear what you are communicating. Briefly state the problem or issue and why it is worth taking time to talk about. Stay away from long-winded explanations, though. Keep it short.

After stating the problem, quickly describe your preferred recommendation and the main benefits that can be expected to result from your recommendation. If your suggestion has efficiency, productivity, or cost benefits, or the prospect of quick results to recommend it, then be sure to emphasize those advantages. But don't go on and on about one benefit after another. After a point, this begins to weaken your case instead of strengthening it. You might begin to sound too "salesy," which can arouse feelings of suspicion or distrust in a decisive.

If you use jokes, do so sparingly at the beginning and end of your discussion, not during the middle. When you are discussing an issue, keep things impersonal and businesslike. Don't expect friendly chitchat while working.

Keep things on a positive footing. Minimize criticisms and discussions of possible failure to achieve your objective. This could turn the whole conversation sour and make your recommendation seem murky and messy.

Be firm in your position, projecting an image of relaxed

confidence. Show confidence in your decisive associate's ability to carry out any part of an agreement that you reach.

Keep in mind that it is unwise to go into a meeting with a decisive without having a recommendation for dealing with whatever problem or issue you will discuss—unless, that is, you are indifferent about what course of action will be taken. If you do go in unarmed with a solution, you will either emerge with a solution handed you quickly by your decisive colleague, or you will risk frustrating him or her with your indecisiveness.

We recall one CEO we dealt with who happened to have an integrative role style but whose operating style was very decisive. He enjoyed kicking around a lot of ideas, but was in the habit of suddenly stopping the conversation and saying, "OK, what do you think we should do—one, two, three?" When he said that, it was very clear that we were expected to be able to respond with a recommendation right then with no further deliberation.

If you are going to make a presentation to a decisive, a good decisive presentation technique is to use a few simple briefing charts with two or three bullets on each chart summarizing major points. Don't try to put all your information on the charts, though. You can always add more information orally if your decisive audience asks for more information. But if you aren't asked, avoid the temptation to offer more.

If you come in with a standard, hierarchic style presentation, prepared with a couple of pounds of briefing charts crammed with facts and data, you can count on losing the attention and interest of your decisive associates. You must capture decisives' attention and interest in the first few moments of a presentation or discussion. Don't try to build up your case with a carefully crafted train of logic that gradually reveals your recommendation. By the time you reach your conclusion, your decisive associates either will have tuned you out or reached their own conclusions.

We saw clearly the difference that presentation style can make in winning over a decisive audience in a situation in which a director of business development presented the executive staff of his company with a long, hierarchic briefing that concluded with his recommendation to invest a sizable chunk of capital in a new business venture. During the presentation his rather decisive audience remained mostly silent, and the meeting broke up with the recommendation neither accepted nor rejected. Several months later, after sizing up a few styles, the director made another briefing on the same topic to the same group with the same recommendation. But for this briefing he made a brisk, decisive presentation with his recommendation up front, using just a few charts, each with only two or three bullets. This time his recommendation was accepted enthusiastically, and he actually received a round of applause.

One last point regarding communication with decisives: be on time for your meetings. Time is precious for decisives, so be careful not to treat theirs or yours casually.

How Flexibles Communicate

Flexibles also like fast-paced discussions about facts, always with a results emphasis. However, they differ from decisives in that they favor talking briefly about a variety of subjects. They strive to keep things light and to keep options open. To keep things from stagnating they may use humor and jokes at any point during a conversation or presentation. They look for and prefer recommendations that can be implemented quickly and that hold the prospect of quickly producing several different kinds of benefits. They especially like recommendations that do not require long-term commitments of capital or other resources.

Flexibles show a distinct preference for open-ended discussions. They use few if any briefing charts, preferring instead to let a discussion or presentation take its natural course. Strict adherence to preestablished agendas feels restrictive to them, as do repeated attempts to steer a conversation back to a particular point or recommendation.

Flexibles do not like arguments and debate, and they avoid recommending or accepting actions that limit future options.

How to Communicate with Flexibles

In communicating with flexibles, as in communicating with decisives, keep things moving. Don't get into volumes of detail and information. Keep the emphasis on options and benefits.

Resist the temptation to bring with you a bunch of neatly prepared briefing charts. They only give the impression that you have already reached a firm conclusion. Oral communication is best. Use flip charts to capture ideas that come up during your discussion, especially regarding alternative courses of action.

In general, keep things on the informal side. Formality strikes flexibles as stuffy and contrived. Don't be afraid to be casual. If you see humor in a discussion, point it out. Jokes are OK as long as they are short.

Be sure to solicit ideas from your flexible associates. Be sure to come armed with several ideas of your own, as well, but try not to get too attached to them. Show a willingness to adapt and modify your ideas. Flexibles admire the ability to quickly generate a profusion of suggestions for alternative ways to handle a problem. Try to keep an open mind.

Although you should not seem unsure of yourself when communicating with flexibles, don't come across as too convinced of your analysis or of the value of your recommendations. Be somewhat tentative. Use *perhaps* or *maybe*. Say *we could* instead of *we should* or *we will.*

If you have a strong preference for a particular course of action, don't get too intense about it, or your flexible associates will think you are trying to coerce them or make them look foolish if they don't go along with your idea. Don't present your preferred suggestion first. Throw out a bunch of ideas, and save your preferred idea for last. Flexibles tend to act on the most recent idea that looks workable. If you sense some resistance to an idea, suggest that "We could just try it out. If it doesn't work, then we can try something else."

Remember to try not to take yourself or your ideas too seriously. Be ready to laugh at yourself a bit.

Also keep in mind that it is important to move quickly to implement a recommendation or set of recommendations after reaching an agreement with your flexible colleagues. Otherwise, as time goes by you run an increasing risk that they will change their minds and opt for a very different solution or simply withdraw their support.

How Hierarchics Communicate

Hierarchics believe in doing their homework, so before taking a stand on some issue, they try to get their facts straight and to sort them out using a method that logically dictates a course of action. For example, in training workshops, we often use a group decision-making simulation in which participants play the roles of a management committee deciding about which of a set of projects to fund. If there is a hierarchic in the group, sooner or later he or she will urge the group to lay out the project proposals in a matrix that allows the merits of each to be weighed objectively and compared to one another.

When making presentations, hierarchics typically present large amounts of organized information about their analyses, factors they took into account, methods they used, and alternatives they considered. Last of all they present a conclusion and a clear recommendation. The sequence and content of their presentations are set up to present their recommendation as the "best course of action." From a hierarchic perspective, best conclusions are those that produce high-quality results. If trade-offs are to be made and hierarchics are free to choose among alternatives, they are naturally inclined to make the trade-offs in favor of quality over costs, efficiencies, and short-term results. Basically, their logic says that "If something is worth doing, it is worth doing right."

How to Communicate with Hierarchics

You will be most successful in your communication with hierarchics if you do your homework just as they do. Don't go into an important discussion with hierarchics with sketchy views and half-baked recommendations. If you do, you will lose their respect and confidence. Once you lose their respect, you may find it next to impossible to regain it.

If a topic or subject is important and your hierarchic colleagues are poorly informed about it, you basically can forget about going into a meeting with them and emerging later from the same meeting with your recommendation accepted, unless, of course, you possess a sterling silver tongue or the meeting lasts all night and part of the next day.

Communicating with and influencing hierarchic colleagues is best thought of as an ongoing process and not an event. You must realize that you are unlikely to persuade or convince hierarchics of anything unless you see to it that they convince themselves in the process. Hierarchics find it virtually impossible to go along with a recommendation unless they are fully convinced in their own minds that it is the best thing to do. To go along with a recommendation without being fully convinced that it is the right one is like shirking one's responsibility.

Your hierarchic associates must be thought of as participants in your analyses if you need their support. But throughout the process, you must maintain your credibility with them. This may mean that you find yourself walking a delicate tightrope. If you do not do your homework and reach high-quality conclusions of your own, you lose your credibility. However, if you present your hierarchic associates with an elaborately documented, watertight case for a particular course of action, you make them feel locked out of the process.

If an important decision is coming up and you have strong views of your own about what should be done, there are several things that you should do. First, let your hierarchic associates know what issue or problem you are working on, and make sure that you and they are in agreement about a main objective. Then give them facts—preferably spaced out over a period of time—and ask also for information from them.

Next, consider tossing them one or two ideas about courses of action that seem to fit the facts you have been considering. Do not push them to accept them. Just toss them out as "food for thought." Do not be surprised or discouraged if they show little or no enthusiasm for your ideas. This may mean that they have not convinced themselves yet. If you let a little time pass for them to "mull things over," you often will find that they come to you and say, "You know, I've got an idea. I think what we should do is . . . "—and out will come your idea, perhaps with a slightly different twist. This is when you should say, "That sounds like a great idea to me! In fact, I've been thinking about something like that myself."

Then you can call a meeting in which you make your hierarchic presentation, with all of your slides and charts and facts, giving credit of course to your hierarchic associate's input and ideas. This, of course, means that you must be able to swallow enough of your own ego to share credit with your colleagues, even if you were the primary originator of the recommendation that you present. For some people, that's a difficult thing to do.

Incidentally, you should not conclude that your hierarchic colleagues who come back to you with your ideas, but with their names on them, are intentionally or knowingly trying to steal your glory. By the time that they have convinced themselves to accept an idea, they may have completely lost sight of where it came from originally.

One last point about communication with hierarchics: avoid getting into public debates with them in which you "win the argument" and cause them to lose face in front of others. This kind of humiliation can cause you to permanently lose their support.

How Integratives Communicate

In communication, integratives face a problem. They have many ideas, but they are equipped with only one mouth by which to communicate them. Consequently, they tend to interrupt themselves a lot, saying such things as, "But on the other hand . . . " or "And, of course we could also . . . " This kind of talk frustrates others with different styles who are trying to follow their integrative colleagues' reasoning. In some people, it also creates the impression that integratives are confused or muddy in their thinking.

When listening to integratives, you can expect to hear them spout a proliferation of facts and observations, as well as ideas about actions to take. By and large, they expect and want the same from others. Integratives, by virtue of their style, are almost compelled to work in groups. Can you see why? People are excellent sources of information and new ideas, so it comes naturally to the integrative to get a group together to chew over some issue and to come up with some new insights and creative ideas. The same need for information and ideas leads them to be good listeners.

In making presentations, integratives may show up with a large stack of briefing charts, but they seldom follow a set plan or agenda. They want the freedom to follow lines of reasoning wherever they may lead. In considering courses of action to follow, integratives tend to be particularly attracted to creative new ideas that may lead to new insights or discoveries.

How to Communicate with Integratives

You should treat your integrative associates as partners in your communication, just as you treat your hierarchic associates. Integratives don't need to be absolutely convinced that a position is the right one or that a course of action is the best; they simply want to have some fun. For integratives, talking about issues, sharing information, and coming up with new ideas is fun.

If integratives are forced into a passive role in communication in which they are expected only to receive information and react to others' ideas, they lose interest. When this happens, they either withdraw or try to stir up some fun anyway. In the latter case, this would likely take the form of frequent interruptions, attempts to change topics, and a barrage of skeptical questions. This might be fun for them, but they may be working at cross purposes with you.

When speaking with integratives, talk first of all about problems and issues. Do not worry too much about making it clear why the problems or issues that you want to talk about are worth considering. For many integratives, any topic is fair game for a conversation.

Try to engage your integrative associates in defining a problem and exploring its parts with you, even if you think you already understand the problem fully. You might learn something new, and you will win their involvement and interest.

In sharing information, talk about information from as many sources as possible. Things do not have to be neat and tidy. Again, enlist their assistance in sorting through the information. Bring it to them as something interesting and intriguing to explore.

Understand, however, that you should be prepared with your own analyses of the information. Integratives, like hierarchics, admire other people's abilities to take messy information and extract insights from it. Just don't go too far in the direction of preparation to the point that you become overcommitted to a particular perspective or position—especially if you are hierarchic or decisive. If your integrative associates suspect that you already have your mind made up about something and your position staked out, they will begin to tune out of the communication process.

Make sure not to push for closure on solutions too fast. Doing so spoils the fun and makes your integrative associates feel uneasy. Basically, integratives feel that they ought to look at more alternative solutions than they will end up deciding to implement. If you try to cut things off too soon, they may end up trying to go in the direction of reopening consideration of all kinds of things that you already have resolved.

Be prepared for some friendly argument and debate, but do not interpret this negatively. Integratives often take the position of devil's advocate by arguing against something you favor or for something that you oppose. Usually, this means that they are just trying to better understand an issue by bringing out opposing points of view. Try doing this yourself with them. They won't mind your playing devil's advocate with them, as long as you don't start becoming truly argumentative and antagonistic.

When an integrative associate appears to take a strong position against some idea, keep in mind that the door is not closed on the issue. With integratives, the door is never closed; reconsideration is always possible, especially if new information comes to light. But this does not mean that you should come back to your integrative associates again and again with the same old position. You must introduce something new—a new version of your idea and new information about it.

If time pressures are compelling you to act but you need the support of your integrative colleagues who seem to be still in exploration mode, suggest a course of action that you could "put into action now, just to get things going." This works best if it leaves open the door for modification or other alternatives that can be implemented later. You will be most successful in selling your integrative associates on this approach if your immediate action promises to generate useful information that can be used later to adjust your plans and strategies.

Patience is a true virtue when dealing with integratives. When you find your patience being strained, it helps to remind yourself that your investment of time with your integrative associates will pay long-term dividends even though the short-term costs for you seem high. The time you invest will win their support and acceptance, you stand to gain new insights and ideas yourself, and you could find yourself becoming a central figure in a powerful decision-making and problem-solving team.

How Systemics Communicate

Much of what we have said about integratives and hierarchics applies also to the systemic style, which includes both of these other two styles. As communicators, systemics like information and analyses and, given a receptive audience, will share a great deal of information, logic, and insight.

When dealing with a new or unfamiliar issue or subject, systemics behave much as integratives do. They take in lots of information, examine issues from different perspectives, and like to entertain a variety of ideas.

But as the process goes on, specific objectives and plans begin to take shape in their minds, and they start to become more hierarchic in their thinking—more rigorous and structured in their analyses and consideration of alternatives. When this happens, they stop asking for others' input and stop responding positively to random ideas. To be considered, information now must be pertinent, and ideas must stack up well against specific criteria and objectives.

Systemics tend to favor long meetings that elicit large amounts of information and bring forth a variety of perspectives and possible courses of action. People with other styles often grow weary of these meetings, but the systemic who called the meeting is usually the last to show signs of fatigue or declining interest.

As we have mentioned before, systemics' tendencies to define problems very broadly—perhaps as sets of interrelated problems, rather than single issues—combined with their propensity to pursue multiple objectives makes it easy for others to lose sight of the problems and objectives that systemics are working on.

So systemics try several different techniques to facilitate communication of their thoughts. One technique they use is to tell stories. These are usually real stories from their own or someone else's experience that hold other people's interest while getting across a lot of information and ideas. In effect, the stories are parables. Then they apply the points the stories make when they suggest perspectives on issues or when they propose strategies.

Another technique that systemics often use is to get information and ideas across to others by asking questions. The questions are intended to cause others to think things through as the systemic has—very broadly and in depth. In systemic-style meetings, the systemic often poses question after question. Sometimes this catches on, and others begin posing questions, too. That's what the systemic prefers to have happen. The questions promote exploration of issues and, if the systemic has already arrived at some conclusions, tend to lead others toward the same conclusions. That the questions are leading somewhere predetermined may be seen by others, but exactly where is seldom clear.

We recall an interesting case of a vice president who convened his staff for an all-day meeting to agree on affirmative action goals and strategies. Throughout the day, he asked question after question, literally pulling information out of his staff. Finally, by evening, the group had reached consensus on their goals and strategies. Later, however, a staff member found several papers that the VP had brought into the meeting with him, and—lo!—written down neatly were the precise numbers and strategies that the group had agreed to by the end of the day.

How to Communicate with Systemics

You can apply many of our suggestions for communicating with hierarchics and integratives to your communication with systemics. Nevertheless, we have some specific recommendations to highlight. First of all, take everything that we have said about making partners of your hierarchic and integrative associates and *underscore* it. If you need the support of your systemic associates, you must communicate with them as partners early in your decision-making or problem-solving process and then frequently throughout the process.

But gaining the interest and involvement of your systemic counterparts cannot be ensured only by early and frequent communication. You must look for connections between what you are trying to do and their particular interests and objectives. Because their interests tend to be broad and their goals many, this should not be too difficult to do. But it is important and means that you must stay in communication even when not working together on any problems or issues.

Be prepared to see your systemic colleagues modify your ideas and suggest alternative or new interpretations of their own. Bend over backwards to incorporate these views. They must see clearly the imprint of their own thoughts on any outcome of your discussions.

You will often find that they want to put their "riders" or conditions on your plans. To systemics, your willingness to include their ideas is fair pay and expected for their involvement. Your best bet is to solicit their ideas before venturing very far in your planning efforts. Do not wait for them to speak up, because they might not do so on without your invitation. If they cannot see their ideas and suggestions reflected in your plans, however, you are unlikely to gain their support.

Be prepared to give credit and recognition to your systemic associates publicly. This should be easy to justify in your own mind, inasmuch as they surely will put their own twist on things—if you succeed in gaining their interest and involvement.

Be certain to present lots of information of your own and your own points of view. Get your information and ideas across early before they start shifting toward the hierarchic side of the systemic style.

Try to sense the shift from integrative to hierarchic mode that systemics undergo as the communication process goes on, and adapt your communication accordingly. Otherwise, you may find that the communication techniques that were working well with a systemic colleague a few days ago are producing negative reactions now.

Most of all, keep the lines of communication open. Maintain the flow of information, thoughts, and ideas. Do not let your systemic colleagues wander into the corner alone with their own thoughts. Otherwise, you may find that they have taken a very different direction to which they have become very committed and which they are reluctant to change. As with integratives, bear in mind that your patience will pay off—especially in the long run. You stand to learn a lot, and if treated with respect as full partners, you will gain the support of some very knowledgeable and capable thinkers.

Adapting to Role Styles and Operating Styles

Earlier we mentioned the need to accurately identify other people's styles to make the appropriate adjustments in your communication. This may mean you may need to adapt your mode of communication to both operating and role styles. Assuming that you have been able to estimate both of these styles in a person with whom you wish to communicate, here are some pointers to help you sense when to adjust to a person's role style and when to adjust to operating style.

> When communicating with people you are very familiar with in "shirtsleeve," side-by-side circumstances, your best bet is to adjust to the person's operating style.
> In formal meetings—especially with a person who does not know you well—begin your communication in a way that suits the person's role style.
> As meetings or conversations progress, people generally move into their operating styles, unless the circumstances are very formal or there is the possibility that they are being evaluated critically by others. Watch for the shift toward operating styles. Sometimes you can feel this intuitively, almost as a change in the atmosphere in the room, or you might sense that another person is reacting to you differently even though your behavior has not changed.
> Watch for coats coming off and ties being loosened as a meeting progresses. These gestures can signal a move toward operating style.
> Watch for behaviors in general that indicate the other person is doing things that he or she ordinarily would not do if

feeling self-conscious or self-aware—such as repeatedly rubbing a mole on his or her face. These behaviors can alert you to the need to start adjusting your behavior to fit the person's operating style.

The main challenge here, of course, is to remain aware not only of how others are behaving but also of how *you* are behaving. If you are attempting to adapt your communication to a style that is greatly different from your own, avoid lengthy meetings and discussions if possible—at least until you become used to this new mode of communication. As discussions and meetings progress and you get wrapped up in issues and ideas, the tendency will be for you to slip back into the communication mode that corresponds to your own operating style. Moreover, the strain of doing something that does not come naturally can be exhausting.

Try your experiments in adapting your communication gradually. Practice frequently. Look for incremental gains in your success in communicating with different styles. Over the long run, small increments can add up to very large gains.

8

Managing with Style

We believe that the style model provides an invaluable management tool. Using style analysis you can identify the nature of each subordinate. The person who "always seems to need direction" can be more fairly understood and managed as a decisive subordinate. Workers with "that God-awful mess" in their offices can be appreciated as integratives.

By diagnosing subordinates' styles using the checklists provided in Chapters Five and Six you can better understand and motivate them. You should diagnose while paying particular attention to the "filter" through which your own style views your subordinates. For instance, if you favor a decisive style, you may be able to replace your belief that a flexible subordinate's habit of agreeing with you is weak with a more accurate understanding that he wishes to support your views while preserving possibly different views for himself. With this new understanding you can work with the flexible's need to please the boss by telling him it is OK to disagree. You may then stimulate more open communication.

We cannot explore all possible combinations of style in bosses and subordinates, but we do examine general rules for succeeding in managing each style, regardless of your style. We also examine what goes wrong most often for each subordinate style and what you can do about it.

Once you diagnose the style of a subordinate, you will find this chapter a useful guide to maximizing his or her potential.

The Decisive Subordinate

Having a subordinate with a dominant decisive style can be a delight if several basic rules are followed and all is going well. The basic rules are

1. Give clear direction.
2. Provide frequent feedback on progress.
3. Avoid over-frequent changes in direction.

The rule on clear direction is essential. One of the most difficult things for a decisive person to tolerate is a confused or rambling directive. A classic confrontation occurs when a decisive subordinate meets with an extremely integrative boss. The latter will explore many "fascinating" ways to tackle a task then tell his quietly desperate underling to "go to it." The decisive leaves the meeting mumbling to himself, "What did he say?"

The decisive's need for clarity is so critical that it is usually a good idea to write down your objectives and operating procedures in a simple format. It is helpful to lay out a schedule with milestones—even to use a graphic technique like a Gantt chart.

Failure to follow this rule often leads to that most frustrating habit of the decisive when confused—the "freeze-up." An overloaded decisive often says nothing to his boss because he dislikes confronting authority. Instead he may block the boss's task from consciousness and focus on other more clearly understood tasks. This freeze can go on for months before the horrified boss finds out that nothing has been done.

This freeze-up problem leads to Rule Two: provide frequent checks and feedback. Laying out too long a plan with too many contingencies for a decisive—a failing of many hierarchic bosses— can be a disaster. The decisive style tends to focus on the immediate. Overcomplex plans are usually "tuned out" after the first two or three steps. A far better approach is to provide a brief action plan with clear checkpoints for not more than six months or a year at most. Even better is a more frequent checking pattern where weekly or even daily feedback can be given as to progress. In the absence of this kind of feedback the decisive loses energy, and his boss may discover that there has been no progress—too late.

If a decisive is going the wrong way, criticism must be direct, quick, and followed by clear directions as to how to correct the situation. Criticism from authority is acceptable to a decisive, but only if it conforms to Rule One—give clear direction.

The final rule is to be wary of frequent and unclear course changes, a particular problem for flexible bosses. If change comes too often and with no clear cause, the decisive begins to lose confidence in the boss. It is preferable to hold off change until a milestone has been reached to allow some sense of closure before shifting direction. In some cases it is actually better to buffer the decisive from change by keeping the planning horizon very short; change can then be introduced without the decisive's being aware of it. Finally, change should always be introduced as being a better way to attain established goals. It is particularly palatable if the change increases efficiency.

If the above rules are followed, the decisive can be a joy to manage—provided that nothing goes wrong. There are two major ways things can go wrong: task mismatch and imperialism. In either case the problem is amplified tremendously by the decisive's tendency to avoid passing bad news to the boss.

Unfortunately, the decisive's dislike of failure and desire to please the boss may result in a disastrous failure to communicate. As noted above, frequent checking may help, but it is equally important to beware of the twin pitfalls of the decisive manager— overload and weak boundaries.

The overload problem relates to the match between person and task. Simply put, the style model proposes that each style is at its best in certain environments and jobs. In positions requiring swift action, where there are clear tasks and well-documented procedures, the decisive style shines.

In management, these conditions are often found in first-level supervision. For instance, a study of first-level supervisors in a state bureaucracy found that decisives were rated better performers and were much more satisfied with their work than those with other styles (Boulgarides, 1973). However, the decisive style is not suited only to first-level management. We recently saw a case where a whole administrative unit was floundering in a sea of confusion. A decisive senior manager was hired to clean up the mess. Within a few weeks, she had fired some misfits, cleaned up procedures, and restored confidence to all levels in the unit.

Problems for a decisive set in when conditions go into overload. This can occur if the complexity of the task gets too high or if the need for a slower, more thorough approach becomes paramount. Under such pressures one hopes decisives have a complex backup style. If not, they are likely to become even more decisive and run into massive problems, which they may try to cover up. Some of the behavior surrounding the Challenger space shuttle disaster illustrates this problem.

The solution is for a boss to monitor the load carried by subordinates. If a temporary complexity/uncertainty increase occurs, it is necessary to buffer the decisive. A standard method is to assign a temporary aide who has a maximizer style to work with the decisive on the problem. Another approach is to simplify the problem's complexity by assigning parts to others. Possibly the worst solution is to assign the decisive to a task force—particularly with integratives—to study the problem. The decisive's dislike of committees is intense.

If it seems that the job is going to permanently change, one can consider either reassignment or a gradual program for shifting style. We discuss such programs in Chapter Ten.

Finally, decisives experience problems when there is a lack of clear task/unit boundaries. This is the opposite of overload. When decisives have "solved all problems" and feel insufficient challenge, they tend toward imperialism. Under these circumstances the decisive looks around for new worlds to conquer—often in other areas in the organization that need "straightening out." If boundaries are not clearly defined, other managers may find an invasion of their territory under way.

Decisives will ask senior management to let them "help out," and before much time is up they will be running a new unit—unless stopped. The boss can try two things in this situation—find a challenge within the decisive's domain and very firmly forbid expansion to other areas. A failure to deal with this tendency can lead to massive and destructive "turf battles."

If you maintain the respect of the decisive subordinate, you can expect full loyalty and dedication. Decisives usually are the last to undercut or compete with their legitimate superiors. They respect authority, and if it is properly used, they can deliver on their commitments with extreme efficiency and enthusiasm.

Managing the Flexible Style

In many ways, the flexible style employee is the easiest style to manage because the employee strongly desires to agree with the boss. The flexible wants the boss to feel good so that his ideas are given support and praise, but this tendency can be the greatest pitfall in managing the flexible when needed objections to the boss's ideas are not strongly voiced and conflicts are downplayed.

We witnessed a company president make every effort to detect either a problem or a clash between a flexible staff person and other staff people, but the flexible softly evaded and minimized each probe. When finally confronted with his evasiveness and with the presence of real conflict between him and others, the flexible staffer smiled and said, "I agree."

Managing this style does not mean "pinning them down." The cardinal rule for managing flexibles is to always allow maneuvering room. This translates into several specific recommendations:

1.   Avoid detailed, commitment-type planning.
2.   Avoid direct orders.
3.   Avoid obvious and frequent control checking.
4.   Keep operating systems as simple and adaptable as possible.

For a flexible person, planning is not just a waste of time, it is downright unproductive. It locks one in and reduces the possibility of improvisation. When planning is needed, a good approach is to discuss objectives, review options, and request prompt action. Giving the flexible person a set of resources (such as financial, people, or technology) and free rein to maneuver with those resources—with some outer limits—produces excellent results.

Direct orders should be avoided. In dealing with the flexible person, suggesting several optional ways to go usually produces outcomes. Direct orders are verbally agreed to but can generate resentment and only nominal compliance.

Controlling the flexible person in a tight, systematic way can be dysfunctional. They often turn this kind of surveillance into a game and try to work around or even "fool" the controls. What does seem to work is the informal conversation to see "how things are going." It is also useful to unobtrusively check for bottom-line outcomes to avoid the possibility of evasive responses to informal questions.

A flexible tendency is to throw a Band-Aid on a problem. Of course, in many relatively simple or nonrecurring problems the flexible Band-Aid may be the most useful solution, but in complex recurring problems, you may need to slow down the flexible to come up with more systematic problem solving. For this type of problem solving the ideal flexible approach is a noncritical brainstorming method. Brainstorming is ideal for the flexible because it minimizes criticism and conflict while allowing freewheeling, intuitive generation of many alternatives. It also fosters humor—a strong flexible stimulant. It may be necessary to delegate more painstaking analyses of these alternatives to less flexible staff persons.

What is most likely to go wrong with a flexible person? As with the decisive, task misfit and interpersonal difficulties are the two most important types of problems.

For a flexible person, the best task fit is with fast-moving unstructured jobs. They can do well in entrepreneurial work as well as sales, promotion, or entertainment activities. They can do well as supervisors in loose, small organizations. Trouble sets in, as with the decisive, when flexibles move into more complex tasks. Having to read complex, detailed reports, sit in on long, involved committee meetings, or engage in long-range planning can be deadly for a flexible who cannot move into a maximizer backup style. To head off this type of task misfit, staffers can work through details and give the flexible person verbal briefings on key issues. Because flexibles can drop in and drop out of meetings with ease, they can be given permission to leave sessions when involved debates are going on and return later when conclusions are imminent. They can even be allowed to bring other tasks to meetings (such as letters) to work on as they drop out and in at will.

On the interpersonal side, flexibles are usually well liked if interaction frequency is low, but over long time periods of close interaction others find that the flexible can wear thin. Decisives resent their lack of commitment, integratives find them shallow, and hierarchics point to both faults.

The best solution is understanding, tolerance, and humor on the part of others. Flexibles tend not to be serious or self-important. They can give and take humorous comments on style—including their own—quite well.

Another tack is to move the flexible person fairly often. They dislike routine and sameness, so rotation of work partners, places, and even work itself is usually welcome. It also reduces the possibility of difficulties with others caused by excessive contact.

If handled right, the flexible employee can be an endless source of adaptability, good humor, and emotional support for a manager. In the right setting they can wheel and deal like no other style.

Managing the Hierarchic Style

The surest way to manage a person of hierarchic thought pattern is to create the feeling that they are the power behind the throne. Hierarchics like to view themselves as experts with very high levels of influence in the system.

If mishandled, they can be a source of serious trouble for a boss. With their penchant for data and detail they can undermine a boss through misinformation. We recall a case where a superdecisive new president of a division ran roughshod over his hierarchic staff. Within six months he had been fired—the victim of elaborately incorrect information given to him by his hierarchic staff for a disastrous presentation at corporate headquarters.

The following rules can lead to successful supervisor-subordinate outcomes in managing the hierarchic:

1. Use well-analyzed data to influence opinion, but allow them to "win."
2. Agree on goals, but permit the hierarchic to design his or her own implementation plan.
3. Set up elaborate, impersonal control systems to monitor progress.
4. Allow the hierarchic to be seen as an influential expert.
5. Work out succession plans such that your advancement leads to their advancement.

Direct orders or even suggestions, without substantiation, are most unconvincing to a hierarchic and can breed disrespect or even contempt over time. To command respect and compliance the manager of a hierarchic must be master of most of the relevant facts. It is also necessary at times to leave some issues on a topic open and ask for the hierarchic's "advice" or to debate some points in a plan and let the hierarchic win. A fine line must be observed between being seen as a lightweight or as too rigid by a hierarchic.

In planning it is essential to reach agreement on objectives and clear-cut goals, but to do a hierarchic's detailed planning for him or her is as demotivating as giving a flexible a direct order. Let hierarchics do their own plans. Once the hierarchic has finished planning, it is essential for the boss to review it and to debate several points in the plan.

Control needs to be exercised via impersonal, objective reports. Computerized systems are ideal hierarchic control mechanisms. The reports should be frequent, detailed, and aimed at very high quality levels.

When things go wrong, be prepared for a debate on causes, which can become a defensive shifting of blame if not handled right. The criticism should be factual and impersonal. The focus should be on correcting the problem—but not on examining the whole system, as one might do with integrative or systemic subordinates.

On a more personal level it is important to deal with the hierarchic's need to feel wise and powerful. Giving them credit for their analysis—especially with higher management—is important. Referring to your need for their advice (especially to peers of the hierarchic) is very helpful.

However, going too far in this direction is dangerous: the hierarchic may upstage you and even threaten your job. If you work out an agreement that your rise will benefit the hierarchic, forming a usually beneficial coalition can benefit everyone involved—especially when the hierarchic style is complementary to your own style. For example, General, then President, Eisenhower may have had such a relationship with his long-term chief of staff General Alfred Gruenther. Gruenther's complex hierarchic analysis was a perfect complement to Eisenhower's decisive finesse at getting things moving.

As with other styles, managing the hierarchic can be far more difficult where there is a mismatch between task and style. The hierarchic can work well whenever there is sufficient structure and complexity in work.

They do well in jobs calling for planning, analyzing complex data, and designing elaborate systems. They fit well in middle-management positions in high-tech or financial organizations that are not building totally new products or sources. We have found them highly concentrated in middle management of a large airline and in some areas of an aerospace firm (Alawi, 1973).

Things can go wrong if tasks become too simple or too unstructured, however. Hierarchics may try to overcomplicate simple tasks or overstructure inherently loose situations. On failing this, they may turn to politics to provide complexity.

Clearly, allowing them to delegate uncongenial tasks to more appropriate others is a good idea. If this is impossible, putting them under time pressure helps because it makes simple tasks more challenging. Allowing them to plan contingencies in advance may help alleviate their negative reaction to unstructured situations.

At the interpersonal level, perhaps the biggest hierarchic problem is overcontrol or its inverse—lack of delegation. The admirable hierarchic tendency toward high quality can lead to perfectionism, which in turn can lead to low trust in others' doing things right. Colleagues or subordinates of the hierarchic may feel lack of trust or that they are being "micromanaged."

The solution here seems to be to build respect in the hierarchic's mind for other people's competencies. This is easiest to do in looser areas where hierarchics feel less sure of their own competence. For instance, in a developmental discussion we attended with a hierarchic subordinate, an executive suggested that the hierarchic not delegate key technical tasks to others but rather delegate some problems involving people issues. His relief at this suggestion was obvious.

In a similar vein, delegation can occur in simpler tasks that are not as valued. The hierarchic can then gradually build confidence in others by delegating more and more complex, important tasks.

When managed appropriately hierarchics can provide invaluable assistance to a manager. Their precision and concern for quality can do much to turn an organization into a center of excellence.

Managing the Integrative Style

Managing the integrative person is a lot like riding a raft on a wild river. Not handled well, the experience can lead to being swamped or drowned; it also can be exhilarating, however.

As with the raft, the integrative needs to be steered but not fought. Tight control is disastrous. The integrative approach is collaborative and participative; hierarchy is seen as a necessary evil. A boss who insists on status or uses raw power is likely to be seen as Neanderthal by the integrative.

As subordinates they deluge a boss with ideas, suggestions, and information. They never see issues as permanently settled. They are always ready to sit down to discuss issues from all points of view—even in a crisis.

To get the best of this kind of employee requires several related approaches:

1. Use consensus-oriented meetings to set goals and define methods. Allow plenty of time.
2. Provide for many points of view in meetings.
3. Use subgroup task assignments to capture and explore new ideas generated at meetings.
4. Control by both elaborate data systems and frequent review meetings.

5. Have other things to do when meetings are planned; do not expect punctuality.
6. Provide job enrichment.

The central themes in this style are creativity and participation. Hence open-ended meetings become a way of life. The process to follow is consensus. This does not mean a voting-type democracy, because this process cuts off discussion. True consensus means exploring all points of view, bringing out conflicts, and creatively resolving them by finding solutions that all agree on.

The consensus process is time-consuming and can get heated. Its great advantages are that all participants feel committed to the outcome and many synergistic ideas may emerge that no one person would offer. Managing a consensual group or even two-way discussions requires skill in observing and managing group process. Integratives are as concerned with group dynamic issues like involvement, dominance, unexpressed feelings, and ideas management as they are with the content of a discussion.

To manage an integrative discussion one must be willing to halt content-oriented talking and at times determine whether everyone is involved and being heard, whether someone is talking too much or not listening, whether someone is silently upset, or whether ideas are getting lost.

Rules Two and Three above illustrate these *process interventions*. To the integrative, agreement prior to hearing several sides or many alternatives is valueless and frustrating. A good manager of integrative groups has different points of view represented at meetings or develops alternatives prior to a meeting.

Sometimes, integrative interactions bog down in what a colleague of ours calls data loops. Differing sides cite incomplete data to support their views and talk around and around. The manager at this point needs to assign someone or a subgroup to procure more data to resolve the issue.

At other times a new idea may emerge as a tangent to the main theme. The greatest temptation for a leader, especially a unifocus leader, is to cut off discussion and get things "back on the topic." For integratives this approach is a straightjacket and produces increasing resentment and boredom. A far better practice is to again assign a subgroup or person to explore the new idea and come back to a later meeting to discuss it further. Keeping a running list of such ideas on a flip chart also helps.

Once consensus is reached in an integrative discussion, actions do follow. Integratives are not victims of "analysis paralysis." They attack a project doing many tasks simultaneously and need control systems to determine how things are going. As with the hierarchic, elaborate data-oriented reporting systems are an answer. Unlike the hierarchic, moving off course is a signal for a "review meeting" in which not only the immediate problem but the entire approach may be revised.

It is clear that meetings are an integrative way of life—yet they are rarely on time for meetings, because most of their interactions tend to go longer than scheduled. The boss can anticipate this and adapt several strategies:

1. Have other work to do.
2. Set meeting times with integratives a half hour or more ahead of the actual time you expect the meeting to begin.
3. Remind the subordinate integrative of the importance of the meeting an hour or so before it is held.

If a boss can tolerate and master integrative meetings, the integrative employee can be enormously productive except for two other pitfalls: job burnout and power game withdrawal.

Job burnout refers to the job-person matching problem. When integratives are placed in complex and varied tasks, all works well—for a while. Even the most challenging jobs in most types of organizations become repetitive—hence boring—to an integrative. There are exceptions in areas such as research and the creative arts, but in managerial work problems do recur.

Solutions include job enrichment and lateral job moves or career spiralling (Driver, 1979b). The manager of integratives needs to plan ways to provide variety and increasing complexity in their work. This can be done by assigning increasingly complex tasks, moving them up in management (usually increasing social complexity), or moving them into new career areas over time.

Moving up in management can be a problem as senior management levels are approached. Here the time pressure increases with complexity. The integrative seems unusually sensitive to time pressure. Hence top management usually is not a good option for integratives who lack some "defense" (as we discuss later in Chapter Nine).

If these burnout protective moves are not taken, integratives can either try to be more decisive with increasing loss of morale or may create their own form of job enrichment—overly complicating their own world and everyone else's.

A second problem concerns politics. In highly competitive political battles, integratives—who are basically cooperative—feel disgusted and may withdraw, to their own and their boss's sorrow. A boss can try to create a more integrative culture by exposing secret plots and raising trust. Failing this, it becomes necessary to "run interference" at times for an overtrusting integrative by giving advice or even acting on others to block destructive moves. Sometimes an integrative can be induced to play at politics like a game for the good of the unit.

In turn, when properly guided in an atmosphere of trust, participation, and creative openness, integratives can be ideal subordinates—in the right job. They have the capacity to inject a new level of organization process and achievement into familiar structures.

Managing the Systemic

In dealing with the systemic subordinate, several guidelines can ensure best results:

1. Do not hurry tasks.
2. Provide adequate support for a thorough analysis of any problem.
3. Use a well-developed, impersonal control system.
4. Treat the systemic with respect as an expert.
5. Provide interaction time, but don't expect agreement.
6. Listen to stories.

In many ways, the systemic, in contrast with satisficing styles, reminds us of the classic tortoise and hare. Systemics often are maddeningly slow and deliberate, yet they very often win the race. If you wish a job done in a thorough yet creative fashion, this style is often your best choice.

This style is often unintentionally deceptive and can be easily misread. Systemics often appear integrative and seem to welcome participation, but as previously noted in Rule Five above, this participation is only a phase in their process. Summarizing during a discussion or assuming that no more will happen after a discussion with a systemic is folly. They have a great need to go away, sort things out their own way, and then come back to you with a proposal for action.

In managing tasks that have been agreed on, it is critical to set long time frames. Of all styles the systemic is most adverse to working fast. Unlike the integrative who gets flustered under time pressure, systemics often ignore it. If something must be done quickly, delegate it to someone else.

Related to this slowness is the mass of analysis this style needs to confront. The systemic style needs financial and human support to operate this type of analysis. The essence of this style is the need to be seen as an original. To do so systemics must be given the data and the opportunity to create unique solutions.

Systemics typically like to plan many projects for simultaneous attacks, but they prioritize the projects in terms of time and resources. Learning what inner system of values guides their priority list is very useful in managing this style.

In controlling progress with this style it is desirable to set up mutually agreed-on, impersonal controls. Frequent checking on progress is resented. Systemics need space as well as time and need to feel in control at a task level.

Socially, you should be prepared for infrequent but lengthy interactions with persons of this style. They seem to delight in telling stories or anecdotes of varying degrees of drollness. Attentive listening seems to be appreciated.

In managing task accomplishment, two primary problems may emerge: hidden agendas and isolation. If trust and respect are not established between you and systemics, they may not reveal their inner value systems to you. You may encounter only the integrative part of their style and assume you understand their thinking. Unfortunately, their priority systems may differ from yours. When un-covered, a boss may complain of hidden agendas. The solution seems to be to think through values and priorities with systemics and allow them to come back later with their priorities for further discussion. Success then lies in using rational analysis to resolve differences.

The isolation problem is more serious. Because they are hard to fathom and may seem slow and even insincere, people may avoid them. They work well alone, but this isolation may be detrimental to team effort and group morale.

One solution is to establish trust so that you can understand their values. You then can help others understand their style and build respect for the systemic's originality and precision.

When properly managed, the systemic style can provide the highest quality of output of any style when facing complex prob-lems. Systemics can provide a solid foundation of ethics and pro-fessionalism in practically all walks of life.

Each of the decision styles has different strengths and weaknesses. If they are understood and managed appropriately, however, each style can make significant, unique contributions. The keys are to assign a particular style to appropriate task environments, and to adapt your management style to coincide with the style's operating nature. Such effective matching can greatly enhance your manage-rial effectiveness as well as your subordinates' satisfaction, produc-tivity, and personal development.

9

Getting Ahead with Style

*T*his chapter takes a deeper look at how career issues are affected by decision style. Everyone wants a successful career. But what does success mean? People have many different meanings for career success. Before discussing how style can help you succeed in your career, we examine four basic definitions of career success to see how style relates to this basic question.

Definition of Career Success: Career Concepts

After studying careers for some time (Driver, 1979a, 1980, 1982, 1985, 1988), we have discovered that most people look at careers in one of four ways:

1. The *steady state career concept* sees a career as a lifelong involvement in an occupation such as law with increasing expertise and respect as signs of success.
2. The *linear career concept* defines a career as a steadily upward movement on some clearly defined ladder. In organizational management careers, success is defined as reaching the top.

3. The *spiral career concept* sees a career as a series of different careers, each lasting about ten years and each building on the strengths of the past but allowing the development of new skills. Success is seen as the development of one's inner potential to its maximum.

4. The *transitory career concept* defines a career as a series of short engagements of one to four years in varied fields with the key being novel challenge. Success is translated into the ability to meet greater challenges.

We have found some clear relationships between decision style and career concepts (Olson, 1979; Prince, 1979; Coombs, 1989). Table 9.1 reflects our findings. Interestingly, decisive style leans toward either steady state or linear careers and integrative toward spiral or steady state careers.

This means that those most focused on a purely linear struggle to get ahead are likely to be decisive or hierarchic style persons. Flexible style individuals are more likely interested in lateral moves, as are purely integrative types. And some decisive or integrative people prefer to find a lifelong vocation and stick with it.

These, of course, are generalizations. There are flexibles who seek to move up linear ladders and hierarchics who want to be steady state experts. In examining your career, however, you should first determine which concept you really want to follow. Once this is clear you can see how style dynamics can help you succeed.

Because most individuals in management careers tend to be linear (Driver and Hoffman, 1979), and because many organizations define success for their managers in a linear manner, this chapter focuses on how style dynamics can be used to aid a linear career.

Table 9.1. Career Concepts and Decision Operating Style.

Career concept	Related style
Steady state	Decisive, integrative
Linear	Hierarchic, decisive
Spiral	Integrative
Transitory	Flexible

Although we take a linear focus here, it is useful to mention the existence of career concept hybrids—combinations of other career concepts with linear. A linear/transitory type moves up by hopping from company to company at a rapid rate—always up. Then there is the linear/spiral who systematically moves around different functional areas at a slower pace—but also keeps moving up. Finally, the linear/steady state pattern climbs the ladder in one area.

Each of these hybrids has a style affinity: the linear/transitory links to flexible, the linear/spiral to integrative, and the linear/steady state to the other two styles. These differences speak to different career strategies that are explored below.

The Organization Fit Issue

There are three essentials in mapping linear success:

1. Find the right organization.
2. Find the right jobs.
3. Find the right boss.

Let's look at the organization fit issue. You can have the right job and the right boss but still feel totally frustrated with your career if the organization culture is wrong. Consider this case of Jim, a bright, young systems engineer. His boss thinks the world of him, his work is going extremely well, yet he is totally discouraged. Why? He is in the wrong type of organization. He is in a very flat, static engineering group with only three layers of management, no lateral moves, and possibly six to seven years for an upward move. He feels trapped. He must now make the right organizational choice. To make right choices we will use some ideas presented in Chapters Five and Six concerning style and organization. Two types of factors are relevant: (1) type of industry and (2) size and structure of organization. Figure 9.1 summarizes our thinking on the type of industry or occupation best suited to each style. The key dimensions are complexity and uncertainty. Industries or occupations of lower complexity and uncertainty are good matches for the decisive style.

A classic example of such a company is a large transportation company specializing in package movement. It prizes efficiency and

Figure 9.1. Industry Type and Decision Style.

	Simple		Complex
Certain	*Decisive* Food Transportation Assembly-type manufacturing Oil Tobacco	*Hierarchic* Pharmaceutical Utilities Financials Chemicals Construction	*Systemic* Aerospace
	Flexible Clothing Public accounting Entertainment Law	*Integrative* Electronics Computers Real estate development Consulting	
Uncertain			

speed, dislikes elaboration, and concentrates power at the top. It offers good opportunities to move up, and the advantage here lies with a person of a decisive style. Less decisive players often get sidetracked into staff positions from which they never return.

Flexible styles work best in relatively simple yet highly unstable areas. A classic illustration is the record business. The decisive person who wants to "lock in" and stick with a particular product here is lost, unless she connects with something like the Beatles. Heavy analytical orientation frequently is a liability in this type of industry, which prizes "gut feel."

In sharp contrast, the stable high technology firms such as chemicals or pharmaceuticals, where change in technology is relatively slow, usually develop elaborate linear ladders that reward technical competence and favor the hierarchic and systemic styles. Many investment firms managed by economists show similar traits.

As one moves into highly uncertain and complex arenas, the systemic and integrative come into their own. A classic example of this is the computer industry, where the emphasis has been on creative innovation and close teamwork in developing new products. Apple Computer started this way, and IBM decentralized its PCM group to adopt a similar style.

Underlying this industry map is a still more basic map of

organization structure and size. Figure 9.2 shows the ideal match pattern.

If you are a flexible person, your best choice is a small, informal organization. Typical examples include law partnerships or a unit in a large organization that sets up informal, temporary teams to handle business. Ideally, a flexible avoids large linear firms in favor of small units where the climb to the top is fast and involves acceptable job hopping. If flexibles do land in large bureaucracies, seeking the most flexible unit will aid their careers, as is discussed below.

An integrative is also better off out of the traditional linear bureaucracy. They do well in participative moderate-size units that deemphasize power and induce maximum involvement. As the popularity of these managerial ideas of high involvement penetrate traditional firms, the integrative style finds higher acceptance and fit. As with the flexible style, integratives in large organizations should seek to advance their careers in pockets of more participative culture.

The traditional organization with its rules and top-down power system is a good fit for decisive and hierarchic styles. The difference is that the decisive does better where the system is decentralized into a set of relatively independent units or baronies where each baron is his own master. Many modern universities fit this pattern. The hierarchic works better when rules and procedures link all units into a complex network of relationships.

Figure 9.2. Organization Structure and Decision Style.

Decisive	Hierarchic		
Small proprietorship or "baronies"	Larger "scientific bureaucracy"	Large matrix structures	Systemic
Small partnerships; loose teams	Larger organic systems		
Flexible	Integrative		

Finally, the systemic is most at home in the fairly common form of the matrix structure where there is a mix of traditional linear authority and participative teamwork. In sum, we suggest that a crucial early task in managing your career is to determine the right culture for your style.

You can use the guidelines provided here to adapt these concepts to variations from the main patterns we have identified. For instance, some highly innovative transportation companies may favor the integrative style.

The central tasks are to examine the economic environment and technology of the organization. Is the economic environment stable or highly turbulent? Is the technology simple or complex, changing or stable? These patterns change considerably. The once stable areas of banking and utilities, for instance, may be growing unstable.

A second way to assess culture is to look at people—especially top people in an organization. By studying interviews, stories, and biographies of key leaders in an organization you can do a "remote" style appraisal of a leader that can tell you much about the culture. In fact, we have found a surprisingly strong relation between leader style and the style culture of organizations. The checklists in Chapters Five and Six can be completed with fair accuracy on key leaders using information found in articles and books.

An astute person can use job interviews to assess culture. One can get information on how groups are organized, how much power is decentralized, what type of person is admired, and so on. This process is particularly useful in dealing with people inside work units as opposed to recruiters.

Using methods outlined here, the ideal move is for each style to select its best match in industry and organization structures. This leaves larger bureaucracies of the traditional type largely to decisive and hierarchic styles and smaller or more participative organizations to flexible and integrative styles.

Because most sizable organizations in the United States today remain traditional, however, the problem of managing a career in such systems is *not* restricted to decisives and hierarchics. We believe that the following task fit guide can help all styles cope with linear careers in traditional bureaucracies.

Task Fit

In traditional linear bureaucracies, decision styles play a crucial role in successful movement up the career ladder. We have found that a consistent style pattern emerges during movement up the managerial ladder. Three layers of management are usually described—supervisory, middle level, and top management—and the tasks performed by these managers are seen as quite distinct. Not surprisingly we find different styles work best at each level.

To illustrate this phenomenon we present in Table 9.2 a tasks analysis of the three main levels of management. This chart is not based on any one company but represents many years of experience doing executive succession planning and managerial selection for a wide range of companies.

Consider the first-level supervisor. This is usually a high-pressure situation with fairly structured procedures. The incumbent does not have to handle complex social situations or complex data

Table 9.2. Tasks Analysis of Managerial Work at Three Levels.

Task dimension	First-level supervisor	Middle manager	Top management
1. Control by rules; boss	High	Medium	Low
2. Routine	High	Medium	Low
3. Complexity of information (reports, etc.)	Low	Medium	High
4. Time pressure	High	Low	High
5. Stress	Medium	Low	Medium-high
6. Rewards	Low	Medium	High
7. Planning horizon	Low	Medium	High
8. Frequency of meetings (committees, etc.)	Low	High	Medium
9. Creativity need	Low	High	Medium
10. Complexity of people dealt with	Low	Medium	High

analysis. Given these position demands it is not surprising that across many industries we find a decisive style works best in first-level supervision. Factors 1, 2, and 9 measure uncertainty in the job, and when low, as for supervisor, they call for a unifocus style. Factors 3, 7, 8, and 10 apply to the complexity of the position; low scores call for satisficing styles. Factors 4, 5, and 6 measure environmental load and, when high, argue for satisficing styles. As you can see, the supervisor job calls for unifocus and almost total satisficing—the decisive style.

Note the shifts in Table 9.2 for middle management. Typically, we find that uncertainty factors increase in middle management, sometimes to high levels. Unifocus shifts possibly to multifocus. Even more pronounced are changes in complexity and load. The middle manager has to read complex reports, deal with long-range planning, sit on endless committees, and deal with subtle, difficult people. At the same time, pressures such as stress and deadlines retreat—environmental load decreases here. The net effect is to move people into a moderate-load condition where multifocus, maximizing styles can flourish. This is the realm of the integrative, systemic, and sometimes hierarchic styles. Our research in many organizations confirms this expectation.

Top management provides a major challenge. Uncertainty continues to increase, as does complexity. Most current studies on leadership (Bennis and Nanus, 1986) stress that the leader must provide a vision for an organization, a vision forged by them out of uncertainty, which can provide certainty to the organization. Top managers actually have to serve as "uncertainty absorbers" for the rest of the organization. Hence we see a strong need for multifocus thinkers at the top. This is further underlined by the need to deal with highly diverse stakeholders.

Complexity demands in top management also escalate. Planning horizons lengthen, meetings become even more complex, as do the people dealt with. Most senior managers handle an enormous mass of information.

Yet load factors like time pressure do *not* continue the downward trend found in middle management. In senior positions time pressure maximizes, as do rewards. Stress actually declines somewhat at the very top but is high for those near the top. The paradox here is that one needs to satisfice to handle load yet maximize to handle complexity. One must be multifocus to create strategy and vision but unifocus to reduce uncertainty in subordinates.

What style can possibly work here? The final verdict is not in, but our current hypothesis is that a decisive/ integrative operating style (with most likely an integrative/decisive role style) works best in top management. We call this pattern the executive style.

Figure 9.3 illustrates this style pattern. At this operating level, the executive style person makes quick decisive decisions except when pressure is moderate, when complex planning and envisioning can occur. Often individuals with the executive style know how to maneuver the environment to produce this integrative window: holding calls and going off-site are two familiar mechanisms they use.

Conversely, in today's "participative" world the executive gives off an aura of participation and creativity (integrative role styles), which is shed only when pressure is high, when the decisive role matches the decisive operating style.

Figure 9.3. Executive Style.

Decisive   Integrative   Decisive

Operating
style
    Low   Moderate   High

Integrative

Role
style
   Decisive   Decisive

    Low   Moderate   High

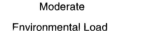

Environmental Load

There are many situations where this model may not apply. For instance, in structured environments a decisive/systemic pattern may appear at the top. However, we believe that this model (the D-I-D model) can serve as a blueprint for mapping linear careers in linear organizations.

The obvious problem here is style transition. The model suggests that the best style for first-level supervision is decisive. Given the prevailing reliance on performance appraisal for promotion, the most decisive supervisor is most likely to be promoted out of supervision into middle management. But an integrative world awaits this person in middle management.

This mismatch has resulted in untold numbers of career disasters—middle managers who just "peaked out," decisives who could not cope with integrative positions.

The problem continues into top management. Here again, based on performance the best integrative is promoted into senior management, only to find a world of massive time pressure and demands for certainty. Even more depressing career wreckage is found at this level: integratives unable to adopt an executive style often are "put on a shelf."

What can you do to survive these obstacles? An obvious answer is that those with decisive/integrative styles have an optimal chance for success in traditional linear organizations. Those with other styles should consider other types of organizations or consider a style modification (see Chapter Ten). Organizations are rarely as simple as the D-I-D paradigm suggests, however. There are important sectors inside traditional linear bureaucracies where the hierarchic and even the flexible patterns often flourish. These areas are "landmines" for the decisive/integratives and "safe refuges" for the hierarchic or flexible.

Table 9.3 shows a highly schematic view of a typical bureaucratic organization's departments at three levels: nonmanagement, supervisory, middle management. In each area we specify an optimal style pattern based on task analysis. This is generalized but is typical of many organizations. In general, note that nonmanagement positions are quite diverse. Only manufacturing or operations favors the decisive style at this level. Hierarchic is favored by finance/accounting and engineering, and integrative shows strongly

Table 9.3. Style Map of Traditional Bureaucracy.

Functional level	Sales		Department marketing	Finance accounting	Manufactur- ing operations	Engineering	Legal	Human resources
	Simple	Complex						
Nonmanagement	F/D	I/H	I	H/F	D/I	H/I S	F/H	I/I
First-level supervision	D/F	D/I	D/I	D/H	D/I	D/H	D/F	D/I
Middle management	F/I	I/H	I/D	H/D	I/D	H/D S/D	F/D	I/□

Executive style: D/I

in marketing and complex sales (*complex sales* refers to selling technically complex products or services with a long sales cycle). Systemic adapts to engineering, and flexible to simple sales, human resources, and legal. At this level a typical bureaucracy can accommodate each style in the right functional area.

Moving to supervision is difficult in some areas. For instance, complex sales and marketing operatives need to acquire a decisive style that directly opposes their integrative style. As Chapter Ten demonstrates, it is no easy task shifting to a decisive mode, especially with no help from the organization.

The style model suggests that transitions of this magnitude are helped immensely by awareness of the problem by both the new supervisor and his or her boss. The new promotee can be given a role model (another supervisor who is operating as an effective decisive) and support by the boss. It also helps if the human resource (HR) department can develop programs stressing decisive behavior (such as time management). In fact, supervisory training programs can facilitate this transition. The military has built some excellent prototypes in their officer candidate programs.

Similar problems attend transitions to middle management. Here the major traumas may be in simple sales, where an integrative style has to be developed from a decisive/flexible pattern. Again, mutual understanding by boss and promotee, plus a human resource middle-manager training program aimed at increasing integrative or hierarchic styles, greatly aid the transition.

Note in Table 9.3 that a critical assumption is that a backup style of integrative or hierarchic is maintained in first-level supervisors. This must be done by making part of their work less time pressured and more complex. In some organizations temporary assignments can attain this goal. Where this assumption is not met and supervisors become superdecisive, the transition to middle management becomes far more difficult.

The final transition in Table 9.3 to top management also has differential problems. For human resources, operations, or marketing, the shift is from a backup to a dominant style, which is relatively easy. For other functions—such as engineering, sales, or finance—the shift is far more demanding and requires a top management training program to facilitate the process.

This general map indicates that the best point of entry for a decisive is operations. The main problem is developing an integrative backup style. One method is to attend outside courses that foster complex, multifocus thinking in a low-pressure setting. MBA programs help here, or human resource departments can set up integrative training programs for would-be managers (as some companies have, in fact, done). Another tactic is for the decisive person to cross-train in and work with nondecisive functions such as marketing on a *gradual* basis.

If the decisive succeeds in acquiring an integrative backup, the next challenge is to maintain it as a first-level supervisor. Overload can burn out the integrative over time. If this happens, work load must at least temporarily be reduced. Often, more delegating can help here. On promotion to middle manager, the decisive/integrative has merely to reverse dominant and backup styles, which we know relatively brief training can accomplish (Driver, 1979a; Driver and Pate, 1989). The shift to top management also requires this reversal process.

For the flexible person, a linear career is more difficult in a traditional bureaucracy. Entry into congenial areas (sales, employee relations, legal) is easy enough, but moving into first-level supervision requires acquiring a decisive style, which, if it is not already a backup style, is not easy. Here again, if the human resource personnel are aware of style dynamics, a decisive training program for first-level managers would greatly help. Note that we have found that this transition often is particularly difficult in human resource departments themselves.

A totally different type of solution for organizations is to hire supervisors from outside when style change demands on employees are too drastic. This, however, does not solve the career problem of flexibles. Perhaps a move to a more flexible type of supervisor would help.

By the time we reach middle management, flexible disappears from human relations (HR) and holds in legal and simpler sales. However, transition to senior management from these two areas seems far more difficult than areas such as marketing or operations. It seems that a flexible person on a linear track in a linear organization needs to ultimately shed this style if his or her goal is top management.

The route to success for a hierarchic or systemic is a bit less thorny in traditional organizations. Classic entry positions are finance and engineering. As with the flexible, a decisive backup needs to be acquired to move into first-level supervision. Special training and assignments stressing timeliness can accomplish this. Moving into middle management is a simple reversal for finance but involves a more integrative development for engineering (except in the most routine technologies). Because this inclusion of integrative style puts engineering middle managers closer to the executive style than typical finance middle managers, the transition to top management is more demanding for finance managers.

For integratives, the best entry positions are complex sales, marketing, and HR. The first two require the addition of a decisive backup for promotion to supervisor. This is more difficult for the integrative than the hierarchic or flexible but can be done. The HR route seems far more difficult and may account for why progress from entry to supervisor in HR is difficult. The next transition to middle manager is easiest in marketing, suggesting that this area is the best route for integratives with linear aspirations. More steady state integratives could do well in complex sales. Linear/spiral integratives might consider rotating into HR at the middle management level only.

One interesting implication of the D-I-D problem is that for nondecisive people, skipping first-level supervision may be an attractive career option. Its danger is that you may not develop the necessary decisive style as a backup.

We believe that you can find a route to success even in organizations alien to your style, if you pay attention to the tasks required and are willing to acquire new styles. The map provided here is one illustration of the process. We suggest that you use the factors in Table 9.2 to analyze jobs in your projected career path to assess your fit and to determine any needed style changes.

Interpersonal Factors

Even with the best fit with organization and tasks, careers can fail. The cause is interpersonal—often called "bad chemistry." We all can recall cases where, despite phenomenal task success and rave reviews by all around, a career is stymied. The person simply did not get along with a boss.

Earlier chapters discussed getting along with subordinates and peers. We conclude this chapter with a discussion of how to get along with superiors.

There is an important difference between getting along with immediate supervisors and getting along with more remote executives who may play a mentor or sponsor role in your careers. Interactions with the higher-level elite require attention to your role style, because with them you are most self-conscious. Your immediate boss usually interacts enough with you to be concerned with both your operating and role styles.

Countless issues are raised by this topic, but we focus on key style problems encountered by each possible combination of boss and subordinate styles. In general, the best strategy seems to be to find a boss not too dissimilar in style. People with similar styles tend to like each other and feel that their chemistry is good. It has even been found that students with styles similar to their professors get better grades than their dissimilar peers.

A glance at Table 9.4 shows that even with similar styles, problems between supervisors and subordinates can emerge. The decisive pair works well if their values don't clash. If you are a decisive working for a decisive boss, we strongly advise you to very carefully avoid value-laden topics (such as religion and politics) unless you learn that you both agree. If you're not careful here, you can have a head-on collision, with you as the loser.

Flexible and integrative pairs get along very well—too well. The danger here is that they bring out their mutual tendencies to bounce among a multitude of topics and get no one thing done. As a subordinate in such a situation you can gain respect by being alert to this tendency and offering to "close in" on a particular action. This will improve both of your images in generally decisive-hierarchic linear organizations.

Systemic pairs have a problem not unlike decisives: because both appear open and keep their inner priorities private, both may assume a nonexistent agreement on goals. As a systemic subordinate

Table 9.4. Key Boss-Subordinate Style Problems.

Subordinate style	Boss style				
	Decisive	Flexible	Hierarchic	Integrative	Systemic
Decisive	Values clash	Too rigid	Not analytic	Rigid	Simplistic
Flexible	Not meeting commitments	Too much fun	No planning; inconsistent	Not confronting	Unreliable
Hierarchic	Too analytic	Too analytic and rigid	Too threatening	Too structured; manipulative	Too rigid
Integrative	Too many ideas (don't get things done)	Too slow	Too creative	Nothing gets done	Too loose
Systemic	Not "upfront"	Too slow	Not "upfront"	Too slow	Values clash

it is vital to work with your boss to lay his priorities out on the table. Differences then can be openly and rationally addressed.

The most difficult like pair are two hierarchics. If not managed carefully, this relationship can turn into a battle of competency, which the subordinate is likely to lose. As a hierarchic subordinate it is vital to gain your hierarchic boss's respect but fatal to be *too* competent. A good strategy is to provide a competency the boss lacks in a way that makes you both look good. It is important to openly acknowledge your boss's competence in his or her areas of strength when dealing with mutual supervisors. In general, trying to build a win-win team approach in competition with others can be quite successful.

Table 9.4 summarizes the major problems we see emerging in cross-style boss-subordinate relationships. For instance, flexibles working for decisives are most often in trouble for agreeing to accomplish something that they subsequently disregard. The flexible subordinate sees a need to change tactics and no need to notify a boss. The decisive boss does not get upset over minor activities but is upset if major goals and milestones are missed. If you are a flexible working for a decisive, be sure to identify key objectives that must be met, as opposed to minor activities that can be shifted. If you think major goals may be missed, it is critical to communicate this so corrective action can be taken.

Decisive bosses tend to like hierarchic subordinates if they do not drown them in too much detail. The decisive boss likes to probe subordinates now and then to see if they're "on their toes," but forcing the decisive to sit through exhaustive analyses can be the kiss of death for a hierarchic subordinate. You must prepare summary briefings and keep the more elaborate analyses on hand—to be produced as needed.

A fairly difficult relationship to manage is the decisive boss-integrative subordinate interface. We have seen many decisive bosses close to despair over integrative subordinates who, with the best will in the world, come in and deluge them with "great new ideas." When this is coupled with the decisive view that integratives don't get things done, the result can be disastrous.

If you are an integrative working for a decisive, it is essential that you respect the decisive boss's time concern. Do not go in for an open-ended chat at just any time. First work over a new idea yourself and test it out on others. Is it really worth your boss's time? If it is, get it summarized into a few key points. Set a meeting with your boss at an unhurried time (such as the end of the day), and avoid running over the time allotted. A few good meetings where you give worthwhile ideas will be welcome, as opposed to a constant barrage.

It is also important to give your decisive boss frequent updates on your accomplishments toward goals. You must counteract the impression that you are all talk and no action.

A systemic working for a decisive is well advised to get his or her more structured side in evidence. It is far better to act more hierarchically and reveal your analytic side than to be seen as an integrative who isn't really integrative. As such you lose on two counts: the decisive dislikes purely integrative process and misreads your complex shifting from integrative to hierarchic as insincerity.

Flexible bosses find decisives (and to some degree hierarchics) too rigid. If you are a decisive working for a flexible, it is important to unobtrusively check on directions at frequent intervals. One way is to drop in often for a discussion of your recent progress. Do not be surprised if directions have changed; make certain it is a real change and not a tentative idea. This can be done by pointing out the costs and benefits of continuing versus changing. If you sense change is real, don't keep fighting for the earlier plan; a brief discussion of costs can often keep your flexible boss on course.

Hierarchics can have considerable difficulty working for a flexible. They are seen as rigid, too mired in detail, and lacking intuition. One way to handle this problem is to use your hierarchic style to anticipate possible moves by your flexible boss and be prepared to go along as he changes course without abandoning overall planning. As with the decisive boss, you must also keep briefings brief—preferably verbal for a flexible boss.

Integratives and systemics can work rather well with flexible bosses if they avoid overdoing discussions. Unlike with a decisive boss, you can "pop in" to a flexible for a discussion, but do so with a preworked idea that you can get across in a few minutes. It is also important not to take too much time to accomplish tasks of high priority to a flexible. It is crucial to move a quick solution into place from time to time. You can always fine-tune it in a more complex way later.

Decisives can work well for a hierarchic boss if they take time to review exactly what the boss wants done. Occasionally taking time to do some homework on a project of great importance to the boss wins respect that you can be analytic when time permits.

A much more difficult situation occurs for flexibles working for a hierarchic. They are seen as scattered and unreliable. We have seen this relationship frequently end in termination. The solution lies in self-discipline. You must avoid "dropping in to talk" without considering how it will be perceived. Does it fit with the boss's agenda? You must determine critical agreements and stick with them. If you feel the need to change tactics, think it out with someone else, get supporting data, then check it out. Never try a spontaneous shift of direction, even in minor areas.

A far easier relationship holds between integrative and hierarchic styles. Mutual respect based on analysis is usually developed. However, the integrative must observe some of the cautions raised in dealing with the decisive boss in this relationship also. Spontaneous chats are not welcome. You should determine their relevance in advance, prepare any relevant data, and schedule a formal meeting. You also need to keep the hierarchic posted on progress.

The systemic-hierarchic relation can work extremely well, especially if systemics reveal their more hierarchic side. The only dangers are in hiding their real values or in being too threatening (discussed previously concerning two hierarchics). Usually the more open manner of the systemic diffuses this competitive tension, so the main issue is to uncover basic values for rational discussion.

Working for integratives may be the easiest to manage because they exhibit empathy and try to understand you. However, decisives working for an integrative often run into severe problems; they are in danger of being seen as "hip shooters" and out of touch with the big picture. As with the hierarchic boss, decisives in this situation must take time to do homework on some projects. They must schedule time for their boss to come in for integrative discussions and be prepared for meetings to run over. Probably the best idea is to be open about differences and work on the complementary nature of your styles. You can be the one who keeps things on track and on time—an asset in a decisive-hierarchic organization.

Flexibles can get along well with integrative bosses if they curb their tendency to smooth over all conflicts. The integrative enjoys getting into conflict and hammering out a consensus; the flexible prefers to gloss over such issues. If this is your situation, you should solve them. Integratives do *not* think ill of you or your subordinates if you are involved in conflicts or problems.

As mentioned, hierarchic-integrative relationships can be quite successful. The hierarchic, however, must plan ahead to cope with the integrative's direction shifts so as to not seem excessively rigid. They must also respect the integrative penchant for openness. Hierarchics can be seen as too Machiavellian if they do not share their thinking frequently with their boss.

Systemic-integrative relations also can go extremely well if values are shared. Another concern is speed. At times the integrative likes to make creative leaps; these must be supported, not criticized, at the time. You should reserve critical analysis for later.

Systemic bosses can be somewhat difficult to understand, particularly for decisive subordinates. The integrative side of the boss may mislead them to miss the real structure in this style. The systemic, in turn, is likely to find the decisive and flexible styles too simplistic. The two satisficing styles in this situation need to occasionally do homework on key issues. They must patiently probe for the systemic's real priorities and focus on them. Flexibles, in turn, must be careful to follow through on key commitments or check with the boss if they feel they must change.

Maximizer styles can get along very well with a systemic boss—if they realize the dual nature of this style and correct for the side of the systemic they least resemble. The hierarchic needs to loosen up, especially in preliminary stages of a problem. The integrative needs to realize that the systemic does want to systematize solutions at some time.

We suggest that finding similar style bosses (except for hierarchics) is often the best way to achieve career success. When it is not possible to control this, avoiding the major pitfalls identified in Table 9.4 and stressing complementarity can help strengthen relationships. In the next chapter we deal with one solution to achieving career success: changing your style.

10

Modifying and Adapting Your Style

So you want to change your style? Perhaps you have concluded that you are too hierarchic and you want to be more flexible, or you feel that you are too decisive and want to be more integrative. These kinds of style change objectives are possible to achieve and may be worthy goals. But before you embark on an ambitious program of style change, let's take a look at what may be in store for you and at some alternatives.

Assessing Your Options and Alternatives

First of all, you should be certain that style change is the appropriate route for you to take. Style change can be extremely challenging. If, for example, you have a highly integrative operating style, and you want to change to a decisive operating style, you can be very sure that making this transition will not simply be a matter of rolling out of bed on a different side in the morning. You probably will be working against many years of experience and reinforcement of your present style. The process could be long and arduous.

If you are contemplating a style change, you should assess both the pros and cons of the change. First, what is leading you to think about changing style? What advantages might you gain in changing style? What are the disadvantages? How big of a gap is there between your current style or styles and the style you want to develop?

Very often, changing styles is clearly a less than ideal way to deal with a bad fit between a style and a situation. Instead, you may be much better off finding ways to take advantage of the style that you are most comfortable using now.

Changing Situations

It's important to keep in mind the very basic idea that styles are neither good nor bad. A style can be thought of as good only if it fits well the demands of a situation. Instead of changing your style to fit your situation, a more appropriate, easier, and realistic action might be to change situations. Rather than become more decisive, why not find yourself a new situation in which being integrative works to your advantage? This allows you to capitalize on and reap the benefits of the years that you have invested in the development of your current style.

Consider the case of Jack Harper. Jack began his career in sales early, as a high school student selling encyclopedias. After high school and college he moved through a series of sales jobs in which he accumulated an impressive track record of success. When we met him, he had been working for a company selling information services for five years. For the first three of the five years, he had been one of the leading sales reps for the company. During the past two years, however, his sales had fallen dramatically, until he was close to the bottom. When we spoke to him, he hadn't closed a single sale in over six months. As far as Jack was concerned, he had "lost it."

During this time, the company had undergone a major shift in strategy away from service contracts to "big ticket" software system sales. Analysis of the sales job and of sales reps' styles and sales records showed clearly that an integrative/hierarchic operating style combination was best for success.

Jack's operating style was very flexible with a decisive backup. This was a good fit with the company's past service sales strategy with its emphasis on cold calls, knocking on doors, getting in and out quick, and closing many deals. But it just did not fit the new big-ticket sales strategy with its lengthy sales cycle and emphasis on closing a few very large sales each year.

Jack hadn't lost it, of course. Instead, the job had changed. Should he have committed to a program for developing an integrative/hierarchic style combination? He wanted—very desperately—to be successful once more, and he saw himself as a sales professional, so the idea of getting out of sales did not appeal to him. On reflection, he really had no particular intrinsic interest in big, complex systems. What he wanted was to close sales—lots of them.

Jack made what was probably the best choice for himself. Instead of struggling with the new sales process and trying to adjust his style, he opted to capitalize on his past experience and go for success as a high producer of service sales for a different company.

Job Redesign

Another way to deal with a misfit between your style and your situation is to modify your situation so that it better fits your style. Redesign of your job makes sense if your current style fits well with most parts of your current responsibilities but misses by a mile one particular aspect of your job. If this is the case, you probably are the occupant of a poorly designed job.

Many jobs are poorly designed in the sense that they fundamentally call for two very different style profiles. Even though most of us are able to shift from primary to backup styles, there are limits to our ability to adapt our styles as we move from one situation or task to another. For example, few of us would be able to move easily from being extremely decisive in one situation to being extremely integrative in another. Yet jobs set up as though this kind of adaptability is easy are not all that uncommon.

One recent example in an aerospace company was the job of program manager with responsibility for winning major new contracts. As the job was set up, the program manager was chiefly responsible for planning and strategizing for capturing and managing demonstration contracts that over a period of years would lead to an award of a contract worth hundreds of millions of dollars.

The target program was still being defined as the initial contracts were being awarded to the competing companies, and there were many, many twists and turns that budgets, politics, and competitors could take to steer the competition in different directions. The program manager had to anticipate these twists and turns and then plan for them or, better yet, influence them favorably for his company.

However, the program manager was also responsible for building, organizing, and managing an organization to handle the competition and the demonstration contracts. He had to keep his team members fully informed of developments, make assignments, coordinate their activities, and monitor performance. These tasks were made even more demanding because the technology involved in the program was relatively new for the company, so personnel and organizational arrangements that had worked well on past programs could not be assumed to yield successful results for the new program.

From a decision style perspective, this program manager position was a "bad design." On the one hand it required long-range thinking, high comfort with ambiguity and uncertainty, creativity in generating new strategies, and in-depth understanding of events and trends in technology and politics. On the other hand, it required frequent and careful attention to immediate organizational problems, budgets, and logistics.

When a job calls for two or more very different styles, you usually find that certain parts of the job are neglected in favor of other parts. This may not be a big deal if the neglected parts are not very important. But if they are all important, as was the case with the program manager job, poor job design spells trouble.

That's what we saw happening. Frank, the incumbent program manager, had a highly integrative operating style with a strong hierarchic backup style. Consequently, he was doing a super job of tracking developments on the program and anticipating and planning for twists and turns that were shaping the course of the competition. He was wowing his customers with his understanding of the technology and his capacity to generate and articulate ideas.

However, internal management of the program organization was suffering. At staff meetings, Frank overwhelmed his people with information and ideas. The meetings were lengthy, but agendas were sometimes unclear and seldom adhered to. People began to resent the loss of "productive time." Although they grew more and more impressed with Frank's command of information, they felt confused about exactly what they should be doing with the information presented at the meetings.

Of course, there are many good reasons for modifying your style, related to a changing work situation, promotion, transfer, or the need to work compatibly with people whose styles differ from yours. There are two basic style change strategies. One strategy involves moderating the intensity of your style. This allows you to continue using the style you have grown accustomed to, but more judiciously than you might have in the past. The second strategy involves fundamentally changing your style from one primary operating style to another. This is the more ambitious of the two strategies, but there are times when the challenge is worth every bit of the effort it requires.

Toning Down Your Style

Each style has its own potential strengths and weaknesses. As a person's style habit becomes stronger, both the strong and weak points of a particular style become more noticeable.

Very often a person can improve his or her style fit with a job or situation by learning to avoid the potential pitfalls of his or her current style. This might be the case where a person simply is too decisive, too hierarchic, or too flexible for a particular job.

Let's imagine that a customer service manager job requires a person to be responsive to the frequently changing and highly varied demands and preferences of customers. A moderate flexible style fits the job well. Now suppose that the current incumbent, Jerry, is extremely flexible. Although Jerry probably is viewed as very fast and responsive, he runs the risk of being seen by his boss as too willing to acquiesce to customer requests, too willing to give away the show, and possibly creating bad precedents for the future with other customers. Some customers love him, but others feel that he jumps too fast to conclusions about what they need or that he promises them the world but often fails to follow through on his commitments. Others may see him as unreliable, maybe even sneaky, because they have heard him saying different things to different customers about the same issue.

Jerry's job requires him to be flexible but not as extremely flexible as his current style. He needs to tone down his flexible style. Rather than trying to be more decisive or hierarchic, Jerry's first task in modifying his style is to back off from the flexible style somewhat by consciously watching out for the dangers of his currently too flexible style.

If Jerry does this, he can naturally decrease the intensity of his flexible style without losing its main advantages. At the same time, he can open a window of opportunity and experiment with other styles that previously were overshadowed by his extreme flexible style.

To tone down your style, of course, you need first to be aware of your style and then to understand what the potential failings of your style are. Table 10.1 lists some of the noteworthy liabilities of each of the five decision styles. Once you clearly see the potential pitfalls that your style may be leading you into, you can devise a program of style change:

1. On a regular basis, think about situations you must deal with soon, anticipate the specific problems your usual style might create, and plan to take actions to avoid those problems.
2. On a regular basis, review situations you have dealt with recently, determine whether you fell into a style-related pitfall, and plan corrective action for the future.

Toning Down the Decisive Style

Despite the many virtues of the decisive style, liabilities begin to show up if it is used more than required.

When decisives run into difficulties in solving problems and decision making, they usually have jumped to a conclusion without sufficient analysis, or they have failed to consider more than one possible course of action for dealing with an issue or a problem. Because it is most likely that they have relied only on tried-and-true

Table 10.1. Potential Negative Images of Each Decision Style.

Decisive	Flexible	Hierarchic	Integrative	Systemic
Impulsive	Too changeable	Dogmatic	Too slow	Too slow
Intolerant of complexity	Lacks commitment	Arrogant	Too unpredictable	Difficult to read
Resistant to change	Too agreeable	Overcontrolling	Overcomplicated	Secretive
Poor listener	Flippant	Too critical	"Debates" too much	Wants too many things
Intolerant of others	Scattered	Perfectionist	Doesn't respect rules	Manipulative
	Insensitive			Too cautious
				Overcomplicates

solutions as possible remedies, the solution they have chosen may not work if the problem is new or unusual. Finding that the usual solutions are unlikely to work, they sometimes conclude that the problem defies solution.

In the eyes of people whose styles are not decisive, this behavior looks unthoughtful and impulsive. They see the decisive as unable to handle complexity, resistant to input, and unwilling to do things in new ways. Moreover, because decisives are steaming ahead while others may still be trying to understand what the problem is all about, they get the reputation of being impatient and poor listeners. This also conveys the feeling that they are indifferent to and hard on people. If your style is decisive and you sense that you are running into these types of difficulties, try some of the following remedies to help tone down your decisiveness:

1. Watch for your feelings of impatience: they are good signals that you are about to shift into hyperdecisive gear. Make a conscious effort to relax. Use any trick you can to get your feelings of impatience under control.
2. Rid yourself of any belief you may have that making quick decisions is a sign of intelligence. Research shows that no decision style has the edge over any other in the intelligence department (Driver, Sundby, and Chulef, 1989).
3. Make an extra effort to listen to what others are saying, and make sure to show that you are listening.
4. When you feel that you have reached a decision, set it aside at least momentarily. See if there is another way of handling the situation. Ask others if they can see a better alternative.

Practicing these remedies will help to eliminate some of the abrasive potential of your decisiveness. You don't have to change your style. You can take these precautionary measures and still retain the advantages of the decisive style.

Toning Down the Flexible Style

Flexibles usually get themselves into trouble when they change their minds once too often. They may take a strong position on some issue but later pursue a very different course of action in response to recent developments. Or they may abandon a whole series of business strategies as difficulties with each become apparent. Consequently, despite a great deal of activity, they may make very little progress.

In their relationships with other people, flexibles sometimes experience problems because they appear vacillating and unreliable. They redefine in their own minds agreements reached with other people, leaving others with the impression that they cannot be trusted. Sometimes flexibles assume that situations have changed so much that old agreements are pointless, yet their less flexible colleagues may still expect explicit commitments to be honored.

Because flexibles emphasize action and alternatives, they generate many ideas rapidly. They are inclined to speak rapidly and to shift quickly from topic to topic. Unless they do a lot of self-censoring, they say things that startle others, giving the impression that they are flippant or insensitive and that they cannot be taken seriously. As this impression grows, those whose styles are less flexible, particularly those whose styles are hierarchic or systemic, began to mentally write them off as lightweights with little to contribute.

If your style is flexible and you are having some of these problems, you may want to experiment with some of the following techniques:

1. If you change your mind about some issue, let others who might be affected by your actions know that you have changed your mind, and give reasons for your change of heart. Don't give the impression that you are behaving arbitrarily or that you simply are caving in to pressure or reacting to only the most recent input of data.

2. When you feel yourself losing interest in, or confidence in, a particular course of action or strategy, find a new strategy that still preserves important features of the one you have been pursuing. Don't leap to some wildly new course of action, even if it looks intriguing. Involve other people in your analysis. This minimizes later confusion and the chances that others will see you simply as "weather-vaning."

The main thing to keep in mind is that changing your mind costs you credibility. You risk confusing others. You lose time and energy overcoming momentum. You incur start-up costs associated with new courses of action. Keep these costs in mind when you find yourself about to shift directions. To make the change worthwhile, the potential benefits clearly should outweigh the costs that you are sure to incur.

Toning Down the Hierarchic Style

People get into trouble using the hierarchic style by doing too much of everything: they analyze too much, lecture too much, give too many instructions, concern themselves with too many details, criticize too much, overcommit too much to a goal and method, and expect too much of themselves and others.

If you need to tone down your hierarchic style, you can make real progress by learning to let go. Here are some tips to keep in mind:

1. Learn to let go a bit. Try striving for a little less perfection. Learn to discriminate problems and issues that really do require exhaustive analysis and exacting solutions from those that are less complicated and critical.
2. Try being a little less demanding of yourself and of others. People inevitably make mistakes, but rather than seeing that tendency as negative, recognize that people often learn from mistakes. In fact, mistakes can lead to truly creative breakthroughs and new insights.
3. Give other people room for discretion. Permit some autonomy. The only way that you can be sure that things will be done precisely as you believe they should is to do them yourself. But you can't do everything, can you? You can't control others' actions totally, but unfortunately, you can all too easily frustrate and alienate people as you try.
4. Find something of value in another's idea—especially if it is very different from your idea. Accept that there can be value in doing things differently than your own preference. You gain

stature when you give another person credit for the value that you see in his or her idea.

Learning to back off from, without abandoning, the hierarchic style can actually be fun. You may find some truly worthwhile new ideas, and you will experience less stress and tension by letting go of nonessential details and objectives. The trick is learning to recognize things that are nonessential.

Toning Down the Integrative Style

When the integrative style gets out of hand, several things usually happen. Time passes without notice, so deadlines are missed and schedules get messed up. Other people become confused by the profusion of ideas and possibilities that integratives talk about and conclude that integratives are confused and "fuzzy headed."

Integratives also generate conflict by seeming to argue or debate too much. Even though they may be arguing different points of view just to better understand an issue, other people whose styles are less integrative seldom realize or appreciate this. Instead, they chafe at the integrative's apparent attempts to overcomplicate issues and possibly to "start trouble."

Integratives also get into trouble by not following rules and procedures. Instead, they may prefer to experiment with a new procedure just for the heck of it. This gives them the image of being unpredictable and disrespectful.

If you need to tone down an overly integrative style, you should become aware of the costs of your style. Then try working with some of the following suggestions:

1. Like the hierarchic, you might benefit from consciously conserving your integrative energy for situations in which your creative breakthroughs are most needed and will be most appreciated. Otherwise, you risk losing credibility that you may need when you encounter a situation that presents a real opportunity for integrative thinking. You also risk creating social distance between you and other people whose inputs you may need some day.

2. Be alert to opportunities to capitalize on your past experience
    to achieve some short-term objectives, even if this means fore-
    going the opportunity to try out a new technique or method.
    These accomplishments will also win you credits that you may
    need some day to make a real deviation from the beaten path.
3. Be a little more direct in your communication. If you can pre-
    pare ahead of time, try pruning your communication of "side
    trips" that add little to the important parts of your message.
    The less extraneous information you give, the less the chance
    that you will be misunderstood or that important ideas will get
    lost.
4. Prioritize your objectives before working on a problem or mak-
    ing a decision. Then make an effort to seriously consider only
    ideas and alternatives that meet those priorities. Beware of chas-
    ing too many ideas that do not fit your immediate priorities.
    Promise yourself that you will implement the first workable
    solution you generate unless you find another that is clearly
    superior. This cuts down on your tendency to procrastinate.

Toning Down the Systemic Style

Systemics run into problems when, by choice or circumstance, their
lines of communication with other people are neglected. Because of
their complexity—their tendency to work on interrelated sets of
problems and to opt for strategies that satisfy many goals simultaneously—it is all too easy for them to get lost in their own private
worlds. They find that few others can or will appreciate their visions and the complex reasoning behind their plans, so they often
stop attempting to communicate what they are trying to do.

Put this together with the systemic's tendency to proceed
slowly while assessing a situation, plus a willingness to search for
a course of action that meets many criteria, and you have the picture
of someone who looks very slow and cautious. If the systemic has
not been communicating about his or her plans, others may begin
to suspect that the person has no plans and nothing to contribute.

Because they put so much effort into their analyses, it is easy
for systemics to become extremely committed to their plans. But
they do not like confrontation and do not like to be seen as control-

ling others. As managers, they may engage in complex tactics aimed at getting others to go along with them without ever issuing an order or fully explaining their plans. This is tricky to bring off successfully, so they sometimes gain reputations for being sneaky and manipulative. Meanwhile, systemics can be extremely reluctant to go along with the plans of others unless they see how others' plans fit with their own.

If your style is systemic, a few rules of thumb can reduce the likelihood that you will experience these kinds of difficulties:

1. Routinely share information with others. You may be putting a great deal of energy into thinking about some issue, and you may be generating some great ideas. But unless you share your thoughts with others, no one can tell that you are thinking about anything at all.
2. Involve others early in your analyses and planning. This may produce useful insights and ideas and will take pressure off your communication and persuasive skills later.
3. As with your hierarchic and integrative cousins, try to conserve your systemic energies for situations that profit most from systemic thinking. Not every decision must be made in systemic fashion. If you use your style more judiciously, you will have more energy and credits to be systemic when you need to be.
4. Be explicit about your preferences and intentions. Avoid the temptation to use pseudoparticipation so that others will go along with you. That can backfire and generate resentment and mistrust.
5. Go out of your way to accommodate others and give them credit for their ideas. Factor into your thinking the interpersonal relationship value of accepting others' ideas and suggestions.

The main theme of these suggestions is "stay connected." Keep things out in the open—communicate with and involve others.

Changing Your Primary Style

You may decide that you want to change your style. You don't just want to tone down a style but instead want to develop a new primary operating style.

As a starting point, keep in mind that whatever style you want to develop, your strategy will involve one or both of the following:

1. Changing the amount of information you typically use
2. Changing the number of problem solutions you generate or respond favorably to

If you are decisive now and want to develop a primary hierarchic style, you need to concentrate your attention on using more information. Basically, you need to acquire a habit of thinking things through more thoroughly before deciding on a course of action.

However, if your primary style is decisive and you want to shift to an integrative primary style, you need to increase *both* your use of information *and* your inclination to generate multiple solutions. Compared to the decisive-to-hierarchic change, this shift is more of a reach, unless integrative is already your backup style.

Switching your primary style to your current backup style is the change of style that is easiest to accomplish. The backup style is familiar to you, and using it won't seem awkward or strange.

Setting Your Expectations

Successfully bringing off an effort to change styles requires a sense of realism about what you are trying to do and a clear understanding of the factors that can limit your success. After you recognize these factors, you can actually turn them to your advantage.

Force of Habit. Changing style means changing habits, but habits can be difficult to change because they are usually unconscious. This makes it easy to slip back unconsciously into old behavior patterns.

Past Reinforcement. A habit can be particularly strong when you have a long history of being rewarded for the habitual behavior. In changing styles you may resist your own efforts because you sense that you are trading in something that, for better or worse, has worked in the past for something else that is new and unfamiliar.

Sense of Awkwardness. When you experiment with methods aimed at changing your style, you are basically asking yourself to act out of character. Unless acting is a special talent of yours, you should expect to feel uncomfortable, awkward, and even downright foolish.

Being aware of these obstacles is important in helping you overcome feelings of being let down and disappointed. Learn to expect them. Know that they will come and go. If you persist with your efforts and you are successful, they gradually will fade. With these thoughts in mind, let's turn our attention to some specific strategies for developing each of the decision styles.

Building Your Decisive Style

"Keep it short and simple"—KISS—is the theme song of the decisive style. Get things done and keep moving. Here are some decisive style-building suggestions:

1. *Stick with the essential facts.* Learn to focus on the few key facts that you need to get a quick handle on a situation. Even if you are now an information maximizer, you probably notice that you can get a basic feel for a problem fairly fast from a relatively small amount of information. To be decisive, you need to stop your analysis as soon as you sense that you have a handle on the problem, even if you know that you could learn more. Resist going after those additional details.

Keep in mind that information analysis is costly. While you are gleaning and evaluating additional information, you could be turning your attention to new problems or tasks that need to be handled.

This is the decisive way of thinking: get the essential facts; zero in on a workable solution; get on with things; keep moving. Keep your productivity high.

2. *Start focused, stay focused.* If your style now is multifocused, you need to cultivate the habit of picking one course of action and staying with it. Here's a suggestion to help you do this: before you wade into a problem, take a few moments to clarify your objective. If several objectives come to mind, jot them down and cross out the ones that would be nice to accomplish but are not necessary.

Concentrate only on the objective that you absolutely must accomplish.

Devise a course of action that satisfies your objective, grab it, and go. Don't tweak your idea to come up with a new alternative that lets you accomplish another objective, too. That can start all the old habits working again. Keep moving!

As a manager, you can use a number of techniques to cultivate a decisive style in dealing with your people. Try some of these ideas:

1. Hold short staff meetings. At each meeting, put out a brief and clear agenda and stick to it in the meeting. Start on time, and stop on time.
2. Reach closure on several items at each meeting. Ensure that everyone understands what decisions are made and what actions are necessary.
3. List decisions that can be delegated, and then delegate them. Tell people exactly what you expect of them and when you expect a product or result.
4. Avoid micromanaging. After stating your expectations, stay out of the details. Leave decisions about methods and techniques for getting work done to the people you are delegating to.
5. Try to accept others' results or decisions with minimal change, as long as they fit your main objective (remember your focus).
6. Set short-term goals and schedules for both yourself and others.

Using suggestions like these will become easier with practice. Be realistic. Don't worry about perfection. That's not the decisive way. Keep moving!

Building Your Hierarchic Style

"Success depends on having a plan" is the hierarchic credo. If you want to be hierarchic, you must clearly focus on what you want to accomplish and develop a clear strategy for accomplishing your goal. From the hierarchic perspective, failure can mean one of two things: either you were confused about goals, or you erred in your analysis of a situation and therefore failed to develop an adequate plan of action.

If you want to develop your hierarchic style, here are a few rules to live by:

1. *Establish clear priorities.* When you approach a situation requiring a decision, establish your priorities before starting your analysis. Otherwise, you run the risk of getting sidetracked. You will spend too much time looking at aspects of the situation that are of little importance and not enough time digging deeply enough to unearth and then organize the important information. Focus on your key objectives at all times.

2. *Develop a plan.* Once your priorities are established, your task is to develop an appropriate plan for analyzing a situation. What information will you need? What will you do with it when you get it? Hierarchics frequently use matrices or decision trees to organize and evaluate information. These help to identify important categories of information and to select a course of action that best fits a high-priority goal.

3. *Do your homework.* "Winging it" is not the hierarchic way. Before you do anything, you must prepare. Try not to be caught in a situation where you find yourself unable to answer important questions or, worse, discussing something unfamiliar.

Hierarchic bosses can be very motivating and yet difficult to work for. Their commitment to a vision for the future is catching, and they are very protective of their people. They tend to be very demanding of others, however, and easily fall into the habit of micromanagement. Be careful if you aim to use this style more in your management activities.

If you plan to be more hierarchic as a manager, here are some tips that may help you capitalize on the strength of the style:

1. Share your plan and vision. Let your goals and your long-term commitment to them be evident.
2. Involve others in developing your plans. This promotes commitment and unity of purpose.

3. Help your people stay focused. Involve them in the development of a mission statement.

4. Encourage your people to develop clear goals and plans themselves.

5. Follow up on action plans. Don't just file the plan until it is time to develop a new one next year. Use the plan as a road map for management.

6. Reward commitment and excellence. Give credit for goal accomplishment—especially when you see that people have overcome obstacles in order to stay true to their goals and produce high-quality work.

Use the hierarchic style where it counts most, on problems and decisions that are most important to you. This will increase your chances of identifying and sticking to high-priority goals. Keep a journal to record your efforts and their results.

Building Your Flexible Style

If you want to develop the flexible style, you need to cultivate a real appreciation for adaptability, the hallmark of the flexible style. Faced with an obstacle, flexibles simply pick a new direction and move. They don't spend time and energy trying to crash through barriers. If you need to make more use of this style, try some of these ideas:

1. *Learn to expect change.* If you want to develop the flexible style, you probably are faced with a frequently changing environment and never quite know what to expect. Approach situations and decisions by expecting that things will change and that you will need to adapt quickly.

2. *Watch for signs of change.* If you anticipate change, you will find it easier (especially if you are an information maximizer) to see the folly of doing lengthy analyses and carefully planning strategies that need to be abandoned or redone when circumstances change. Quickly size up situations until you have a good enough grasp on things to see some options for how to proceed. Then be ready to shift directions if necessary.

3. *Avoid becoming overcommitted.* Don't be trapped into overcommitment to either an interpretation of a situation or a way of dealing with it. People who do not use the flexible style sometimes cause unnecessary conflicts about inconsequential issues because they become so heavily invested in their own views and methods. They lose sight of the fact that they can more effectively accomplish their goals if they overlook nonessentials.

4. *Practice generating alternatives.* When a situation changes, you may need to shift rapidly to a different course of action. You can do this more successfully if you make a habit of outlining several possible courses of action whenever you make decisions. Then you will already have a useful alternative when you need one.

If you are a manager of a unit that needs to be responsive to shifting currents and unpredictable demands, you may find the flexible style essential. Certain kinds of sales and customer service departments fit this description. However, be careful not to overdo it, or you may find yourself getting labeled as "wishy-washy" by your subordinates. As one very hierarchic subordinate was heard complaining loudly about his very flexible boss, "Every time the phone rings around here, we reorganize!"

Here are some tips on how to use the flexible style effectively as a boss:

1. Make clear to your people that you value responsiveness and adaptability by rewarding your key innovators.
2. When situations require change, get your people involved early in generating ideas for new courses of action.
3. Avoid fixed rules and regulations. Instead, make liberal use of task forces or special teams to reach agreements on objectives and methods.
4. Stay away from lengthy and detailed job descriptions that cause people to define their responsibilities narrowly and create "turf wars." Encourage job rotation and cooperation. Accustom your people to performing different roles. Create the feeling of being part of a team.
5. Rely more heavily on intuition than past plans and procedures.

Building Your Integrative Style

Curiosity is an important part of the integrative style. Integratives enjoy information for its own sake and appreciate opportunities to explore new ideas to see where they might lead. If your aim is to become more integrative, try letting your curiosity lead the way. Here are some ideas to help get you started:

1. *Set action implications aside.* Try approaching problems that need decisions with the attitude that you will not be satisfied until you discover at least several things about the situation that surprise you—things you never would have guessed about it. This will help keep you in the information-gathering mode where your goal is discovery rather than finding a solution. The surest way to short-circuit the integrative process is to start thinking about implications for action and solutions every time you come across a new piece of information. Return to exploratory mode, stimulate your curiosity, and promise that you will return to action implications later. If you fear that you will lose a good idea, note down your idea and set it aside for later reference.

2. *Practice open-ended listening skills.* Compared to other styles, the integrative style is least guilty of bad listening habits. This, of course, meshes with the curiosity that was just mentioned. When someone speaks, an integrative's sense of curiosity leads him or her to want to find out more about what the person has to say and why.

Open-ended listening is the process of listening to fully understand what someone is saying, without jumping ahead to anticipate where the person is going. When you start thinking ahead, you miss important points and nuances, which could cause you to misinterpret what the person has to say.

A number of good, active techniques can help you practice open-ended listening. Try periodically checking with the person you are speaking with to make sure you understand his or her meaning. For example, you might say something like, "So you are saying . . . ," followed by a paraphrase (not the exact words) of what you think you have heard. Punctuate your paraphrase with a question like, "Is that right?"

Make it clear that you are listening to understand, not to refute, debate, or find a flaw in the other person's argument. As you gain skill with these techniques, you will learn more about what people are thinking, win points (most people appreciate being understood), and help others develop and clarify their own thoughts.

3. *Generate multiple solutions.* When you turn your attention to generating ideas about courses of action for handling a situation, guard against locking onto one idea without considering other options. Remain tentative about any idea you come up with. The more you feel convinced that you have come up with the "right way" to handle a problem, the more you need to remind yourself to be tentative. Consciously put your great idea aside for a moment while you look at other ideas. You can always return to your original idea later.

Ask others for their ideas. Human diversity being what it is, you can be certain that they will give you some ideas that are different from your own. This is why few integratives want to work alone: other people are a rich source of information and ideas.

There are many ways to use the integrative style as a manager, but if you go too far you can confuse and frustrate your people with what they may see as "endless cycling" on the same ideas and unrealistic thinking. Here are some ways to keep the accent on the positive side of the integrative style:

1. Familiarize your people with the integrative style. Help them understand the strengths of the style and the role it can play in promoting a cooperative, creative, and team-oriented work situation.

2. When you know you are going into integrative mode, let your people know, particularly if they are unused to dealing with this style. Recently, we saw a management team used to dealing with a very structured and autocratic boss become almost paralyzed by their confused and anxious reactions to a new boss who was very integrative. The team members just couldn't figure out what he wanted them to say and do. It took them a long while to comprehend that he truly wanted them to be not fol-

lowers but full partners with him in developing ideas and plans.

3. Use groups and teams as much as possible to generate new ideas and develop action plans. With practice, and perhaps some training, your groups can become creative "idea machines" in which people feel real ownership in the ideas that are generated.

4. Signal that even oddball ideas are legitimate topics for discussion. Discourage self-censoring on the part of your team members. Encourage people to voice different, even apparently conflicting, viewpoints. Try to counter the pressures that promote conformity and caution in groups.

Keeping in mind the relationship between style and environmental load, make sure that you practice using the integrative style under moderate pressure. In particular, avoid high-pressure situations. Don't try to be integrative when the telephone is ringing off the hook and you have half a dozen people milling around outside your door waiting to see you.

If your office is always like that, you may have to escape for your experiments with the integrative style—perhaps to a hideout in a different part of your building or an off-site location. You should pick problems that are important but not too important—especially at the early stages of your experiments. High pressure may defeat your success with the integrative style and discourage you from staying with your program of style change.

Building Your Systemic Style

Appreciation for the "big picture" is an important part of the systemic style. Systemics look at issues as sets of issues: no problem exists by itself, and no one course of action affects one situation without also affecting others.

If you want to develop the systemic style, you need to get in touch with this basic philosophy of interrelatedness. You need to develop and maintain the patience necessary to dig deeply into issues until you understand their parts and the dynamics between the parts. Then you need the perseverance to produce plans that deal with all or most of the parts.

To develop the systemic style, you can use many of the techniques that have been mentioned as useful for developing the integrative and hierarchic styles. The trick is to move smoothly between the less structured integrative techniques and the more structured hierarchic techniques without allowing them to cancel out each other. In other words, to be systemic you need to be both highly structured and unstructured—not just some middle-of-the-road average.

Here are some suggestions to help develop this complex style:

1. *Develop a broad but sharply defined set of goals.* Systemics know what they want, and they want a lot. So don't compromise in establishing your goals. Be unwilling to settle for too many trade-offs. This commitment to many objectives will help you to sustain the effort required to do systemic style analyses.

2. *Approach problems in integrative mode.* Once you have clearly established your goals, set them temporarily aside and approach a situation in the exploratory frame of mind of the integrative style. This promotes the fullest, least biased understanding of the situation. Look especially for interrelationships between the immediate problem and other problems or situations you know about or might be dealing with now. Try to develop the fullest possible picture of the problem.

3. *Organize your picture of the situation.* As your insights into a situation grow, organize them in a way that reflects the parts of the situation and their dynamics. For example, we find that systemics often use flow charts to develop a graphic representation of a situation (we have seen these charts covering entire walls). This helps keep the big picture and its dynamics in full view and also helps them avoid fixating on one part of the situation to the exclusion of others.

4. *Be demanding of solutions.* Don't let yourself off the hook until you find several action strategies that deal with the situation as a whole and satisfy most or, better yet, all of your criteria. Here again, be wary of trade-offs that might be unnecessary with more analysis and persistence. Fortify your patience with the conviction that your persistence will be rewarded in the long run by accom-

plishing more of your goals than you would if you caved in to pressures to make trade-offs. Just as hierarchics tend to use matrices to aid in identifying solutions, so can you as a practicing systemic. Just be sure to do justice to your decision criteria by representing all of your goals in the matrix.

5. *Build composite strategies.* Rarely does the systemic approach find that a single course of action satisfies all criteria. Instead, several strategies composed of many courses of action are required and include backup solutions that can be used to meet different contingencies that might arise.

In management, the systemic style is ideally suited for the development of highly organized and controllable plans, such as launching a new business segment or planning for a major investment in a new plant where decisions will have major long-term consequences. The complexity of the style can easily overwhelm others, however. With these thoughts in mind, here are some suggestions for getting the most out of the systemic style in your management activities:

1. Encourage your people to be ambitious in setting their own goals. Initiate frequent planning meetings to review goals, surface new goals, and assess progress.
2. Include others' goals in your own plans. Show that you are willing to be uncompromising in protecting their plans and promoting their success.
3. Publicize goal attainment. Identify and make highly visible measures or barometers of goal attainment. Give recognition for persistence and success. Do not dwell on failure.
4. Promote the view that strategies must be reviewed and revised frequently. Make this process as visible as possible and include as many people in it as possible.
5. Place a high premium on sharing of information. Avoid doing anything that penalizes people for sharing information. For example, do not penalize people when they report information showing that they are not meeting their goals. Instead, thank them for being open and offer resources and assistance to help

them improve performance. When their performance turns around, use them as examples of success for others to follow.

Your best bet for developing the systemic style and using it effectively is to begin with issues that are complicated and touch on many other people. The issues should be important to many people and should have significant consequences.

However, don't try using the style to put out raging fires—too many things will get burned before you make progress. Instead, try using the style with a compatible group of people to plan and manage a strategy for handling a new opportunity that is likely to produce important benefits for you and the others.

Managing Your Style Change Program

In setting out to change your style, it is best to think of yourself as a project manager embarking on a new project. The project happens to be an important self-development project. Your strategy for managing this project depends on the particular style that you intend to develop, but regardless of your specific style objective, try following these few simple project management rules:

Practice Frequently

Your project involves changing a habit, and habits increase with repetition. So to shed your old style habit and build a new one, frequently practice using the style you wish to develop. Think of yourself as developing a new skill, as you did when as a child you learned to ride a bicycle. Eventually, habit will work to your advantage: your old style will lose its force, and your new style will begin to feel natural.

Try for Gradual Change

If you expect overnight success in changing your style, you simply are setting yourself up for frustration that will eat into your commitment to change styles. Instead, look for incremental results. For example, if you are attempting to boost both your use of information and your generation of multiple solutions, you might want to note first any changes you see in your use of information and not worry at all for a while about solution generation.

If, at some point, you begin to feel overwhelmed by your style change efforts or just tired of the whole process, then back off a bit and try to go slower. Pushing too far and too fast can have a boomerang effect. Sometimes going slowly can actually lead to more progress in the long run.

Arrange for Some Rewards

Success in your efforts to change your style should be rewarding in and of itself. But don't skimp on rewards. Make sure to reward your efforts. Be sure to take note of favorable consequences that seem to result from your efforts—such as compliments from a boss or better relationships with customers or coworkers. Such outcomes powerfully reinforce your style change. To add some extra reinforcement, take yourself out to dinner, or plan a special vacation to reward yourself for success. In fact, reward yourself if for nothing more than your efforts, even before you see any outcomes. Lavish yourself with rewards.

Build Supportive Relationships

Try also to find supportive people to be your allies in your style change efforts. These people should already be using the style that you are shooting for, so they will be sympathetic with your intentions. Let them know what you are doing and why, and ask for feedback. They can be of tremendous value by helping you track your progress, alerting you to any drift back to your old style, providing suggestions, acting as role models, and generally by validating socially the legitimacy and worth of your efforts to change your style.

Changing your decision style is a challenging undertaking that requires considerable investment of time and energy. Before embarking on such a transition, consider in depth why you want to change and whether there are alternatives. What are you trying to accomplish by a style change? Might it be more appropriate to change situations or redesign your job? If these are not options, you might consider undertaking a less ambitious course of action, like toning down your style to avoid its weaknesses, while building on its strengths.

If you decide to change your primary decision style, don't expect immense differences overnight. Be prepared for investing a lot of energy in constantly being aware of what you are doing and forcing yourself to process information in unfamiliar ways that are appropriate to your goals. It is helpful if colleagues can be enlisted to provide you with feedback about your progress and to reinforce you with praise as you exhibit your desired style.

As you increase your awareness, modify your behavior, and receive reinforcement, the new style will become more natural and comfortable. The sense of satisfaction and the increased effectiveness of your new style can be worth every bit of your effort.

11

Using Styles for Success in Work Groups

*P*erhaps you have noticed that you can spend most of a day calling people on the telephone without speaking to a single person you wanted to reach. You might hear these refrains: "I'm sorry, but she's in a meeting" or "He has some people with him right now and he has another meeting to go to in fifteen minutes." How much time do you spend working in groups or in meetings with at least two other people? Include in your estimate all the time you spend in staff meetings, project meetings, planning meetings, board meetings, and so on. Don't be surprised to find that you spend 80 percent or more of your time on the job working in a group of one kind or another. That's the way it is for managers in today's business organizations.

In many ways this is a very good thing: organizations cannot function without group work and meetings. They ensure coordination and agreement on task assignments and divisions of labor. And groups can be powerful tools for stimulating ideas and creativity and for generating feelings of involvement and ownership in decisions.

But against these benefits must be weighed the potential disadvantages. Working in groups and meetings is costly; it disposes of the time of many people in large chunks. The realities are that process problems cut deeply into work group effectiveness—to the point that some groups literally are better off if they never get together at all. No doubt you can recall a few instances when you suspected that this might be true of a group of which you were a part. What we mean by *process problems* are the misunderstandings, frustrations, and outright conflicts that occur when groups fail to effectively handle such issues as decision-making procedures, stages of problem solving, individuals' roles, and levels of participation and influence.

Decision Styles and Small Group Behavior

You probably can see that decision style differences—and even similarities—are important contributors to group process problems. At any point during a group meeting, people with different styles often have completely different perceptions of the meeting's specific purpose and even of the issue currently under discussion. For instance, we once intervened in a group discussion that seemed to be going nowhere and asked each of the ten people present to state the topic they believed they were discussing. To their amazement, they discovered that they held five completely different views of the topic being discussed.

You can better manage work group effectiveness by understanding how different decision styles are displayed in individual behavior in small group settings—groups that range in size from three to twelve participants.

Table 11.1 summarizes the major characteristics of the behavior of different decision styles in groups. The table shows that decision styles can affect behavior in groups in many ways, ranging from when and how much people with different styles talk, to methods for determining courses of action. Let's take a closer look at these style-related behaviors. As you read, you may want to refer occasionally to the table.

Communication

People with different styles differ in their frequency of communication in groups and also communicate about different things. For

Table 11.1. A Summary of Style Behavior in Small Groups.

	Decisive	Flexible	Hierarchic	Integrative	Systemic
Communication volume	Low	High	Low (at first)	High	Varies (high to low)
Communication style	Terse; task oriented	Many topics; light and humorous	Data-filled speeches	High involvement; "spin-off" comments; some process comments	Questions; stories
Leadership	Task oriented; directive	Social; emotional	Intellectual; expert; status	Intellectual; process facilitation	Information; leading questions
Number of goals	One	Many and changing	One major goal plus subordinated others	Many	Many
Key types of goals	Efficiency; productivity	Survivability; cordial relations	Quality; business growth	Creativity; learning	Systems development; thoroughness
Involvement of others	When needed by tasks; delegates tasks outside group	For interpersonal relationships; for diversity and versatility	For knowledge and expertise	For varied information and ideas	For information and commitment
Decision	Voting; established rules; leader decides	Compromise; most current idea	Structured method (e.g., decision matrix); best documentation and logic; expertise	Participation; approximate consensus	Full consensus

example, the typical decisive pattern is to communicate with short, task-oriented comments, particularly at the beginning of a meeting. Compared to those with other styles, decisives are most concerned about having a clear agenda and keeping the discussion on track. Usually decisives have most to say at the beginning and end of meetings and less during the middle of a discussion. They tend to jump into a discussion with lots of energy, clarifying the agenda and topic and what the group needs to do. Before long they begin to call attention to the time and press for closure on discussions and for concrete decisions about actions. If the group is unwilling to reach early closure on discussions, as often is the case when the group includes many people with styles other than decisive, decisives tend to withdraw from the discussion. This often signifies growing frustration and impatience on their part and the general feeling that "We're never going to get anywhere with this rambling discussion, and I'm sure as heck not going to contribute to more confusion by opening my mouth!"

Flexibles also tend to communicate with short comments. But compared to their decisive counterparts, they tend to communicate more frequently and more evenly throughout the meeting. Moreover, their comments tend to be on the light side, and they generally cover a wide range of topics. To others, they may appear to be hopping all over the place. We often find that the group jokester has a flexible style. When discussions begin to get heavy and detailed, flexibles often try to lighten things up and move the discussion along to other topics by making a humorous comment.

Hierarchics communicate with a much different pattern. Generally, their level of participation picks up as the discussion progresses. At first, they may remain rather quiet until they fully grasp an issue and topic and develop a point of view that they feel comfortable voicing. They tend to begin by asking a few careful, well-chosen questions but gradually make more and more long, data-filled comments or speeches that advocate a particular point of view or course of action for the group.

Integratives tend to stay involved in a discussion throughout a meeting. They typically ask a lot of questions and generally try to elicit information and points of view from others. They also tend to make a lot of spin-off comments that build on others' ideas

("That's an interesting thought. Maybe we could . . .") and suggest new perspectives or courses of action ("If we think about what Jim and Joan just said, there's another way of looking at this whole issue"). When among people with different styles, the integrative is most likely to try to clarify or get elaboration on others' points of view ("If I understand you, you seem to be saying that . . .").

Systemics' communication tends to vary between the hierarchic and integrative patterns. If they lean more toward the integrative pattern, they ask many questions and make many comments—often telling stories about similar situations they have seen in the past. Usually, however, their comments are lengthier than the typical integrative comment. If, on the other hand, they lean more toward the hierarchic pattern, they might have almost nothing to say throughout a group discussion until the very end, when they come out with an extremely long-winded discourse that tries to weave together nearly everything that has been said and that culminates with an elaborate proposal for future action. Prior to making a pitch for any course of action, however, systemics usually can be counted on to ask questions that produce answers pointing in the direction that they end up advocating.

Influence Basis

People vary a lot in how they try to influence and sway others. Even the most innocuous group meeting can run into tensions around influence and control. Many of the differences in techniques that people use to gain influence spring from differences in decision styles. For example, decisives try to influence things by structuring agendas, tasks, and assignments or by direct or indirect references to any formal authority that might be associated with their office or position. Flexibles use very different and less direct techniques. They influence by nurturing the social and emotional experience of the group. If someone is attacked, they come to the person's defense or make a joke to ease the sting. If someone becomes aggressive, they sometimes shoot a "zinger" in that person's direction that turns things around or eases the tension. They tend to compliment others liberally and generally try to get the group to feel good about itself.

This tends to gain them acceptance and the power to influence levels of participation of others.

Hierarchics have several influence techniques in their tool chest. Their most frequently used techniques are expertise or command of information and logic, and association with high status. When they want to sway the group in a particular direction, their tendency is to cite information that either indicates their greater expertise through past experience ("I know a lot about computers. I've programmed in Fortran, Cobol, and APL") or demonstrates on-the-spot superior knowledge of a topic. They often use logic to organize and tie together statements of others that support a particular point of view or that expose flaws in a position that they oppose. Where these techniques fail or when they opt for a short-cut to influence, they tend to make comments that associate themselves with people who are in positions of high status and authority ("I was talking to the chairman yesterday, and he said . . .").

Integratives gain influence by taking on the role of intellectual leader and by becoming a process leader for the group. As intellectual leaders, they gain points by offering new and sometimes esoteric items of information and by generating new and creative ideas. This role often overlaps with the process leader role that they sometimes unofficially adopt as they encourage others to speak up, help clarify communication, and resolve conflicts. For example, when two group members enter a debate, a typical integrative intervention is to say something like, "It seems to me that the two of you really are talking about two different things . . . ," followed by an elaboration of what the underlying ideas and issues seem to be.

Systemics rely almost exclusively on expertise and command of information to gain influence. However, they tend to be more subtle and less direct in the way that they use these techniques than their hierarchic and integrative counterparts. For example, instead of directly stating information that they possess in a meeting, they often ask questions of others that are phrased in a way that allows specific items of information to surface. Or instead of summing up things themselves and articulating the logic of a point of view, their tendency is to keep asking questions and prompting others to respond to information that has surfaced until the logic emerges from the group discussion. To help things along, they might share a few

anecdotes that illustrate some points of logic but do not necessarily
point out the logic themselves.

Goals and Objectives

Groups often run into conflicts and confusion about goals and
objectives. After hours of meeting time, participants may discover
that different people have had different goals in mind all along.
Decision styles influence both the number and types of goals that
group members are inclined to pursue.

Decisives are inclined to identify one specific goal or objective. The particular objective they stress often has efficiency, productivity, or cost reduction overtones to it. Flexibles, on the other
hand, may have many possible objectives in mind that may change.
It is possible that during the course of a group discussion they may
drop one in favor of a very different objective. If there is a constant
theme to their goals, it is likely to be survivability or adaptability.

Hierarchics, on the other hand, are inclined to strongly emphasize one particular goal—usually one that favors quality of performance or that emphasizes growth of market share or profits.
Subordinate to this overarching goal may be a host of other objectives such as boosting customer satisfaction, improving product designs, better identification of high-potential customers, and so on,
as long as they serve the main goal.

Integratives are usually open to a variety of goals. If a potential course of action fits more than one important goal, so much the
better. They feel uncomfortable with any course of action that satisfies just one goal, even if it is an important one. If forced to make
trade-offs, they are most inclined to adopt goals that involve opportunities for themselves and others to do things in new and different
ways and thereby gain new knowledge and experience. To always
pursue the same goal is definitely not the integrative's idea of a good
time, even if the group is getting better and better in its ability to
achieve the goal. Whereas hierarchics might be satisfied as long as
the group is improving the quality of its output and generating
more profits, integratives might feel bored and restless.

Like integratives, systemics are inclined to emphasize multiple goals. However, they are more like their hierarchic counterparts

in being precise about what those goals are and in being very demanding about goal attainment. In a sense, systemics aim to maximize performance simultaneously on numerous goals, whereas hierarchics want to maximize attainment of one particular goal and integratives are satisfied by any course of action that allows them to do well on several goals and at least acceptably on some other goals that they value.

Involvement of Others

The styles also differ in their purposes for including other people in groups. Decisives get others involved when tasks clearly require the assistance of other people. Group meetings then revolve around identifying specific tasks that must be accomplished, identifying decisions that must be made, and dividing the labor among the group participants. Frequently, decisives want to make some quick decisions on key issues and then delegate the rest of the work to individuals or subgroups to be done outside the group meeting. Generally speaking, groups put together by decisives will be smaller and have shorter meetings than groups set up by people with other styles.

Although flexibles also involve other people in group meetings when tasks require the assistance of others, they are also inclined to include people simply to stimulate the feeling of involvement on the part of others and create opportunities for interaction between group members. This gives an added measure of versatility to the group that can be useful if something unexpected emerges during a group meeting. Groups put together by flexibles may include some people who do not have any specific functional responsibility or even expertise related to the group's agenda or charter.

Hierarchics typically involve others in groups and meetings to get information from a variety of sources. They are inclined to include anyone who can reasonably be expected to have some useful information to offer. Meetings set up and orchestrated by hierarchics often take the form of "show and tell" meetings in which each participant in turn makes an elaborate, information-rich presentation on the particular aspect of a problem or issue about which he or she has special knowledge or expertise. Most commonly, one spokesperson per issue or topic is selected from among others as the most knowledgeable.

Integratives also involve others in groups and meetings in order to collect information from a variety of sources. They also want to get diverse ideas, even conflicting ideas, in order to stimulate creativity and new insights, so they intentionally involve people known to have strongly differing views on a particular topic. This can mean that they invite nonexperts for a new perspective and some fresh ideas. Instead of using meetings for presentation of reports, they are inclined to use them as active, problem-solving sessions that generate creative solutions and produce consensus about actions to be taken.

Systemics involve people, as do integratives and hierarchics, for their information, knowledge, and expertise. However, they are somewhat more likely to include people who may not have much to contribute directly to the issues that are being addressed but whose commitment to decisions that are taken is needed to carry them out.

Decision Methods

In a typical decisive meeting, final decisions are made unilaterally by the leader, by following preestablished rules or by taking a simple vote. Can you see why voting is favored by decisives? It gets decisions made and issues resolved neatly, quickly, and fairly without messy, unpleasant, and lengthy debates. It also produces a very definite feeling of closure and finality, which of course is appreciated by decisives.

One of the potential problems with voting is that it produces losers who may walk away with feelings of resentment. Consequently, flexibles look for ways to work out compromises that minimize resentments and preserve harmony. If there are no real conflicts over preferred solutions, then flexibles are likely to go with whatever course of action has been discussed most recently and seems to have a reasonable amount of support in the group. They steer away from highly controversial ideas that create divisions within the group. Of course, a decision is final only in the sense that the group generally agrees to try it out to see if it works. If it doesn't work well, the group will get back together soon to pick another idea.

Hierarchics prefer to make decisions "rationally" by selecting the best-documented idea. Ideally, facts, data, and logic should make the decision for the group. Consequently, when meetings are called for the explicit purpose of making a decision, as opposed to simply reporting information, hierarchics like to use methods that organize facts in some structured way that makes obvious the best course of action. In meetings it is very common to hear a hierarchic participant suggest using a decision matrix that allows the specific merits of various options to be weighed and compared objectively. The presumption is that the idea that gets the "best score" also will get the support of the group.

Integratives and systemics both prefer that decisions be made by consensus. By and large, integratives are less strict about this than are systemics, in that they are comfortable with decisions that are supported by the vast majority of group participants. Systemics are more inclined to hold out for absolute 100 percent consensus and often seem uncomfortable as long as any dissenting views remain. Consequently, strategies tend to be reworked until all agree that the strategies have a high probability of meeting the group's established goals.

Integratives, on the other hand, are inclined to deal with dissenting group members by agreeing not to agree and perhaps by adopting several different strategies rather than pushing for one unified strategy or grand compromise.

Aligning Styles with Roles in Groups

The inclination of people with different styles to behave differently in groups is at once a major stumbling block and a major opportunity for most groups. It is a stumbling block, for example, when a decisive group member is trying to get closure on an issue by pushing for a vote at the same time that an integrative member is trying to stimulate discussion in order to see the pros and cons of different points of view. But the presence of different styles in a group can be a real asset if group members understand their own and others' styles and learn how to divide tasks among group members according to their styles.

Each style can play one or more special roles in a group, although individuals should not be confined to these roles. For example, decisives can play particularly useful roles by taking the lead in identifying tasks that need to be accomplished, getting discussions started, keeping track of time, and eventually pushing for closure on issues before time runs out. Flexibles can help keep a group from getting bogged down in unproductive analyses and polarizing debates by introducing humor when energy begins to fall off or when tensions reach high levels. They can also keep things moving by quickly throwing out new ideas when the group is blocked by some obstacle. In effect, flexibles can play a socioemotional leadership role in their groups.

Hierarchics can help by organizing analyses and introducing methods for narrowing choices in a logical way when a group must adhere to established requirements or when resource constraints limit the number of courses of action a group can implement. Because of their penchant for doing "the right thing the right way," they can also perform a useful quality-control role in their groups.

Integratives are naturally inclined toward cooperation and collaboration in groups, and they value the varied information and ideas that groups have the potential to generate. Consequently, they can act as facilitators of group discussions and thereby encourage high participation among members and bring out information that existed in the group but otherwise may never have been brought to light. They can also help prevent misunderstandings from hampering the group and from generating conflicts by pointing out similarities and differences in group members' points of view. Their interest in creativity and exploration can also help groups avoid falling into ruts of thinking by encouraging members to express unusual or differing points of view.

Systemics generally take the broadest view of problems and situations. They can help groups to avoid the trap of solving one problem only to create another. They can also help to keep their groups from fixating inappropriately on only one aspect of a problem and from mechanically applying the same solution over and over again to different kinds of problems.

Managing Groups with Style

Most groups consist of people with a variety of styles, but in some groups a majority of the members share a particular style. This leaning toward a particular style gives the group a particular personality associated with that style. A group where the decisive style has the edge will behave differently from a group with a large number of hierarchics, and both will behave differently from an integrative group.

If you are working with a group with a decision style mix that favors a particular style, or if you are in a position to put together such a group, you can take advantage of these differences in group dynamics to produce different kinds of results. Let's have a brief look at the dynamics of groups with different style mixes, and at the kinds of tasks and situations for which they are best suited, as well as some pitfalls that can hamper their performance.

Decisive Group Behavior

A quick glance at the decisive column of Table 11.1 provides an overview of the behavior that is expected of small groups in which the decisive style dominates. They are task-oriented and efficiency-minded groups that get things done quickly. When decisive groups are working well, you can expect to see the following kinds of behaviors. First, you can expect to see a clear and concise agenda for each meeting. The group does not get together simply to kick around some ideas. Meetings begin promptly with not much time spent on "the friendlies," although you might hear a few jokes poking fun at team members, the team itself, or the assignment. Then the group gets down to business.

In a decisive group, getting down to business means quickly defining the problem and the tasks that need to be done. Usually, this takes the form of an oral briefing, with perhaps a couple of briefing charts each with two or three bullets highlighting key issues. Most of this definitional work has been done, probably by the group leader, before the meeting.

This may be followed by a short question-and-answer exchange, during which members seek to clarify the problem and task requirements. Rarely do you hear comments that challenge the way the problem has been defined. The conversation quickly turns to issues revolving around who is going to do what and when tasks should be completed. The tasks are then assigned to individuals and subgroups to accomplish on their own outside the larger group.

You can expect to see most decisions during the group meeting made either by the group leader or by a vote. Most decisions, however, revolve around assignments and schedules. Most of the real problem solving takes place outside the group meeting. Subsequent meetings are scheduled to report back on findings or results of the tasks that have been assigned. This may lead to a quick examination of implications for action and an attempt to find the most expedient course of action for dealing with the problem facing the group. Here again, after a relatively brief discussion, any remaining differences of opinion are resolved by the group leader or by a vote.

Advantages of Decisive Groups. Decisive groups shine under time constraints and when there is a need for speed. This is particularly true when unexpected problems arise and the tasks that need to be accomplished are relatively clear and can be subdivided easily and given to individuals or smaller subgroups to accomplish independently.

For example, suppose that an equipment failure has greatly limited production in one of your company's manufacturing facilities, and in order to meet commitments to customers you need to decide how to redistribute production to other facilities while the equipment is repaired. If data about current capacities and schedules can be gathered quickly from each facility, a decisive group composed of operations managers from each location can meet to decide how to allocate the work.

Disadvantages of Decisive Groups. There are no guarantees, of course, that decisive groups will work as efficiently and effectively as we have just described. Certain process problems tend to plague decisive groups, just as other process problems trouble groups with a different mix of styles.

In decisive groups, listening can be a major problem. Group

members sometimes become so concerned about time or so preoccupied with their own thoughts about implications for action that they stop listening to their fellow members' comments. For the same reason, problems may receive such a superficial analysis that critical issues remain unidentified and unresolved, causing the group to return again and again to a recurring problem.

Self-censoring can inhibit the group's effectiveness also. Because of the group's high emphasis on forward motion and task accomplishment, group members who have important information or useful points of view that either cannot be articulated succinctly, or that question basic premises on which the group is acting, may feel reluctant to do anything that slows down the group or that introduces "a wrinkle" that might be seen as throwing the group off track.

Other problems occur when new information seems to contradict other information that the group has already absorbed, or when it becomes apparent that the pieces of the puzzle do not fit together well. In its haste to move forward, it is easy for a decisive group to conveniently ignore discrepant information and attempt a force-fit solution that becomes at best a distant, patchwork approximation of what the problem really requires.

Decisive individuals, of course, are quite capable of disagreeing with other decisive individuals. So decisive group meetings sometimes generate heated arguments over which of several courses of action is best for the group to adopt. Decisives generally do not like lengthy debates, however, so arguments tend to be cut short by the group leader or by other members who have grown impatient with the disagreeing members.

For the most part these problems are unlikely to hamper the performance of a decisive group when the nature of the problem fits the decisive group process. When process problems do occur in a decisive group, they should be taken seriously as a warning that the problem may not lend itself well to decisive group process. For example, discrepant information, pieces of the puzzle failing to fit together well, and debates over what should be done may indicate that the problem is not as simple as it may have seemed at first. These could be symptoms of a complex problem that requires thorough group analysis leading, perhaps, to new or unusual solutions that themselves may be quite complex.

Flexible Group Behavior

A glance down the flexible column of Table 11.1 provides clues to the behavior that you can expect to see in a flexible group. In contrast to the orderly process of their decisive counterparts, flexible groups are very loose and informal.

You can expect to hear humor throughout group meetings, especially when discussions stall. This is when someone tells a joke that basically stops the analysis of a problem or an aspect of a problem that has hung up the group and moves the discussion to a different problem or topic.

Flexible group meetings seldom follow a fixed agenda. If an agenda has been established, it is ignored. After starting a meeting with a specific issue or problem in mind, a flexible group tends to let whatever happens just happen. Usually, this means visiting many topics in quick succession. If a topic deals with a problem facing the group, a brief discussion of the problem is likely to lead quickly to a series of suggested courses of action for dealing with the problem.

Unlike decisive groups, flexible groups tend to shun divisions of labor. They make few attempts to identify and assign specific tasks to group members. Anyone can comment on anything, regardless of his or her job title or formal role.

Flexible groups particularly stand out from others in their "idea flow" or the rate at which they produce ideas. Among groups with a particular style mix, flexible groups are capable of producing the highest volume of ideas per unit of time.

Advantages of Flexible Groups. Because of their speed, adaptability, and high idea flow, flexible groups are well suited for dealing with problems or situations in which many obstacles must be surmounted quickly, in which the preferences of different parties must be satisfied by the solutions generated or in which novel solutions are needed to deal with a new or unusual situation.

Flexible groups are well suited for situations in which conflict potential is high, particularly when the factors giving rise to the conflict are subjective and revolve around matters of preference and habit more than technical issues and logic. Flexibles dislike conflict, so they are highly motivated to find ways to diffuse tensions. They are unlikely to get hung up on minor details or tradition and past practices, so they are willing to bend and compromise. Moreover, their high idea flow allows them to see a number of different ways of getting around problems.

We saw this clearly in a recent corporate merger. Mergers usually are highly charged with conflict. The merging organizations have many decisions to make in the process of integrating policies, setting operating procedures, and defining roles, and each of these decisions is loaded with conflict potential. In the merger we observed, the only people who remained on the executive staff of the combined organization eighteen months after the merger were those with primary or backup flexible styles. The hierarchics and decisives were nowhere to be seen, regardless of which of the predecessor companies they had come from.

Flexible groups are right for situations that call for breaking out of patterns of thinking and behaving. They make great forums for brainstorming in the purest sense, in which many different ideas are generated quickly without being critically evaluated. Consequently, they generate a variety of viewpoints and ideas that can later be used by other, nonflexible groups to work out details and deal with the complexities of planning and logistics. For example, a flexible group can supply a strategic planning group with information about future trends in markets and technology and ideas for new products or product lines.

Disadvantages of Flexible Groups. Most of the problems that plague flexible groups revolve around their tendency to become so scattered and disorganized that they accomplish either nothing or the wrong things. These groups can fall apart when members fail to get on the same track at the same time. When each goes off in a different direction, members cease to operate as a group. Sometimes their good humor and emphasis on easy interpersonal relationships distracts attention from the problems or tasks at hand, and productivity suffers.

Usually, a little gentle nudging or calling attention to key issues or tasks overcomes these problems. However, if you are in the position of managing a flexible group and your style is not flexible, be careful not to become overbearing and highly directive. This squelches the flexible process and causes the group to lose energy.

Long meetings should be avoided. Flexibles find them tedious. They work best in relatively short bursts. So try to keep meetings on the short side. Anything more than ninety minutes without a significant break or diversion is pushing things.

Keep in mind that if scatter and lack of productivity plague a flexible group, the group may be working on the wrong problems or tasks. Their job should be to quickly produce a variety of ideas, solutions, or recommendations when there is a need for such things. Detailed planning, control, and implementation are not the strong suits of flexible groups, so they should not be used for these purposes.

Hierarchic Group Behavior

The behavior of hierarchic groups is quite different from decisive groups and especially flexible groups. How a hierarchic group behaves is influenced heavily by the presence or absence of a hierarchic leader. When a hierarchic group leader is present, meetings tend to take on the show-and-tell quality mentioned earlier, in which team members make lengthy and orderly presentations to the leader without much interaction with one another. Group members may ask each other a few questions from time to time, but for the most part, they comment on each other's presentations only if called on to do so by the leader.

When hierarchic groups follow their own natural tendencies without the direction of a hierarchic leader, their tendency is to become increasingly structured in the way they operate over the course of a meeting. For example, in a meeting to deal with a new and unfamiliar problem, a hierarchic group's first tendency is to ask a lot of questions and offer opinions aimed at defining the problem. Next comes a period in which individual group members begin to develop positions about courses of action that they start to advocate and defend. If there are many different points of view, the group at some point seeks a means of objectively evaluating the relative merits of the various points.

This is the point at which the group's process begins to become quite structured. For example, someone may suggest that each person comment on the strengths and weaknesses of each course of action being considered, or the group may decide to lay out the different courses of action in a matrix that allows each to be compared to the others on key criteria.

After what may amount to considerable debate about the pros and cons of the different courses of action, the decision usually goes to the one that ends up with the best and most convincing support on key criteria. Seldom does a hierarchic group vote to decide an issue.

As Table 11.1 suggests, the only times that hierarchic groups willingly deviate from objective analysis as the decision method is when an issue clearly falls so squarely within the expertise of a particular individual, and outside the areas of expertise of the rest, that the group defers to the judgment of one person.

Once the group has selected the course of action that it considers best, it shifts its attention to the development of plans for carrying it out. Most typically, this involves constructing something approximating a "pert chart" with detailed timelines and milestones.

Like decisive groups, hierarchic groups establish divisions of labor. However, unlike decisive groups, where most of the problem-solving work goes on outside group meetings, hierarchic groups prefer to keep the problem solving and decision making inside the group as a regular part of group process. The only tasks that are subdivided and delegated to individuals or subgroups are research projects or implementation tasks decided by the full group.

Advantages of Hierarchic Groups. With their attention to data, logic, and planning, hierarchic groups work well on tasks or problem-solving assignments with firmly established goals and decision criteria, whose successful completion depends on assembling and systematically evaluating information from different sources. This is true especially when the actions that are likely to result from a group's deliberations have major, long-term consequences for the organization.

Hierarchic groups persist with an analysis until they are convinced that they know what they should do and when they will do it. They do not leave jobs half done. You will not find them lurching and thrashing about. When they act, it is with a plan.

Many task categories are suitable for hierarchic groups, including evaluating new business opportunities for fit with the organization's strategic plan, developing plans for a shift in business strategies, deciding about investments in new plant and equipment, and selecting locations for new facilities. These tasks require assembly and objective analysis of information to select courses of action that meet established criteria or goals.

For similar reasons, hierarchic groups often serve well as "courts of last resort" for parties that are unable to resolve conflicts by any other means. They ensure at least that disputes are settled fairly and objectively, if not to the complete satisfaction of the parties in conflict.

Disadvantages of Hierarchic Groups. Like other types of groups, a hierarchic group runs the risk of encountering a number of process problems that greatly reduce its ability to perform effectively. The potential for hierarchic group meetings to degenerate into debates or outright arguments over smaller and smaller details always lurks just around the corner. People using the hierarchic style eventually develop very strong feelings of conviction about the wisdom of their viewpoints, based on their evaluation of information, and it is very easy for a few people with equally strong but slightly different points of view to "get sideways" with one another.

Of course, disagreements can lead to new insights and creative ideas, but when disagreements give way to heated debate they become polarizing and nonproductive. In hierarchic groups, debates usually do not occur until group members have had time to take in information about a problem or situation and develop their individual points of view. You can hear this starting to happen as individuals' comments become longer and longer and start sounding like speeches, while others listen quietly only to respond with, "Yes, but . . . ," followed by equally lengthy speeches. Listening becomes less listening to understand than listening to refute or to find a chink in another person's position. When this occurs, the name of the game has become winning the debate. The objective of finding a high-quality solution for a problem has fallen by the wayside.

Hierarchic groups can avoid this pitfall in several ways. One way is for a leader or another member designated as a discussion leader to act as a "process cop" by intervening when debates occur. The discussion leader can also reduce the frequency of debates by helping to structure the discussion. For example, the discussion leader can ensure that each member has the opportunity to comment on proposed solutions or can call for the use of a structured method such as a decision matrix to help objectively evaluate different courses of action.

Adding structure to the group's process helps keep proceedings on an objective, analytic footing, but too much structure can squelch the group and take the energy out of a discussion. Consequently, finding the right balance of structure and spontaneity is an important challenge in managing a hierarchic group.

Integrative Group Behavior

The integrative group process is highly participative and exploratory, with a high exchange of information and ideas. Disagreements occur, but compared to other types of groups, disagreement does not lead to polarization and conflict. In many cases, disagreements stimulate further exploration and the discovery of new or creative insights.

Integrative group discussions generate comments such as, "That's interesting. I've never thought of that before," or "That gives me an idea. How about if . . . ," or "What you just said reminds me of . . ." As these comments indicate, integrative groups tend to pool information and ideas in such a way that solutions generated by the group often differ markedly from those that individual members might have come up with if they had worked on their own.

Agendas do not carry much weight in integrative groups, except to set the general topic areas to be discussed. Discussions do not hop from topic to topic quite as freely as they do in flexible groups, but the tendency still is to go wherever the discussion leads, even if this means departing from the immediate topic the group has been discussing. The primary topic is not abandoned completely but may be set aside momentarily to be returned to later or modified somewhat. Usually, the topic is expanded to include additional issues that the group believes to be relevant.

Delegation of decisions to individuals or subgroups is not characteristic of integrative groups. Most of the analysis and problem solving goes on in group meetings, even though members may do some individual research and idea generating outside the group itself. In fact, in a truly integrative group, members are encouraged to bring in conflicting information and new or unusual points of view.

A unique feature of the integrative group process is the tendency for members to occasionally comment on the group's own process while it is happening. This does not happen all of the time, but integrative groups make spontaneous comments about group process as it is occurring (such as, "Jim, we haven't heard much from you for a while. What are your thoughts on this issue?" or "Let's think about how we are going to do this"). In most groups, the only time you are likely to hear any comments about the group's process is after the meeting ("Jim sure was quiet. I wonder what was bothering him?" or "That sure was a waste of time. I felt like we were spinning our wheels all afternoon"). This tendency of integrative groups to monitor the process helps them stay coordinated without relying on a leader or on a structured method of analysis or decision making. Integrative groups might experiment with structured methods, but they are not likely to use the same methods repeatedly.

Advantages of Integrative Groups. Integrative groups have several unique advantages. First, the open, exploratory nature of their process is well suited for creative problem solving, especially when problems are complex and have many parts. Integrative groups literally integrate a lot of information from diverse sources and explore different ways of putting the information together. This sets the stage for generating new ideas that group members are unlikely to produce working alone.

In other words, integrative groups have high potential for

synergy, the basic foundation for creativity and the source of the adage "two heads are better than one." As you probably already know from your own experience, very few groups actually create. Process problems revolving around domination, conformity, debates, and conflict too often obstruct groups and keep them far from anything approaching synergy and its outcome, creativity. Yet integrative groups, by virtue of their style of thinking and problem solving, lean naturally in the direction of synergy.

Integrative groups can also be effective forums for resolving conflicts and promoting cooperation and collaboration. Instead of either taking hard, uncompromising stands on issues or tenaciously avoiding disagreement, individuals in integrative groups actively engage in finding ways to build on each other's ideas and take advantage of different points of view. Disagreements are viewed with interest and curiosity and often lead to further probing about the underlying factors giving rise to different points of view. What appeared to be a conflict is frequently recognized as merely the result of individuals perceiving different facets of a problem. The outcomes are less conflict and a better understanding of problems facing the group.

The integrative group process finds another useful application in the participative decision making and high-involvement work teams increasingly emphasized throughout industry. In many ways, integrative group behavior is synonymous with participation and high involvement. To work effectively in a participative mode, groups need to make high use of ideas and information held by group members. The members of a group need to think together and feel actively involved in discussions, without getting stymied by process problems such as dominance and conformity. For participation to work, group members must understand and feel ownership for decisions taken by the group. These outcomes occur naturally when the integrative process is at work in a group.

Disadvantages of Integrative Groups. Integrative groups have their share of disadvantages. Lack of closure is a common problem. Integrative groups generate creative ideas but sometimes encounter problems in narrowing things to a set of solutions that can be applied practically. They may produce more ideas than they can even act on yet find it nearly impossible to discard some.

Integrative groups also encounter time management problems. They have so much fun exploring different aspects of a problem and playing with ideas that they can fail to decide on courses of action before circumstances dictate that they move on to other issues. When this tendency gets out of hand, problems are solved by default and the advantages of the integrative process are lost.

In some cases, integrative groups devise solutions that are overly complex and unusual and consequently very difficult to explain to others. This problem is compounded when the reasoning that led to the solutions is very complex and was never recorded or documented by the group. Others who are expected to implement the group's decisions can be confused and left wondering what exactly they are supposed to do.

To offset these potential difficulties, integrative groups need to periodically "reality check" their process. For example, the group may find itself poised to go down another newly discovered avenue of thinking. Before venturing down this avenue, the group needs to summarize its progress on its main topic up to this point and then make a decision about whether embarking on the new line of reasoning makes sense. This often leads to the realization that the new avenue actually represents working on a new topic that, if important enough, might warrant a separate discussion at another time.

Another reality-checking technique is testing the group's decisions on outsiders who have not been involved in the group discussions before making formal recommendations or announcements about decisions. This helps the group avoid confusing or misleading others.

Periodic progress and time checks also help integrative groups from straying too far afield of important problems and from losing sight of the need to bring their discussions to a useful point of closure before running out of time.

Fortunately, these process management techniques are relatively easy for integrative groups to implement, because their members are naturally process aware. The one exception is making periodic time checks. This does not come naturally. When in integrative mode, the natural tendency for groups and individuals is to lose sight of, and sometimes even to resist keeping track of, the passage of time. Nevertheless, doing so can help to win the credits that they need to go on to be integrative on yet another day.

Some Thoughts About Systemic Groups

We have yet to see a group that fairly could be classified as systemic, and there may be good reasons for this. Chief among these is that systemic groups probably would be very unstable and short-lived.

Imagine the behavior of a group populated by individuals who characteristically see things in very complex ways and who are each committed to the achievement of a complicated set of goals. Unless they all happened to place the same values on the same goals, the potential for fragmentation and conflict, if not outright warfare, would be very high.

Systemics can play productive roles in both hierarchic and integrative groups, however. They can help by adding structure to the integrative process and by broadening a hierarchic group's frame of reference and sensitivity to situations not directly related to the problem facing the group but nonetheless affected by the group's actions. However, when systemics deal with other systemics, they easily begin working at cross purposes and spending much more time persuading each other of the wisdom of their analyses and ideas than they spend working on problems and tasks.

Potentially, systemic groups could be put together and managed effectively, and an entire book could be devoted to that topic. Inasmuch as we have yet to encounter a systemic group, however, and in view of the special challenges such a group would face, we reserve further discussion of them for another time and place.

As you can see, groups that lean toward a particular style can be used with advantage for a variety of problem-solving and decision-making tasks. However, the situational nature of their effectiveness must be kept in mind. If these groups are assigned to tasks that do not fit their particular style, advantages can quickly turn into weaknesses and liabilities. Groups, like individuals, should not be expected to be wonderful in every possible way. Success is the outcome of fit with goals and tasks, not of unrealistic or unconsidered expectations for superior performance in all situations.

12

Team Building

*M*ajor Product Industries (MPI) evolved from a $300 million railroad company into a multinational corporation with operations in a wide array of commercial products. In 1984, MPI accomplished ten divestitures and made several strategic acquisitions, which propelled the Fortune 500 conglomerate into the dynamic areas of aerospace and electronics. In 1985, additional acquisitions to strengthen the aerospace companies included Numero Company and Uno, Incorporated. Both companies were placed under tremendous pressure from their parent corporation to streamline operations, and they improved productivity by 10 percent. Further improvement was mandated in 1986, however, through the integration of functions and elimination of duplicate facilities.

The prescribed strategic plan for the newly merged Numero Uno Company was to concentrate on aerospace, defense, and selected industrial products; withdraw from mature industrial businesses; and develop new technologies, while continuing to streamline operations and improve productivity. These ambitious goals and overwhelming changes put tremendous pressure on Numero Uno's president and chief executive officer, who called us for help in restructuring the pieces of the newly merged company

215

and developing a team from the chaos that could persevere and accomplish its assigned mission.

The president explained to us that the Numero Uno merger created a multitude of significant structural and interpersonal changes that the financial engineers of the merger had not even contemplated, including (1) considerable redundancy in management personnel and structure, (2) a new CEO with ambiguous power and goals, (3) changing operating procedures and responsibilities, and (4) uncertain reward systems and career paths. These externally initiated changes led to a multitude of internal changes in organizational culture, interpersonal relationships, structural uncertainty, and career opportunities. The executive staffs were extremely competent in their areas of expertise but depended on each other to make the organization function effectively. The different styles of staff members, coupled with the anxiety and resentment that rapidly developed regarding the ambiguity of careers and power bases, led to minimal communication, distrust of others' intentions, disorganization, and low productivity. The merger had transformed two effectively functioning teams into a group of disorganized and competing individuals that threatened to reverse previous progress and possibly destroy the new company and everyone in it.

This was especially true of the executive staff, which was made up of the president, vice president, subsidiary company presidents, financial and legal division directors, and their immediate staffs. The need to streamline and increase productivity meant that all of the current group, which represented officers of both the previous Numero and Uno companies, would not remain at the end of the year because of considerable redundancies. The politics, lack of trust and openness, fear and hostility, and considerable differences in previous corporate cultures and decision styles had created a group of territorial infighters. Clearly the Numero Uno corporate staff was not a team.

The Team-Building Process

Teams are intact, relatively permanent work groups at any level in an organization that are made up of peers and their immediate supervisor. Team members share a common charter or reason for working together and are usually accountable as a functioning unit within a larger organizational context. Although members typically have a variety of decision styles, they are interdependent and need each others' experience and strengths to be most effective. Consequently, they are committed to working together as a group in order to make better decisions and accomplish their objectives.

Major team fragmentation can occur during mergers like the Numero Uno situation, but even minor interpersonal and task-versus-style mismatches can quite often severely impede a task group's functioning. Team building includes all activities aimed at improving the problem-solving ability among group members by working through task and interpersonal issues that impede the team's functioning.

The objective of team building is to develop a cohesive, mutually supportive, and trusting group that holds high expectations for task accomplishment and at the same time respects individual differences in values, decision styles, and skills. Successful team building nurtures individual potential and unique style strengths and does not foster conformity to smooth over differences. More specific team-building goals include the following:

1. Understanding each member's decision styles and how to manage them most effectively
2. Understanding the team's charter or purpose in the total functioning of the organization (where its primary focus is)
3. Increasing and improving the effectiveness of communication among team members by adapting messages to the receiver's style preference
4. Providing greater support of group members through increased awareness and acceptance of the need for contributions from all the different decision styles
5. Understanding group processes
6. Developing effective ways of working through group problems by applying style-coping guidelines
7. Using conflict originating in toxic relationships in positive, creative ways that promote positive changes

8. Fostering collaboration and not competition among team members

9. Increasing the ability of the group to work productively with other groups in the organization through increased understanding and empathy for their different styles and task priorities

10. Supporting interdependence among group members by showing how an individual's style weaknesses can be counterbalanced by a different style's strengths

11. Understanding the team's required roles and how different decision styles fit different roles

To accomplish these goals, several chronological team-building steps are required. First, a needs assessment is necessary to determine the specific assessments and interventions required and the planning and design of the program. Next, team commitment must be established, and individuals must feel comfortable enough with the program and facilitator to openly share and receive feedback from other members. A variety of assessment devices can be administered to increase participants' awareness of interaction problems, including paper and pencil inventories, exercises, and simulations. The information gained from the assessments and exercises is used to identify team problems, which are analyzed, prioritized, and assigned to task groups to solve. Finally, ongoing follow-up is required to ensure that problems are solved, solutions are implemented, and the team continues to monitor itself on an ongoing basis. These steps are diagrammed in Figure 12.1 and are described more fully in the remainder of this chapter.

It is the team leader's responsibility to keep the team functioning effectively. Because many managers have not been trained in the process of data gathering, diagnosis, decision making, and action planning, a consultant who possesses specialized knowledge and skills, an objective perspective, and references to similar situations for a comparison base often facilitates the process.

Our role with Numero Uno was to work with the executive staff until the group was capable of monitoring and correcting its own process and the president had implemented team building as an ongoing activity. It was made clear from the beginning that we

Figure 12.1. The Team-Building Process.

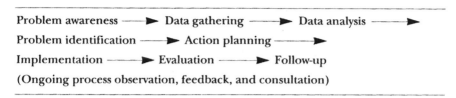

Problem awareness ———▶ Data gathering ———▶ Data analysis ———▶

Problem identification ———▶ Action planning ———▶

Implementation ———▶ Evaluation ———▶ Follow-up

(Ongoing process observation, feedback, and consultation)

were responsible to the entire group and not aligned only with the president or any particular subset of individuals. In order to best enhance and facilitate the team's problem-solving capability, we needed to be free to respond equally to each member of the executive staff and help the group be as creative as possible. Special private consulting with the president was essential in setting the stage for our role and coaching the president about his own role in the process.

We planned not to directly solve the group's problems for them but to help the team learn to solve its own problems by making members more aware of existing decision styles, current group processes, consequences, and alternatives. As the group became better at coping with its own style difficulties and job mismatches, these successes would lead to enhanced positive feelings and understanding among members of a more effective team. At that point we would have worked ourselves out of a job. Following is a summary of how the team-building process was used at Numero Uno.

Needs Assessment

A team-building program is usually initiated because someone (the leader, a higher-level manager, a team member, or a consultant) recognizes that the group is having problems working productively as a team. The president of Numero Uno recognized the serious difficulties his team was encountering and began the process. At Numero Uno the president had noticed the following symptoms:

Overt hostilities between team members
Chronic lateness or absenteeism at meetings

Low quantity and quality of production

Negative gossip and rumors about each other

Decisions not carried out because of misunderstandings and
lack of willingness to take responsibility

Apathy and lack of interest in helping others on the executive
staff

These factors were clearly symptoms of underlying problems
that needed to be determined through data gathering and analysis.
For example, the loss of productivity could have been a symptom
of role ambiguity, inadequate resources, or interpersonal hostilities.

We explained that the success of a team development program depended on the accurate identification of the group's specific
needs and problems. Depending on what the initial needs assessment determined, different approaches and interventions could be
more or less appropriate. It would make little sense, for example,
to apply interventions aimed at increasing trust and openness if the
primary problem encountered by the executive staff was centered on
job ambiguity and role conflict.

The first step was to gather data about the team situation so
that the correct diagnosis could be made. The group was already
experiencing considerable pain, as indicated by a variety of symptoms such as decreased output, hostile sentiments, and interpersonal conflicts. The task now was to determine why these negative
factors existed and what could be done about them. Data gathering
took a variety of forms.

Interviews

It was decided that the best sensing method for identifying the problems was to privately interview each team member, assuring confidentiality. Common and significant problems would later be shared
with the team, but who mentioned them would not be disclosed.

We started the interviews with a set of common questions
concerning factors such as these:

1.   What do you like best and least about the team?

2. What factors keep you from being as productive as you could be?
3. What are some of the strengths and weaknesses of the CEO and each of the members?
4. What changes could make you and your team more effective?

As the interview progressed, however, other factors were investigated as they were revealed by the interviewees in an attempt to identify and understand all significant problems.

In each case, we explained to the interviewees how the interview process would be conducted, how the data would be used to diagnose problems and facilitate team building, and how confidentiality would be honored, although all relevant information would be shared. Taking notes was helpful so that we could recall the reasons for certain comments and provide actual quotes when appropriate. Opportunities also arose to build rapport, trust, and credibility with participants as well as increase their psychological ownership of the information that later would be used in the team-building meetings.

Questionnaires

An alternative to face-to-face interviews would have been to distribute written questionnaires to team members and ask them to complete them anonymously or signed, depending on the climate and content of the questionnaire. We administered the Driver Decision Style Exercise and the Driver-Streufert Complexity Index to obtain data on individual, group, and organizational operating and role styles, respectively (see Appendixes B, C, and D).

Data Analysis

We performed a content analysis of the interview data to identify the common and significant problems, major themes, and suggested solutions. These results were then summarized for presentation to team members in written notebooks and also on transparencies for open sharing of data at the forthcoming team-building meeting.

It was determined that some of the group's problems were caused by scarce resources, job ambiguity, role conflict, unrealistic workloads, or other factors not directly related to how individuals function as a team. In these cases, other activities like job redesign, allocation of additional resources, and job profiling and person matching were recommended. It was apparent that significant individual and cultural decision style differences existed, and we planned a meeting of the team to analyze the data and generate action plans to address the primary decision-making, interaction, and job fit concerns.

Planning and Design

It is important that team members understand clearly the sort of experience they are in for. We described the experience to the leader and members during data-gathering interviews but repeated the plan at a general orientation meeting. Our goals were to ensure that expectations were congruent with the probable experience and to motivate participants to make a commitment to fully involve themselves in the process. Any hesitations or expectation gaps were worked through and clarified as we attempted to build trust and credibility with the team.

We were granted three uninterrupted days, away from day-to-day distractions, in order to generate the climate and energy that would allow us to investigate and improve team interaction. The physical setting was informal, and participants were told to dress casually to enhance feelings of informality and openness.

Sensing

We also reviewed the data analysis gathered from the initial decision style inventories and determined that interpersonal difficulties attributable to different decision styles of team members were a primary problem for the executive staff. Consequently, before the team-building meeting itself, we allocated time for individual feedback and interpretation sessions so that each person understood the ramifications of his or her individual role and operating styles, as well as the dynamics that occur when interacting with the other styles. We also presented the decision style model to the group at one time, followed by questions and application sessions.

Data Preparation for Feedback

Decision style scores were listed on charts for use as overhead transparencies and handouts. Both operating and role styles for each team member were noted for all participants to observe.

A content analysis of the broader-scale team data collected in the initial probe was conducted to determine patterns from the different perspectives revealed. Data were grouped by common themes under descriptive headings using quotes and related comments to clarify and elaborate on the problem areas. These groupings were illustrated on posters, overhead transparencies, and flip charts for presentation at the meeting. Delineations were made between problem areas that the team could realistically do something about versus those that were out of its control and consequently not appropriate for the team-building session.

Team Leader Coaching

The team leader, whether the company CEO or work group supervisor, has a different power base than other group members, and particularly when the leader has practiced a more autocratic style, he or she should be coached to be more participative and supportive of others' ideas and inputs so that all the relevant data will be shared honestly. This can be facilitated by having the leader listen first and share his or her perspectives later to avoid the suppression of important input in deference to the leader.

The leader also usually has the most to gain or lose from the team-building experience. He or she is, after all, responsible for developing an effective team and most likely to receive feedback, especially regarding behaviors that the team has not had the courage to confront him or her with in the normal work situation. The leader's reactions to feedback sets the example for how freely group members continue to give and receive feedback themselves. Consequently, nondefensive listening followed by clarifying questions is recommended until all the data are on the table. If the leader responds defensively or in a punitive manner, the session cannot succeed.

We did not want the president of Numero Uno to be surprised by this experience because it could destroy his trust in us and develop into a negative experience for all involved. A leader who expects nothing but positive strokes and instead is inundated with negative feedback can easily develop hurt feelings, defensiveness, and a desire to retaliate—the opposite of the team-building goals. Consequently, we coached the president on what to expect and how to react to the feedback in order to get the most benefit from it. We also structured the process so that negative feedback was always phrased in a constructive manner and followed a healthy dose of positive feedback.

The president understood that our role was to facilitate the most positive outcome for the entire team, including soliciting feedback regarding how his own behavior could be improved. When the emphasis is on the entire team, it sometimes involves changing leadership behavior, which can be difficult to accept, especially when the leader's original concept is that the team building will "fix them."

The Team-Building Meeting

We opened the team-building session with an explanation of what would be happening and what expectations were for participants. Our role as facilitators to help the team understand its own process and solve its own problems was made clear. Team members were given an opportunity to share their concerns, ask questions, and clarify their roles. Mutual goal setting about what could realistically be accomplished was discussed and agreed on. The result was a psychological contract about participant contributions and most-likely outcomes.

Next, we made a brief conceptual presentation about the dynamics of the team-building process. This included an explanation of the two primary team-building tools of self-disclosure and solicitation of feedback and how decision style differences needed to be understood, treated differentially, and matched with appropriate assignments.

Self-disclosure and solicitation of feedback were emphasized as primary learning tools. To accomplish the goals of team building, individuals must be made aware of how their behaviors affect others and how they can aim those behaviors in a more productive direction. Because people often are not aware of what they do that causes negative reactions in others, this information must be actively sought out, and others should constructively disclose their feelings and perceptions of what is happening and its consequences.

When information is disclosed that is known to both parties, mutually shared perceptions regarding it confirm both parties' previous understandings. People do not always share everything they know, however, because they may be afraid that others will think less of them, will use the knowledge to their advantage, will chastise them, or will be hurt. Information of this nature includes hidden agendas and things we are ashamed of. On the other hand, certain things about us are apparent to others but not to ourselves, either because no one has ever told us about them or because we defensively block them out. We all have blind spots that make us less effective in our interactions with others.

When individuals feel secure enough to ask others about how they perceive their behaviors and provide suggestions for improvement, participants can self-disclose their perceptions and reactions in constructive and supportive ways and help others become more effective as their blind spots are eliminated. Through these self-disclosures, team members trust each other more, become more open, are less afraid to reveal things previously hidden, and take some risks in self-disclosing information helpful to the group but previously withheld because it was potentially harmful to themselves. As this process develops, group members feel better about others in the group, and the team-building process begins.

Sharing the Sensing Data

Once the participants understand what will happen in the team-building meeting, have realistic role expectations, and have accepted the norms of self-disclosure and soliciting feedback, it is time to publish the sensing data previously gathered through questionnaires and interviews. For major problem areas, flip charts or transparencies, each containing one major theme with related points and quotes listed, can be presented. The consultant should read and explain each area and encourage participants to ask for clarification so that everyone understands the essence and ramifications of the problems. At this point, however, the group members should not begin to process the data; the goal is awareness and understanding.

Flip charts, transparencies, and duplicate handouts also can be used to publish the participants' decision style data. These scores should not be shared until all participants have received feedback about their personal scores, the conceptual decision style framework, and the ramifications of their own styles. When the decision style information is shared, the facilitator can begin processing the data by asking team members about predominant score patterns, obvious contrasts, person-job complexity matches, and so forth to help participants understand the ramifications of similarities and differences in decision styles.

After all the data are available, the facilitator and group can begin to determine what is workable and which issues are most important. To ensure that everything is now on the table before diagnosis begins, the facilitator might call for open sharing of any additional data. At this time anything that helps clarify the issues already identified can be shared, and new issues can be added. Whatever keeps the group from being as effective as possible is fair game, as are things participants like or dislike about the group or its members.

Diagnosis and Evaluation

The next task is to set priorities and determine the group's agenda for the time it still has available. It is vital that only those issues that the team can realistically do something about be included on the agenda so that the group can accomplish something positive and start to feel good about itself and its problem-solving abilities. Issues might first be broken down into (1) issues that can be worked on in the meeting, (2) issues that the group cannot influence and must live with, (3) issues that should be delegated to someone else to act on.

The first set of items should next be ranked in order of importance to be addressed during this session. The group next needs to determine what coping mechanisms, if any, are available to make life with the second set of items a little easier. The final set of items involves the participation of outside groups or individuals, and plans regarding how to solicit their involvement should be developed.

Problem Solving

There are several alternatives for analyzing and generating solutions to the major problem areas. If the team is relatively large, the top three or four issues can be assigned to teams of concerned and qualified individuals to work on in subgroups that later share their recommendations with the entire team for further processing. For small groups, the prioritized agenda can be worked on item by item to develop action plans. In either case, action plans should be posted on newsprint and should include a statement of the problem, solution recommended, people responsible for implementing action, and deadlines for results.

During these problem-solving sessions, the facilitator serves as process observer and helper. If several subgroups are working simultaneously, one observer should be assigned to each group. During the sessions, the process observer mentions behaviors that help and hinder the group and may call for or suggest alternative actions. At the end of the session, the process observer reviews with the group the major positive and negative behaviors observed and helps it explore why they occurred and how they should be altered in the future.

Process observation is something that the group should learn to perform continually on its own. Team members should be invited to become process observer-commenters as the group continues to work through the remaining issues. At the end of each problem session, the group takes more and more responsibility for critiquing its immediately finished process before it advances to the next issue. This way, team members build the habit of reinforcing constructive comments and working through destructive behaviors.

Planning Implementation and Follow-Up

The problem-solving phase establishes action plans, people responsible for implementing the actions, and dates for results to be accomplished. If these plans are to make any difference, they must be carried out and evaluated. Within a month of the team-building session, a follow-up meeting should be scheduled to determine how successful the action plans have been and what needs to be done at this point.

The team leader needs to make a clear commitment to check on progress every week before the follow-up meeting to demonstrate that the organization is serious about improving the team. Otherwise, the enthusiasm following the team-building retreat is likely to dwindle as participants return to their daily routines. Although a consultant may be on call as a resource during the implementation, the team leader should demonstrate the initiative and commitment to obtain the agreed-on results.

At the next meeting, the work accomplished can be reviewed and the next steps determined. Thus far, the team has dealt with issues of immediate concern in the classic problem-solving mode. All too often, however, if action plans fail, groups give up and call the whole team-building effort a waste of time. If action plans are successful, the team may feel positive about the experience but ride on its laurels until the next set of dilemmas arises. These outcomes are in contrast to the major goal of team building, which is to see the process become ongoing in the work group.

Ongoing Group Process Development

After the major problems of the group have been successfully dealt with, the team usually continues to have a number of interpersonal issues that hinder it from being as effective a team as it could be. Such issues can center on things like toxic style relationships, misunderstanding of intentions, task assignments incongruent with decision style strengths, and goal conflicts. Other process issues may center around group norms, roles, and values. These interpersonal and group process issues can be dealt with in open feedback sessions, debriefing of decision style and team fit inventories, or exercise and simulation debriefings.

Open feedback sessions use the tools of soliciting and giving feedback to eliminate blind spots and enhance understanding. It is possible, for example, that one person may unknowingly have a decision style that impedes several other team members in accomplishing their own tasks. The objective is to share information so that feelings and consequences can be better understood and performance of all individuals on the team can be enhanced.

Feedback should be given and solicited in the spirit of helping all involved grow. It is critical to have a trained facilitator present if there is any possibility that the session will degenerate into name calling, griping, blaming, or punishing.

In completely open sessions, group members solicit or give feedback spontaneously, usually according to how urgent they feel the issues are. Someone may solicit feedback by saying, "John, I need to work with you to complete project proposals effectively. I find myself resisting, though, because when we work together, you are always late meeting deadlines that are crucial to having clients accept and consider our proposals. Is there anything that I or we can do to ensure your valuable input on these projects within the necessary time frame?" A group process comment might be something like this: "It really frustrates me when I show up at the agreed-on starting time for these meetings, and Bob and I are the only ones present until the rest of you trickle in fifteen to twenty minutes later. What can we do to ensure we all arrive on schedule?"

Semistructured methods to facilitate the sharing of similar data when group members are more reticent include the following:

1. Post pieces of newsprint for each individual on the walls and have group members write perceived decision style strengths and barriers. Each individual then reads them off to the group and receives clarification.
2. The same data as in item one, but instead of on newsprint, write this information on slips of paper and have each participant share and ask for clarification only of information not understood.
3. The same as item one, only for the team as a whole.

Personal profiles based on self-assessment inventories can be helpful on the individual and interpersonal levels. Many decision-making and interpersonal insights can be determined from analysis and discussion of decision style scores and their interaction implications. Other instruments that may be appropriate if concerns center around relationships or feelings are the Fundamental Interpersonal Relations Orientation (FIRO) Inventory (Schutz, 1958) and the Emotional Reactions Inventory (Driver, 1984).

As illustrated in the Numero Uno case, participants can complete the Driver Decision Style Exercise and the Driver-Streufert Complexity Index, receive a lecture on role and operating decision styles, receive their scores and individual interpretations, and then have everyone's scores published for the group to see. The job of the team, with the aid of a knowledgeable facilitator, is to analyze the published scores to better understand why others prefer certain ways of doing things and behave as they do. Congruencies between person and task assignments can be discussed, as can the predictable toxic relationships and what can be done to manage them most appropriately.

As with open feedback sessions, individuals can share feedback with each other regarding interaction difficulties based on style differences and work out contracts to better interact together. Semistructured techniques can also be helpful and applied as described above. For example, strengths and weaknesses of each style can be posted, and team members with a certain style can stand beneath the poster while others confirm the various characteristics and their ramifications. Similarly, the guidelines for coping with different styles (Chapter Seven) can be posted, and individuals with a specific style can confirm which strategies work with them.

If the facilitator or someone else is assigned to take notes during this process, a written guide for improved teamwork can be developed to help participants deal productively with each other by reducing the potential for misunderstandings. A personal synopsis of each person's style preferences can include things like (1) how to gain Mike's support, (2) how to coordinate and share information with Mike, (3) how to identify and solve problems with Mike. An example of the last area might run as follows: "Learn what excites and intrigues Mike. Then use that interest to the team benefit. Mike's systemic backup style may lead him to explore endless possibilities to correct a problem. He doesn't like ambiguity, so explain the complete nature of problems and specific negative ramifica-tions. Be as clear as possible about the impact. Give him wide lati-tude to develop unorthodox solutions. He will sort through them and generate a precise, orderly approach to solve the problem. Be prepared to let him take charge and run with the ball."

Sharing decision style scores can also be used to determine where each team member's strengths can best be applied to the problem-solving meetings. For example, decisive individuals can be assigned to start, close, and keep the group on the agenda during the meeting. For brainstorming alternatives, however, the floor may be best held by flexibles and integratives. Finally, hierarchics and systemics can lead the group in analyzing the data and reaching solid conclusions.

Exercises and simulations can be used to solicit behavior for analysis in a nonthreatening—that is, not directly work-related—setting. Behaviors that help and hinder goal accomplishment and team development in the exercise or simulation can then be dis-cussed in terms of how they might affect individual or team perfor-mance on the job.

One example simulation is the Luna I Moon Colony, which places individuals on project management teams in the moon's first manned colony (Driver and Hunsaker, 1972). Teams can be com-posed of individuals with different decision styles to demonstrate what interaction patterns develop, or homogeneous teams can be compared with those of different styles to show performance strengths and weaknesses.

The teams are given problems of varying environmental complexity to solve, and their solutions and methods of interacting are videotaped and observed. Performance data can later be com-pared, and team process data can be observed and discussed to give individuals and the team feedback on their strengths, weaknesses, and interaction idiosyncracies.

Summary of General Team-Building Procedure

Improving team effectiveness within the decision-making context usually includes needs assessments via in-depth interviews, data analysis and problem solving, training workshops, simulation exercises, team member assessments, individual and group feedback, and interpersonal relations coaching. Although each team-building program should be tailored to specific circumstances, each program generally follows this flow of events:

1. Diagnostic interviews with the team leader and separately with individual team members to build rapport and gather data
2. Identification of sources of current and potential conflict
3. Workshops for team members to deal with conflict issues; activities include
    a. Assessing team members' personal and interpersonal decision style characteristics through paper and pencil inventories
    b. Videotaping problem-solving exercises involving team members working in groups
    c. Presenting relevant personal, interpersonal, and group dynamics concepts (such as a decision style model)
    d. Providing individual feedback and interpretation of assessment results
    e. Facilitating group sharing of assessment results and discussion of relationships that have evolved
    f. Fostering group analysis of videotaped exercises
    g. Providing training in group process
4. Follow-up coaching for individual team members or for subgroups of team members as needed

Team-building programs improve working relationships among team members by stimulating insights into oneself, other team members, and the factors that create dysfunctional relationships and unnecessary tensions. Team members also learn a new language for identifying and discussing interpersonal issues. Finally, individual team members gain a broader understanding of their own and others' roles as members of an effectively functioning management team.

Appendixes

A

The Development of Decision Dynamics Theory

*T*he origin of this model was Sigmund Freud's interest in strategies that our conscious ego uses to defend itself against pressures from the unconscious. Freud (1947) believed that the conscious ego constantly strives to balance primitive lusts and furies emerging from our biological unconscious id with social morals he placed in the superego or conscience. In this struggle the ego is often threatened by the superego with guilt and self-punishment if it permits "evil" id impulses to surface, so it builds *defense mechanisms* to protect itself. These defense mechanisms include *repression, projection* (blaming others), and *reaction formations* (rigid adherence to moralistic behaviors).

Following the cataclysm of World War II, Freudian-oriented psychoanalysts sought explanations for how fascism could pervade apparently civilized and intelligent groups within Nazi Germany. They turned to defense mechanisms and noted that under severe child rearing or economic circumstances some people develop an extreme personality called *authoritarian*. This type identified with power, projected blame onto minorities, and showed extremely simple, black-and-white thinking (Adorno, Frenkel-Brunswik, Levinson, and Sanford, [1950] 1964).

In the late 1950s the authoritarian personality had a distinctly negative reputation, unlike the complex and tolerant *democratic personality*. Milton Rokeach (1960) in the United States and Hans Eysenck (1954) in the United Kingdom noted that the type of simplistic thinking attributed to fascist personalities also could be found in those on the extreme left of the political spectrum. In his book *The Open and Closed Mind* (1960), Rokeach also elaborated on the idea of a thinking process that could be complex but closed to input not related to centrally held values; he termed this process *dogmatism*.

A parallel development at this time was research on *conformity* and *independence*. Interest developed in the underlying thought patterns that enabled some people to develop their own ideas versus those who either fought control (counterdependence) or took ideas from authorities (dependence) (Adorno and others, [1950] 1964).

A third line of research developed the idea of *cognitive style*. Witkin and others (1962), for instance, built a model of field-dependent versus field-independent thinkers, where the independent type tended toward analytic thought and the dependent type used a more global, simplistic approach.

Building on these ideas in the book *Conceptual Systems and Personality Organization*, Harvey, Hunt, and Schroder (1961) proposed a four-stage personality model in which level I was a simplistic, dependent, global, and closed true-believer type, akin to the authoritarian personality. Level IV was a complex, independent, open-style thinker. Levels II and III were less clear in terms of thinking style. Level II was akin to the counterdependent, anti-authority type, while level III was an open yet conformist person lacking the complexity of level IV.

The next step was taken in the book *Human Information Processing* by Schroder, Driver, and Streufert (1967). Based on a series of laboratory experiments, the environmental load model was developed. It was found that information complexity, noxity (negative input), and eucity (positive input) each affected information use in a systemic inverted-U pattern (see Figure A.1). The research also established that complex (level IV) types had inverted-U curves that were higher than those of simpler (level I) types. At this point

Figure A.1. The Environmental Load Model.

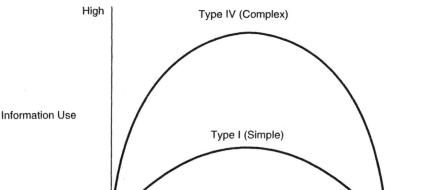

Information complexity:
Noxity (negative input)
Eucity (positive input)

two important developments emerged. First the model focused solely on the complexity of information processing or cognitive style; types II and III disappeared along with concern with the content of ideas. Then it was established that different styles are characterized by patterns of information use that change predictably over environmental conditions. Streufert and his colleagues (Streufert and Streufert, 1978) have continued to elaborate on this model, conducting extensive studies on the effects of threat and success on style and, more recently, on the prevalence of complex thinking styles among senior executives. Future work is planned at using the decision style model to build integrated human resource systems that link unit strategy to style and systematically select, assign, train, evaluate, and reward people in style in appropriate ways.

Interest also exists in developing programs for style change and for linking style theory to models of executive leadership. A third dimension of style—*filtering*, or how people select the most relevant data for use—is under study. This is a dynamic model whose future expansion in use and in theoretical reach is expected to benefit by both new research and application.

An article by Driver and Streufert (1969) introduced a new direction for management research. Two distinguishable types of complex styles were noted: one was open and loose, the other tight and focused, much like Rokeach's dogmatic personality. This was the origin of the *hierarchic* and *integrative* styles. This line of thought leads to the emergence of a second style dimension. The concept of *focus*, or the tendency to organize data around one or many views, emerged along with *amount of information use* as the two key dimensions in the decision style model.

The first full-scale development of the present model was formulated by Driver and Lintott (1972) and was tested empirically in a series of laboratory studies by Driver and Mock (1975b), as well as in an array of other studies. Important field tests of the model by Boulgarides (1973), Alawi (1973), Testerman (1975), Athey (1976), and Hager (1977) showed its value in relating to real-world phenomena during the 1970s. The model predicted performance as a selection instrument in a variety of jobs in an insurance company (Driver and Sundby, 1978).

Decision style has subsequently been used for training and selection in an array of organizations in fields as diverse as aerospace, real estate, international trade, utilities, computers, energy, and government (Brousseau, 1987). The measures of style have been translated for use in Japan, Europe, and the Middle East, where they show great promise as a personnel selection and development tool.

The model also is being used as a powerful tool in the area of job analysis (Meshkati, 1983). There are interesting applications in the areas of work-design performance appraisal and organization culture change. For instance, a current project is exploring a use of integrative role style training to enhance a more participative management style in a previously very decisive company.

B

Driver Decision Style Exercise (Form C1)

Instructions

This exercise looks at how people make decisions. It consists of two parts. Part One is a short case in which a situation in a fictional company is described. Following the description, some additional facts are given.

Part Two asks some questions about the case. First, you make a decision based on the information from Part One. Then indicate how you used the additional facts in reaching your decision. Next, you make another decision based on some new facts. Finally, indicate how you used the new facts in reaching the new decision.

There are no right or wrong answers. No one response is better than another. Work quickly and answer whatever comes into your mind first. There is no time limit.

Please read each question, then circle on your answer sheet (see Appendix D) the one number from the scale that best indicates how you rate each item. Please be certain that all forty-five questions are answered and that only one answer is marked in each space. No stray marks should be made on the answer sheet.

Part One: Case

Please read the following case and additional items of information carefully. When you have finished, proceed to Part Two.

The vice president in charge of personnel has just told you that you have been transferred from a position in the home office of Rush Drugs, Inc., to a managing position in the Halerville branch. Nominally, the two positions are of exactly equal importance, but you have cause to wonder why you should have been transferred. About four months ago you made a decision for the company that was essentially a risky gamble and it came off well. You were never able to find out exactly what your superiors thought of your move, but you do know that they do not all agree in their opinion of it. You are wondering whether your transfer constitutes a reprimand or an encouragement. The facts at your disposal are

Item A	Halerville is a large city with, as yet, small drug sales.
Item B	The previous branch manager of Halerville, who was a man of strong decisions, was very much liked by his employees. They seem to think that "there's no one like him."
Item C	Sales to smaller towns around Halerville are very badly organized. It is with just such a problem that you took your gamble.
Item D	There is a probability of a trucking strike in Halerville. This would involve long, drawn-out negotiations for transportation.
Item E	You have heard the second vice president say that what the Halerville branch needed was "a good strong hand."
Item F	This change in position involves a salary cut of one thousand dollars but there is a slight possibility of making this up or even exceeding it on a commission basis.

Part Two: Questions on the Case.

1. Do you think the transfer is an encouragement?   A ___
                          a reprimand?   B ___

2. How confident do you feel about the choice you made in question 1?

Extremely certain	1	2	3	4	5	6	7	Extremely uncertain

How relevant do you think the items are to your choice in question 1?

	Completely irrelevant					Very relevant	
3. Item A	1	2	3	4	5	6	7
4. Item B	1	2	3	4	5	6	7
5. Item C	1	2	3	4	5	6	7
6. Item D	1	2	3	4	5	6	7
7. Item E	1	2	3	4	5	6	7
8. Item F	1	2	3	4	5	6	7

To what degree do you feel that these items support your choice in question 1?

	Strongly opposes my view					Strongly supports my view	
9. Item A	1	2	3	4	5	6	7
10. Item B	1	2	3	4	5	6	7
11. Item C	1	2	3	4	5	6	7
12. Item D	1	2	3	4	5	6	7
13. Item E	1	2	3	4	5	6	7
14. Item F	1	2	3	4	5	6	7

To what degree do you feel that these items could be used to support *either* choice in question 1?

	Could easily support *both* choices—mine and the other					Could only support *one* choice—mine or the other	
15. Item A	1	2	3	4	5	6	7
16. Item B	1	2	3	4	5	6	7
17. Item C	1	2	3	4	5	6	7
18. Item D	1	2	3	4	5	6	7
19. Item E	1	2	3	4	5	6	7
20. Item F	1	2	3	4	5	6	7

How similar do you think these pairs of items are in the information they gave you about the problem in Part One? For example, if two items seem to say nearly the same thing about the case, you would rate them either 1 or 2; if they imply very different things, you would rate them either 6 or 7.

		Highly similar					Highly dissimilar	
21.	Items A and B	1	2	3	4	5	6	7
22.	Items A and C	1	2	3	4	5	6	7
23.	Items A and D	1	2	3	4	5	6	7
24.	Items A and E	1	2	3	4	5	6	7
25.	Items A and F	1	2	3	4	5	6	7
26.	Items B and C	1	2	3	4	5	6	7
27.	Items B and D	1	2	3	4	5	6	7
28.	Items B and E	1	2	3	4	5	6	7
29.	Items B and F	1	2	3	4	5	6	7
30.	Items C and D	1	2	3	4	5	6	7
31.	Items C and E	1	2	3	4	5	6	7
32.	Items C and F	1	2	3	4	5	6	7
33.	Items D and E	1	2	3	4	5	6	7
34.	Items D and F	1	2	3	4	5	6	7
35.	Items E and F	1	2	3	4	5	6	7

Please Note:

If you regard the transfer as a reprimand (and you chose B on question 1), go to "You See the Transfer as a Reprimand."

If you regard the transfer as an encouragement (and you chose A on question 1), read items G and H below and answer the following questions.

You See the Transfer as an Encouragement

Item G   The vice president in charge of personnel strongly favors conservative policies.

Item H   The operations manager of the branch is known to be extremely stubborn and is supposed to be in almost complete control.

36. Given the new information as well as the original items (you may wish to refer back to Part One), do you still see the transfer as an encouragement?

Yes (A) ___   No (B) ___

37. How confident do you feel about the choice you just made?

Extremely certain		1	2	3	4	5	6	7	Extremely uncertain

Without consulting your previous ratings, how relevant do you think all information items are to your choice in question 36?

		Completely irrelevant					Very relevant	
38.	Item A	1	2	3	4	5	6	7
39.	Item B	1	2	3	4	5	6	7
40.	Item C	1	2	3	4	5	6	7
41.	Item D	1	2	3	4	5	6	7
42.	Item E	1	2	3	4	5	6	7
43.	Item F	1	2	3	4	5	6	7
44.	Item G	1	2	3	4	5	6	7
45.	Item H	1	2	3	4	5	6	7

END OF EXERCISE

(Do not answer any more questions.)

You See the Transfer as a Reprimand

Read items G and H below, then answer questions 36–45.

Item G   The previous branch manager had established good relations with the trucking company.

Item H   The submanagers who will be working under you feel (unlike the rest of the employees) that the previous manager was removed due to some inefficiency and lack of initiative.

36. Given this new information as well as the original items (you may wish to refer back to Part One), do you still see the transfer as a reprimand?

Yes (A) ____   No (B) ____

37. How confident do you feel about the choice you just made?

Extremely certain		1	2	3	4	5	6	7	Extremely uncertain

Without consulting your previous ratings, how relevant do you think all information items are to your choice in question 36?

	Completely irrelevant					Very relevant	
38. Item A	1	2	3	4	5	6	7
39. Item B	1	2	3	4	5	6	7
40. Item C	1	2	3	4	5	6	7
41. Item D	1	2	3	4	5	6	7
42. Item E	1	2	3	4	5	6	7
43. Item F	1	2	3	4	5	6	7
44. Item G	1	2	3	4	5	6	7
45. Item H	1	2	3	4	5	6	7

END OF EXERCISE

C

Driver-Streufert Complexity Index

*T*his questionnaire consists of a series of phrases describing various points of view and ways of behaving. Some of the descriptions you will immediately identify as being extremely characteristic of your behavior. Others you will have the exact opposite reaction to, feeling that the description does not fit you at all. And a number of the phrases may strike you as being somewhere in between these two extremes (as being moderately characteristic or uncharacteristic of yourself).

Please read each description, then circle on your answer sheet (see Appendix D) the one number from the scale to the right that best indicates how characteristic that description is of you.

	How characteristic of you				
	Not at all characteristic of me			*Extremely characteristic of me*	
1. My motives and plans are complicated compared to those of the average person.	1	2	3	4	5
2. I feel we have little control over what happens to us.	1	2	3	4	5

	How characteristic of you				
	Not at all characteristic of me				*Extremely characteristic of me*
3. I feel one can develop successful personal qualities and, at times, influence events and people that strongly affect one's career.	1	2	3	4	5
4. In forming impressions of others, I use basically the same few, reliable categories.	1	2	3	4	5
5. In forming impressions of others, I use many categories that vary from person to person.	1	2	3	4	5
6. In solving problems, I function extremely well when both the problems and the solutions are clear-cut.	1	2	3	4	5
7. In solving problems, I function extremely well when neither problem nor solution is clear.	1	2	3	4	5
8. I tend to view the world as being too simple.	1	2	3	4	5
9. I tend to view the world as being as complex as I like it.	1	2	3	4	5
10. I am strongly attracted to very complicated people.	1	2	3	4	5
11. I am strongly attracted to somewhat uncomplicated people.	1	2	3	4	5
12. I am strongly attracted to very uncomplicated people.	1	2	3	4	5
13. I enjoy being in groups with few fixed rules and many diverse personalities.	1	2	3	4	5
14. I enjoy being in groups with relatively fixed rules but diverse personalities.	1	2	3	4	5
15. I enjoy being in groups with relatively fixed rules and similar personalities.	1	2	3	4	5
16. In considering problems and situations, I hesitate to solve problems that involve many points of view.	1	2	3	4	5
17. In considering problems and situations, I am moderately attracted to problems that involve many points of view.	1	2	3	4	5

| | How characteristic of you | | | | |
| | Not at all characteristic of me | | | Extremely characteristic of me | |

18. In considering problems and situations, I greatly enjoy and seek out problems that require many points of view.

1   2   3   4   5

19. In confusing or ambiguous situations, I put off decisions indefinitely.

1   2   3   4   5

20. In confusing or ambiguous situations, I consider all aspects of the problem, then reach a tentative decision, which might change as I reconsider the problem.

1   2   3   4   5

21. I feel extremely happy when I have a large number of related but distinct projects under way.

1   2   3   4   5

22. I feel extremely happy when I have many distinct, unrelated projects going.

1   2   3   4   5

23. I feel extremely happy when I have a few related projects under way.

1   2   3   4   5

24. In social activities, at gatherings, and at work, I like dealing with one person at a time, and preferably with a person like myself.

1   2   3   4   5

25. In social activities, at gatherings, and at work, I like dealing with people one at a time, but each can be quite different.

1   2   3   4   5

26. In social activities, at gatherings, and at work, I like trying to blend people who are quite different.

1   2   3   4   5

27. In social activities, at gatherings, and at work, I like mixing individuals of vastly different makeups in the same situation.

1   2   3   4   5

28. When someone suggests that I should change my behavior, I listen, sometimes out of courtesy, but rarely do anything about it, because most people are not justified in their criticisms.

1   2   3   4   5

29. When someone suggests that I should change my behavior, I change if I think the other person is justified or has the proper authority; otherwise I reject it.

1   2   3   4   5

| | How characteristic of you | | | |
	Not at all characteristic of me			Extremely characteristic of me

30. When someone suggests that I should change my behavior, I go along if, after careful consideration of the various interpretations of what he said, it makes sense in terms of my view. 1 2 3 4 5

31. If two people are disagreeing with each other, I tend to point out to the participants that if they saw the parts of their argument more objectively they would find that the parts add up to the real solution. 1 2 3 4 5

32. If two people are disagreeing with each other, I tend to try settling it as quickly as I can in order to avoid people's feelings being hurt. 1 2 3 4 5

33. In evaluating a new or changed situation, I generally avoid discussing the situation with people who have different points of view, since this just clouds the issue. 1 2 3 4 5

34. In evaluating a new or changed situation, I look for diverse points of view and often form several possible judgments which may or may not modify my previous outlook. 1 2 3 4 5

35. When a considerable amount of new and apparently contradictory information becomes available on a topic about which I have a strong opinion, I pay little attention, because when I have a strong opinion it is usually well founded. 1 2 3 4 5

36. When a considerable amount of new and apparently contradictory information becomes available on a topic about which I have a strong opinion, I am not affected by the new information, since I rarely take strong positions in any area. 1 2 3 4 5

37. When a considerable amount of new and apparently contradictory informa-

	How characteristic of you			
	Not at all characteristic of me		Extremely characteristic of me	

tion becomes available on a topic about which I have a strong opinion, I use the information to generate even more points of view about the issue, which could lead to seeing the issue in a new light.

    1   2   3   4   5

38. I easily sense the way in which the motives and ideas of others operate.

    1   2   3   4   5

39. I understand the motives and ideas of others only after thinking about them for a long time.

    1   2   3   4   5

40. I have considerable difficulty in understanding the motives and ideas of others.

    1   2   3   4   5

41. In making friends, I prefer those who are similar to me in values and opinions.

    1   2   3   4   5

42. In making friends, I prefer those who are somewhat unlike me in values and opinions.

    1   2   3   4   5

43. In making friends, I prefer those who are quite dissimilar from me in values and opinions.

    1   2   3   4   5

44. In making friends, I prefer a mix of some similar and some dissimilar in values and opinions.

    1   2   3   4   5

45. In making friends, I use many criteria, with similarity in values and opinions not being of great consequence for me.

    1   2   3   4   5

46. In selecting acquaintances, I enjoy being with individuals somewhat like myself in personality.

    1   2   3   4   5

47. In selecting acquaintances, I enjoy being with individuals quite dissimilar in personality.

    1   2   3   4   5

48. In selecting acquaintances, I enjoy being with some similar, some quite dissimilar.

    1   2   3   4   5

	How characteristic of you			
	Not at all characteristic of me			Extremely characteristic of me

49. In selecting acquaintances, I use many criteria, similarity in personality not being of great consequence to me.   1   2   3   4   5

50. In a discussion, I like taking a different point of view from my own. I learn more about my own view as well as others in this way.   1   2   3   4   5

51. I feel it is all right for different people to have different views. However, I feel they should keep these views to themselves and not bother others with them.   1   2   3   4   5

52. I prefer situations where there is a single problem with one possible solution.   1   2   3   4   5

53. I prefer situations where there is a single problem with a number of possible solutions.   1   2   3   4   5

54. I prefer situations where there are a number of different kinds of problems, each with more than one possible solution.   1   2   3   4   5

55. I prefer situations where there are a number of different kinds of problems that can be solved in the same basic manner.   1   2   3   4   5

56. Given that I had an opportunity to take an executive position with an organization that had many departments, each of which had different and sometimes irreconcilable conflicting interests, needs, and personalities (assuming my income is unaffected by this decision), I would like to have responsibility for the entire organization.   1   2   3   4   5

57. Given that I had an opportunity to take an executive position with an organization that had many departments, each of which had different and sometimes irreconcilable conflicting interests, needs,

	How characteristic of you	
	Not at all characteristic of me	*Extremely characteristic of me*

and personalities (assuming my income is unaffected by this decision), I would like to run one department and represent this department on many interdepartmental committees. 1   2   3   4   5

58. Given that I had an opportunity to take an executive position with an organization that had many departments, each of which had different and sometimes irreconcilable conflicting interests, needs, and personalities (assuming my income is unaffected by this decision), I would like to run one department with no participation in interdepartmental committees. 1   2   3   4   5

59. In the field of international affairs, I agree that my country should maintain sufficient power to ensure that its interests are protected in all areas. 1   2   3   4   5

60. In doing work, I have liked having no direct supervision but someone to talk over problems with. 1   2   3   4   5

D

Decision Style Self-Assessment: Answer Sheet and Instructions for Completing Assessments

Please follow these instructions carefully to ensure that your assessment results will accurately reflect your styles.

First, photocopy the answer sheet printed front and back on the same sheet of paper. Fill in the background information on the answer sheet. Other than your name and address, giving us this information is optional. We need it to keep our database current. We will release no personal information that could identify you to anyone other than you. We will keep your name and address in our records so that we can send you information about new developments in the future. However, we will not sell or give your name to anyone outside our organization.

Be sure that you will not be interrupted or distracted while completing the assessments. This is very important. Interruptions or other distractions can influence your results. There are two assessment instruments (questionnaires), the Driver Decision Style Exercise (DDSE), and the Driver-Streufert Complexity Index (DSCI). Most people complete each instrument within twenty to thirty minutes, so you should set aside at least one hour to complete both instruments (in addition to the time needed to enter the background information).

Complete the DDSE first and then do the DSCI. The DDSE presents you with a short case scenario and some additional items of information about the scenario. Then you are asked to respond to a series of questions about the case and the information. There are a total of forty-five questions. Indicate your answers by circling numbers on the scales on the answer sheet. Please do not leave any answers blank because this will make it impossible for us to compute scores for you.

The DSCI asks you to respond to sixty items. Each item makes a statement about your behavior or your preferences. Select a number from the scale next to each item to indicate how characteristic that statement is of you, and then circle the number on the answer sheet.

After you have finished both instruments, double-check to make sure that you have circled numbers for each question. Then mail the completed answer sheet along with a check for $19.95 payable to Decision Dynamics Corporation, 12301 Wilshire Boulevard, Suite 403, Los Angeles, California 90025.

We will compute your scores and return them to you. Your results will indicate the strength of each decision style and they will identify your primary and backup operating styles and role styles.

DECISION STYLE ASSESSMENT ANSWER SHEET

NAME: _____
FIRST | MIDDLE | LAST

ADDRESS: _____

CITY: _____ STATE: _____ ZIP: _____

JOB TITLE: _____ Years in job: _____ Social Sec. #: _____

DATE: _____ AGE: _____ Years of Education: _____ SEX: _____

FIELD OF STUDY (Highest field of study completed)	REGION (place lived longest)	ETHNICITY	OCCUPATION	ORG. LEVEL (Level of your current position)
__ Liberal Arts	__ West Coast	__ American Indian	__ Professional	__ Nonmanagement (labor)
__ Science, Math	__ Northwest		__ Management	__ Nonmanagement (clerical)
__ Business	__ Southwest		__ Technical, Craft	__ Nonmanagement (technical, staff)
__ Education	__ Rocky Mountains	__ Asian	__ Clerical	__ First-level supervision
__ Engineering	__ North Central		__ Staff: Finance, Accounting, DP, etc.	__ Mid. management
__ Social Sciences	__ South Central	__ Black	__ Staff: Personnel, Marketing, Cust. Relations, etc.	__ Sr. management
__ Law	__ Southeast		__ Sales	__ Other ____
__ Medicine, Health	__ Northeast	__ Caucasian	__ Homemaker	
__ Public Admin.	__ Middle Atlantic		__ Semi-skilled	
__ Social Work	__ Canada	__ Hispanic	__ Student	
__ Other ____	__ Mexico		__ Other ____	
	__ Centrl./So. America	__ Other ____		
	__ Europe			
	__ Middle East			
	__ Africa			
	__ Asia			

—— Australia
—— Pacific Islands

DRIVER DECISION STYLE EXERCISE

(Use reverse side for *Driver-Streufert Complexity Index*)

CIRCLE ONE RESPONSE FOR EACH ITEM

	A				B		
1.	1	2	3	4	5	6	7
2.	1	2	3	4	5	6	7
3.	1	2	3	4	5	6	7
4.	1	2	3	4	5	6	7
5.	1	2	3	4	5	6	7
6.	1	2	3	4	5	6	7
7.	1	2	3	4	5	6	7
8.	1	2	3	4	5	6	7
9.	1	2	3	4	5	6	7
10.	1	2	3	4	5	6	7
11.	1	2	3	4	5	6	7
12.	1	2	3	4	5	6	7
13.	1	2	3	4	5	6	7
14.	1	2	3	4	5	6	7

15.	1	2	3	4	5	6	7
16.	1	2	3	4	5	6	7
17.	1	2	3	4	5	6	7
18.	1	2	3	4	5	6	7
19.	1	2	3	4	5	6	7
20.	1	2	3	4	5	6	7
21.	1	2	3	4	5	6	7
22.	1	2	3	4	5	6	7
23.	1	2	3	4	5	6	7
24.	1	2	3	4	5	6	7
25.	1	2	3	4	5	6	7
26.	1	2	3	4	5	6	7
27.	1	2	3	4	5	6	7
28.	1	2	3	4	5	6	7
29.	1	2	3	4	5	6	7
30.	1	2	3	4	5	6	7
31.	1	2	3	4	5	6	7
32.	1	2	3	4	5	6	7
33.	1	2	3	4	5	6	7
34.	1	2	3	4	5	6	7
35.	1	2	3	4	5	6	7

	A			B			
36.	1	2	3	4	5	6	7
37.	1	2	3	4	5	6	7
38.	1	2	3	4	5	6	7
39.	1	2	3	4	5	6	7
40.	1	2	3	4	5	6	7
41.	1	2	3	4	5	6	7
42.	1	2	3	4	5	6	7
43.	1	2	3	4	5	6	7
44.	1	2	3	4	5	6	7
45.	1	2	3	4	5	6	7

DRIVER-STREUFERT COMPLEXITY INDEX

Answer Sheet

CIRCLE A NUMBER FOR EACH ITEM

1.	1	2	3	4	5		21.	1	2	3	4	5		41.	1	2	3	4	5

	1	2	3	4	5			1	2	3	4	5			1	2	3	4	5
1.	1	2	3	4	5		21.	1	2	3	4	5		41.	1	2	3	4	5
2.	1	2	3	4	5		22.	1	2	3	4	5		42.	1	2	3	4	5
3.	1	2	3	4	5		23.	1	2	3	4	5		43.	1	2	3	4	5
4.	1	2	3	4	5		24.	1	2	3	4	5		44.	1	2	3	4	5
5.	1	2	3	4	5		25.	1	2	3	4	5		45.	1	2	3	4	5
6.	1	2	3	4	5		26.	1	2	3	4	5		46.	1	2	3	4	5
7.	1	2	3	4	5		27.	1	2	3	4	5		47.	1	2	3	4	5
8.	1	2	3	4	5		28.	1	2	3	4	5		48.	1	2	3	4	5
9.	1	2	3	4	5		29.	1	2	3	4	5		49.	1	2	3	4	5
10.	1	2	3	4	5		30.	1	2	3	4	5		50.	1	2	3	4	5
11.	1	2	3	4	5		31.	1	2	3	4	5		51.	1	2	3	4	5
12.	1	2	3	4	5		32.	1	2	3	4	5		52.	1	2	3	4	5
13.	1	2	3	4	5		33.	1	2	3	4	5		53.	1	2	3	4	5
14.	1	2	3	4	5		34.	1	2	3	4	5		54.	1	2	3	4	5
15.	1	2	3	4	5		35.	1	2	3	4	5		55.	1	2	3	4	5
16.	1	2	3	4	5		36.	1	2	3	4	5		56.	1	2	3	4	5
17.	1	2	3	4	5		37.	1	2	3	4	5		57.	1	2	3	4	5
18.	1	2	3	4	5		38.	1	2	3	4	5		58.	1	2	3	4	5
19.	1	2	3	4	5		39.	1	2	3	4	5		59.	1	2	3	4	5
20.	1	2	3	4	5		40.	1	2	3	4	5		60.	1	2	3	4	5

USE OTHER SIDE FOR *DRIVER DECISION STYLE EXERCISE*

PLEASE DOUBLE-CHECK
to make sure that you have

References

Adorno, T. W., Frenkel-Brunswik, E., Levinson, D. J., & Sanford, R. N. (1964). *The authoritarian personality*. New York: Wiley. (Original work published 1950)

Alawi, H. (1973). *Cognitive task and organizational complexities in relation to information processing behavior in business managers*. Unpublished doctoral dissertation. University of Southern California, Graduate School of Business Administration, Los Angeles.

Athey, T. (1976). *The development and testing of a seminar for increasing the cognitive complexity of individuals*. Unpublished doctoral dissertation. University of Southern California, Graduate School of Business Administration, Los Angeles.

Bennis, W., & Nanus, B. (1986). *Leaders*. New York: HarperCollins.

Boddy, J. (1978). *Brain systems and psychological concepts*. New York: Wiley.

Boulgarides, J. (1973). *Decision style, values and biographical factors in relation to satisfaction and performance*. Unpublished doctoral dissertation. University of Southern California, Graduate School of Business Administration, Los Angeles.

Brousseau, K. R. (1984). Job-person dynamics and career development. In K. Rowland & G. Ferris (Eds.), *Research in personnel and human resources* (Vol. 2, pp. 125–154). Greenwich, Conn.: JAI Press.

Brousseau, K. R. (1987). *Profiling sales success.* Los Angeles: Decision Dynamics.

Coombs, M. W. (1989). *Measuring career concepts: An examination of the concepts, constructs, and validity of the Career Concept Questionnaire.* Unpublished doctoral dissertation. University of Southern California, Los Angeles.

D'Antoni, J. (1973). *Content oriented and process oriented value systems.* Unpublished doctoral dissertation. University of Southern California, Graduate School of Business Administration, Los Angeles.

Driver, M. J. (1970). *Decision style and decision process in a technical management simulation (Luna I).* Unpublished manuscript. University of Southern California, Graduate School of Business Administration, Department of Management and Organization, Los Angeles.

Driver, M. J. (1979a). Career concepts and career management in organizations. In C. Cooper (Ed.), *Behavioral problems in organizations* (pp. 5–17). Englewood Cliffs, N.J.: Prentice-Hall.

Driver, M. J. (1979b). Individual decision making and creativity. In S. Kerr (Ed.), *Organizational behavior* (pp. 59–91). Columbus, Ohio: Grid Publishing.

Driver, M. J. (1980). Career concepts and organizational change. In C. B. Derr (Ed.), *Work, family and the career.* New York: Praeger.

Driver, M. J. (1981). *Person-environment metastability. 1: Decision style reliability.* Unpublished manuscript. University of Southern California, Graduate School of Business Administration, Department of Management and Organization, Los Angeles.

Driver, M. J. (1982). Career concepts—A new approach to career research. In R. Katz (Ed.), *Career issues in human resource management.* Englewood Cliffs, N.J.: Prentice-Hall.

Driver, M. J. (1984). *The emotional reaction inventory, II.* Los Angeles: Decision Dynamics.

Driver, M. J. (1985, December). Demographic and societal factors affecting the linear career crisis. *Canadian Journal of Administrative Science* 2, pp. 245–263.

Driver, M. J. (1988). Careers: A review of personal and organizational research. In C. L. Cooper and I. Robertson (Eds.), *International Review of Industrial and Organizational Psychology* (pp. 245–277). London: Wiley & Sons.

Driver, M. J., & Hoffman, R. (1979). *Triggers for self renewal among executives.* Paper presented at the meeting of the Academy of Management, Detroit, Mich.

Driver, M. J., & Hunsaker, P. L. (1972). The Luna I moon colony: A programmed simulation for the analysis of individual and group decision making. *Psychological Reports, 31,* 879–888.

Driver, M. J., & Lintott, J. (1972). *Managerial decision diagnostics.* Unpublished manuscript. University of Southern California, Graduate School of Business Administration, Department of Management and Organization, Los Angeles.

Driver, M. J., & Mock, T. J. (1975b, November). *Some experimental results in MIS, human information processing, and tailored information systems.* Paper presented at the joint national meeting of ORSA/TIMS, Las Vegas.

Driver, M. J., & Pate, L. E. (1989, August). *Efficacy of the four aces decision making technique for changing cognitive style.* Paper submitted to the Academy of Management, Management Education and Development Division, Washington, D.C.

Driver, M. J., & Prince, J. B. (1981). *Person environment metastability: 2. Affective and motivational correlates of decisions style in varied work and educational environments.* Paper presented at the meeting of the Academy of Management, San Diego, Calif.

Driver, M. J., & Streufert, S. (1969). Integrative complexity. *Administrative Science Quarterly, 14,* 272–285.

Driver, M. J., & Sundby, D. Y. (1978). *Validation of prediction batteries for jobs in an insurance company: 1. Batteries for underwriter and claims representatives jobs* (Technical report). Los Angeles: University of Southern California, Graduate School of Business Administration, Department of Management and Organization.

Driver, M. J., Sundby, D. Y., & Chulef, A. S. (1989). *Technical manual for Driver Decision Style Exercise.* Los Angeles: Decision Dynamics.

Driver, M. J., & Testerman, W. (1979a). *Validation in company: 5. Selection for management potential* (Technical report). Los Angeles: University of Southern California, Graduate School of Business Administration, Department of Management and Organization.

Driver, M. J., & Testerman, W. (1979b). *Validation of prediction batteries for jobs in an insurance company: 3. A cross validation study* (Technical report). Los Angeles: University of Southern California, Graduate School of Business Administration, Department of Management and Organization.

Eysenck, H. (1954). *The psychology of politics.* New York: Routledge & Kegan Paul.

Freud, S. (1947). *The ego and the id.* London: Hogarth Press.

Hager, J. (1977). *The feasibility of using decision making style as a criterion for career assignment in the U.S. Air Force.* Unpublished doctoral dissertation. University of Southern California, Graduate School of Business Administration, Department of Management and Organization, Los Angeles.

Harvey, O. J., Hunt, D., & Schroder, H. (1961). *Conceptual systems and personality organization.* New York: Wiley.

Kohn, M., & Schooler, C. (1981). Job conditions and personality. *American Journal of Sociology, 87,* 1257–86.

Meshkati, N. (1983). *A conceptual model for the assessment of mental workload based on individual decision styles.* Unpublished doctoral dissertation. University of Southern California, Los Angeles.

Miner, J. (1988). *Organization behavior.* New York: Random House.

Mock, T, J., & Driver, M. J. (1975). An experimental study of alternate accounting feedback systems and differences in cognitive style of information processing. Proceedings of the Annual American Accounting Society Meeting, Tucson, Ariz.

Olson, T. (1979). *Career concepts and decision styles.* Paper presented at the meeting of the Academy of Management, Atlanta.

Penfield, W. (1952). Memory mechanisms. *Archives of Neurological Psychiatry, 67,* 178–198.

Prince, J. B. (1979). *An investigation of career concepts and career* members. Paper presented at the meeting of the Western Academy of Management, Portland, Oreg.

Ridgeway, C. L. (1977). Patterns of environmental adjustments underlying measured cognitive complexity and field independence in men and women. *Perceptual and Motor Skills 44,* 99–112.

Rokeach, M. (1960). *The open and closed mind.* New York: Basic Books.

Schroder, H., Driver, M. J., & Streufert, S. (1967). *Human information processing.* Troy, Mo.: Holt, Rinehart & Winston.

Schutt, D. (1976). *Myers Briggs Jungian typology and decision style.* Unpublished manuscript. University of Southern California, Graduate School of Business Administration, Department of Management and Organization, Los Angeles.

Schutz, W. C. (1958). *FIRO: A three-dimensional theory of interpersonal behavior.* Troy, Mo.: Holt, Rinehart & Winston.

Secord, P., & Backman, C. (1964). *Social psychology.* New York: McGraw-Hill.

Streufert, S., & Streufert, S. (1978). *Behavior in the complex environment.* Washington, D.C.: Winston-Wiley.

Sundby, D. (1978). *Financial analyst study report* (Technical report). Los Angeles: University of Southern California, Graduate School of Business Administration, Department of Management and Organization.

Testerman, W. (1975). *Decision style and job selection in the computer industry.* Unpublished doctoral dissertation. University of Southern California, Graduate School of Business Administration, Los Angeles.

Witkin, H., Dyk, R., Batterson, H., Goodenough, D., & Karp, S. (1962). *Psychological differentiation.* New York: Wiley.

Index

Printed in the United States
46533LVS00003BA/46-69